JavaScript™

FOR

DUMMIES®

4TH EDITION

JavaScript™
FOR
DUMMIES®
4TH EDITION

by Emily Vander Veer

WILEY

Wiley Publishing, Inc.

JavaScript™ For Dummies,® 4th Edition

Published by
Wiley Publishing, Inc.
111 River Street
Hoboken, NJ 07030-5774

Copyright © 2005 by Wiley Publishing, Inc., Indianapolis, Indiana

Published by Wiley Publishing, Inc., Indianapolis, Indiana

Published simultaneously in Canada

For general information on our other products and services, please contact our Customer Care Department within the U.S. at 800-762-2974, outside the U.S. at 317-572-3993, or fax 317-572-4002.

For technical support, please visit www.wiley.com/techsupport.

Wiley also publishes its books in a variety of electronic formats. Some content that appears in print may not be available in electronic books.

Library of Congress Control Number: 2004107963

ISBN: 0-7645-7659-3

Manufactured in the United States of America

10 9 8 7 6 5 4 3 2 1

4B/QS/RR/QU/IN

WILEY

About the Author

Freelance author and Web guru Emily A. Vander Veer has penned several books and countless articles on Internet-related technologies and trends. You can e-mail her at eav@outtech.com.

Dedication

For the D.

Author's Acknowledgments

Many thanks to Gareth Hancock for giving me the opportunity to write the very first edition of this book; to Craig Lukasik, who reviewed this book for technical accuracy; and to all of the other tireless professionals at Wiley, without whom this book wouldn't have been possible.

Publisher's Acknowledgments

We're proud of this book; please send us your comments through our online registration form located at www.dummies.com/register.

Some of the people who helped bring this book to market include the following:

Acquisitions, Editorial, and Media Development

Project Editor: Pat O'Brien

Acquisitions Editor: Steven Hayes

Copy Editor: Virginia Sanders

Technical Editor: Craig Lukasik

Editorial Manager: Kevin Kirschner

Media Development Manager: Laura VanWinkle

Media Development Supervisor: Richard Graves

Editorial Assistant: Amanda Foxworth

Cartoons: Rich Tennant (www.the5thwave.com)

Composition

Project Coordinator: Erin Smith

Layout and Graphics: Andrea Dahl, Joyce Haughey, Jacque Roth, Heather Ryan

Special Art:

Proofreaders: Carl Pierce, Joe Niesen, TECHBOOKS Production Services

Indexer: TECHBOOKS Production Services

Publishing and Editorial for Technology Dummies

    Richard Swadley, Vice President and Executive Group Publisher

    Andy Cummings, Vice President and Publisher

    Mary Bednarek, Executive Acquisitions Director

    Mary C. Corder, Editorial Director

Publishing for Consumer Dummies

    Diane Graves Steele, Vice President and Publisher

    Joyce Pepple, Acquisitions Director

Composition Services

    Gerry Fahey, Vice President of Production Services

    Debbie Stailey, Director of Composition Services

Contents at a Glance

Table of Contents

Introduction

• •

*W*elcome to the wonderful world of Web programming with JavaScript. If you've worked with HTML before but want to add more flexibility and punch to your pages, or even if you've never written a stick of code in your life but are eager to hop on the Infobahn-wagon, this book's for you.

Although I don't assume that you know HTML, much of what you want to do with JavaScript is interact with objects created by using HTML — so you understand the examples in this book that much quicker if you have a good HTML reference handy. One to consider is HTML 4 For Dummies, 4th Edition, by Ed Tittel (Wiley Publishing, Inc.).

I do my best to describe how JavaScript works by using real-world examples — and not a foo (bar) in sight. When explaining things in formal notation makes sense, I do that, but not without a recap in plain English. Most importantly, I include tons of sample programs that illustrate the kinds of things you may want to do in your own pages.

Along with this book comes a companion CD-ROM. This CD-ROM contains all the sample code listings covered in the text along with many other interesting scripts, examples, and development tools. From experience, I can tell you that the best way to get familiar with JavaScript is to load the scripts and interact with them as you read through each chapter. If it's feasible for you, I suggest installing the contents of the CD right away, before you dig into the chapters. Then, when you come across a listing in the book, all you have to do is double-click on the corresponding HTML file you've already installed. Doing so helps reinforce your understanding of each JavaScript concept described in this book. For more information and instructions on installing the CD-ROM, see the About the CD appendix in the back of this book.

System Requirements

Here's what you need to get the most out of this book and the enclosed CD-ROM:

- ✔ A computer with a CD-ROM drive and a modem
- ✔ A sound card (okay, this one's strictly optional, but it's a lot of fun!)

✔ Windows XT[s1] or Macintosh already installed with the following:

- A Pentium or faster processor, at least 16MB of RAM, and at least 25MB of free hard drive space if you're running Windows XT

- A PowerPC or faster processor, at least 16MB of RAM, and at least 10MB of free hard drive space for Macintosh users

- A copy of either Netscape Navigator 7.0 or Microsoft Internet Explorer 6.0 (Chapter 1 tells you how to get a copy, if you haven't already)

About This Book

Think of this book as a good friend who started at the beginning, learned the ropes the hard way, and now wants to help you get up to speed. In this book, you can find everything from JavaScript basics and common pitfalls to answers to embarrassingly silly questions (and some really cool tricks, too), all of which I explain from a first-time JavaScript programmer's point of view. Although you don't find explanations of HTML in this book, you do find working examples on the companion CD complete with all the HTML you need to understand how JavaScript works.

Some sample topics you can find in this book are:

✔ Creating interactive Web pages

✔ Validating user input with JavaScript

✔ Testing and debugging your JavaScript scripts

✔ Adapting your scripts for cross-browser issues

✔ Integrating JavaScript with other technologies, such as Java applets, Netscape plug-ins, and ActiveX components

Building intelligent Web pages with JavaScript can be overwhelming — if you let it. You can do so much with JavaScript! To keep the deluge to a minimum, this book concentrates on the practical considerations you need to get your interactive pages up and running in the least amount of time possible.

Conventions Used in This Book

The rules are pretty simple. All code appears in monospaced font, like this HTML line:

```
TITLEJavaScript For DummiesTITLE
```

Make sure you follow the examples' syntax exactly. Sometimes your scripts work if you add or delete spaces or type your keywords in a different case, but sometimes they don't — and you want to spend your time on more interesting bugs than those caused by spacing errors. (If you're like me, you copy and paste working code examples directly from the CD to cut down syntax errors even more!)

Type anything you see in `code font` letter for letter. These items are generally JavaScript keywords, and they need to be exact. Directives in *italics* are placeholders, and you can substitute other values for them. For example, in the following line of code, you can replace *state* and *confusion* and leave the equal sign out entirely, but you need to type `var` the way that it's shown.

```
var state = "confusion"
```

Due to the margins of this book, sometimes code examples are wrapped from one line to another. You can copy the code exactly the way it appears; JavaScript doesn't have a line continuation character. JavaScript has only one place where you can't break a line and still have the code work — between two quotes. For example, the following line is invalid:

```
. . .
var fullName = "George
Washington"
```

And, when you see ellipses in the code (like this: . . .) you know I've omitted a part of the script to help you focus on just the part I'm talking about. Or, I've placed more code (like the HTML around the JavaScript) on the CD to save paper.

All the URLs listed in this book are accurate at the time of this writing. Because the Internet is such a dynamic medium, however, a few might be inaccessible by the time you get around to trying them. If so, try using a search engine, such as Yahoo! or Google, to help you find the slippery Web site you're looking for.

What You're Not to Read

Okay, you can read the text next to the Technical Stuff icons, but you don't have to understand what's going on! Technical Stuff icons point out in-depth information that explains why things work as they do (interesting if you're in the mood, but not necessary to get the most out of the JavaScript examples I present).

Foolish Assumptions

Everybody's got to start somewhere, right? I'm starting out with the following assumptions about you, the reader:

✔ You know how to navigate through an application with a mouse and a keyboard.

✔ You want to build interactive Web pages for fun, for profit, or because building them is part of your job.

✔ You have, or can get, a working connection to the Internet.

✔ You have, or can get, a copy of Netscape Navigator 7.0 or Microsoft Internet Explorer 6.0.

How This Book Is Organized

This book contains five major parts. Each part contains several chapters, and each chapter contains several sections. You can read the book from start to finish if you like, or you can dive in whenever you need help on a particular topic. (If you're brand-new to JavaScript, however, skimming through Part I first sure couldn't hurt.) Here's a breakdown of what you can find in each of the five parts.

Part I: Building Killer Web Pages for Fun and Profit

This part explains how to turn JavaScript from an abstract concept to something happening on the screen in front of you. It takes you step by step through obtaining your choice of Netscape Navigator or Microsoft Internet Explorer, discovering how to access and modify the document object model, and writing and testing your first script. Part I also includes an overview of the JavaScript language itself.

Part II: Creating Dynamic Web Pages

In this part, I demonstrate practical ways to create Web pages that appear differently to different users. By the time you finish Part II, you'll have seen sample code for such common applications as detecting your users' browsers on-the-fly, formatting and displaying times and dates, and storing information for repeat visitors by using cookies.

Part III: Making Your Site Easy for Visitors to Navigate and Use

The chapters in Part III are devoted to helping you create Web pages that visitors can interact with easily and efficiently. You find out how to use JavaScript's event model and function declaration support to create hot buttons, clickable images, mouse rollovers, and intelligent (automatically validated) HTML forms.

Part IV: Interacting with Users

JavaScript is evolving by leaps and bounds, and Part IV keeps you up-to-date with the latest and greatest feats you can accomplish with JavaScript, including brand-new support for dynamic HTML and cascading style sheets. In this part you also find a double handful of the most popular JavaScript and DHTML effects, including pull-down menus, expandable site maps, and custom tooltips.

Part V: The Part of Tens

The concluding part pulls together tidbits from the rest of the book, organized in lists of ten. The categories include great JavaScript-related online resources, common mistakes, and debugging tips.

Part VI: Appendixes

At the back of the book you find a handful of indispensable references, including JavaScript reserved words, color values, document objects, and special characters. There's also a nifty how-to section that describes all the cool tools you find on the companion CD.

Icons Used in This Book

Ever get in one of those moods when you're reading along and get really excited, and you just wish there was a way to cut to the chase and absorb an entire chapter all at once? Well, if so, you're in luck! Not only is this book organized in nice, easily digestible chunks, with real-life figures and code examples, but there's an extra added value, too: eye-catching icons to give you a heads-up on the most useful tidbits, categorized so that you can tell at a glance what's coming up.

Take just a second to become familiar with the kind of information you can expect from each icon:

This icon flags some of the cool stuff you can find on the CD-ROM included in the back of this book. Because all the JavaScript source code listings are on the CD (plus lots more), you can load up the scripts for each section and follow along while you read if you want.

This icon lets you know that some really nerdy technical information is coming your way. You can skip it if you want; reading through isn't absolutely necessary if you're after the bare-bones basics, but it does give you a little show-off material!

Next to the tip icon you can find handy little tricks and techniques for getting the most bang out of your JavaScript buck.

These little gems can help you figure things out, so pay attention.

Before you jump in and start applying the information in any given section, check out the text next to these babies — chances are they'll save you a lot of time and hassle!

The browser icon alerts you to an important difference between the way Netscape Navigator implements JavaScript and the way Internet Explorer implements JavaScript.

Where to Go from Here

So what are you waiting for? Pick a topic, any topic, and dive in. Or, if you're like me, begin at the beginning and read until you get so excited you have to put the book down and try stuff out for yourself. And remember: From now on, your life will be divided into two major time periods — before you mastered JavaScript and after you mastered JavaScript. Enjoy!

Part I

Building Killer Web Pages for Fun and Profit

The 5th Wave   By Rich Tennant

AT THE REAL PROGRAMMERS DATING BAR

Whoa! Look at the pocket protectors on this one!

In this part . . .

*J*avaScript is one of the coolest Web tools around — and its use is spreading like wildfire. An extension to Hypertext Markup Language (HTML), JavaScript enables you to access and manipulate all the components that make up a Web page. With JavaScript, you can create cool graphic effects and build what are known as intelligent Web pages: pages that verify input, calculate it, and make presentation decisions based on it. You can create all this, all on the client, without having to learn an industrial-strength language, such as C or C++!

Part I introduces you to JavaScript and then walks you step by step through the process of creating your first script. Finally, this part acquaints you with basic JavaScript programming concepts, including everything you need to know to create sophisticated custom scripts, from syntax to the document object model.

Chapter 1

All You Ever Wanted to Know about JavaScript (But Were Afraid to Ask!)

In This Chapter

▶ Understanding a working definition of JavaScript

▶ Dispelling common JavaScript misconceptions

▶ Getting started with JavaScript tools

▶ Finding information online

Maybe you've surfed to a Web site that incorporates really cool features, such as

- Images that change when you move your mouse over them
- Slideshow animations
- Input forms with pop-up messages that help you fill in fields correctly
- Customized messages that welcome repeat visitors

By using JavaScript and the book you're reading right now you can create all these effects and many more! The Web page in Figure 1-1 shows you an example of the kinds of things that you can look forward to creating for your own site.

A lot has changed since the previous edition of JavaScript For Dummies came out. Perhaps the biggest change is the evolution of DHTML, or dynamic HTML. DHTML refers to JavaScript combined with HTML and cascading style sheets, and it's a powerful combination you can use to create even more breathtakingly cool Web sites than ever before.

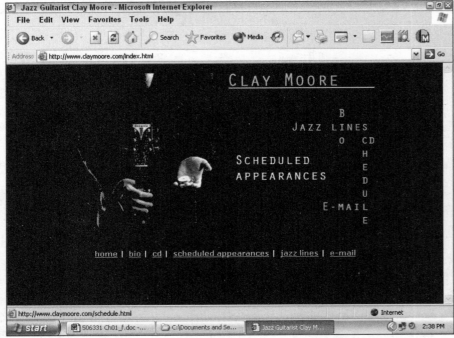

Figure 1-1:
JavaScript
lets you add
interactive
features to
your Web
site quickly
and easily.

Along with this increased power comes increased complexity, unfortunately — but that's where this new, improved, better-tasting edition of JavaScript For Dummies comes in! Even if you're not a crackerjack programmer, you can use the techniques and sample scripts in this book to create interactive Web pages bursting with animated effects.

Before you hit the JavaScript code slopes, though, you might want to take a minute to familiarize yourself with the basics that I cover in this chapter. Here I give you all the background that you need to get started using JavaScript as quickly as possible!

What Is JavaScript? (Hint: It's Not the Same Thing as Java!)

JavaScript is a scripting language you can use — in conjunction with HTML — to create interactive Web pages. A scripting language is a programming language that's designed to give folks easy access to prebuilt components. In the case of JavaScript, those prebuilt components are the building blocks that make up a Web page (links, images, plug-ins, HTML form elements, browser configuration details, and so on).

You don't need to know anything about HTML to put this book to good use; I explain all the HTML you need to know to create and use the JavaScript examples that you see in this book. If you're interested in discovering more about HTML, I suggest checking out a good book devoted to the subject. A good one to try is HTML 4 For Dummies, 4th Edition, by Ed Tittel and Natanya Pitts (Wiley Publishing, Inc.).

It's easy! (Sort of)

JavaScript has a reputation of being easy to use because

- ✔ The bulk of the document object model (the portion of the language that defines what kind of components, or objects, you can manipulate in JavaScript) is pretty straightforward.

- ✔ For example, if you want to trigger some kind of event when a person clicks a button, you access the onClick event handler associated with the button object; if you want to trigger an event when an HTML form is submitted, you access the onSubmit event handler associated with the form object. (You become familiar with the JavaScript object model in this book by examining and experimenting with working scripts. You can also check out Appendix C, which lists all the objects that make up the document object model.)

- ✔ When you load a cool Web page into your browser and wonder how the author created the effect in JavaScript, 99 times out of a 100 all you have to do to satisfy your curiosity is click to view the source code (choose View⇨Page Source in Navigator or choose View⇨Source in Internet Explorer). (Chapter 3 describes the .js files that are responsible for that 100th time.) This source code free-for-all, which is simply impossible with compiled programming languages such as Java, helps you decipher JavaScript programming by example.

However, becoming proficient in JavaScript isn't exactly a no-brainer. One of the biggest factors contributing to the language's growing complexity is the fact that the two major JavaScript-supporting browsers on the market (Netscape Navigator and Microsoft Internet Explorer) implement JavaScript differently. Netscape supports JavaScript directly — hardly a surprise because Netscape was the one that came up with JavaScript in the first place! Internet Explorer, on the other hand, supports JavaScript indirectly by providing support for JScript, its very own JavaScript-compatible language. And despite claims by both Netscape and Microsoft that JavaScript and JScript, respectively, are "open, standardized scripting languages," neither company offers explicit, comprehensive, all-in-one-place details describing all of the following:

- ✓ Precisely which version of JavaScript (or JScript) is implemented in each of their browser releases.

- ✓ Precisely which programming features are included and which objects are accessible in each version of JavaScript and JScript.

- ✓ How each version of JavaScript compares to each version of JScript. (As you see in Chapter 4, JavaScript and JScript differ substantially.)

The upshot is that creating cross-browser, JavaScript-enabled Web pages now falls somewhere around 6 on a difficulty scale of 1 to 10 (1 being the easiest technology in the world to master and 10 being the hardest).

Fear not, however. Armed with an understanding of HTML and the tips and sample scripts that you find in this book, you can become a JavaScript jockey in no time flat!

What's in a name?

A long time ago, JavaScript was called *LiveScript*. In a classic "if you can't dazzle them with brilliance, baffle them with marketing" move, Netscape changed the name to take advantage of the burgeoning interest in Java (another programming language that Netscape partner Sun Microsystems was developing at the time). By all accounts, the strategy worked. Unfortunately, many newbies still mistake JavaScript for Java, and vice versa.

Here's the scoop: Java is similar to JavaScript in that they're both object-based languages developed for the Web. Without going into the nitty-gritty details of syntax, interpreters, variable typing, and just-in-time compilers, all you have to remember about the difference in usage between JavaScript and Java is this: On the gigantic client/server application that is the Web, JavaScript lets you access *Web clients* (otherwise known as *browsers*), and Java lets you access *Web servers.* (Note: In some cases, you can also use Java for Web client development.)

This difference might seem esoteric, but it can help you determine which language to use to create the Web site of your dreams. If what you want to accomplish can be achieved inside the confines of a Web client (in other words, by interacting with HTML, browser plug-ins, and Java applets), JavaScript is your best bet. But if you want to do something fancier — say, interact with a server-side database — you need to look into Java or some other server-side alternative.

It's speedy!

Besides being relatively easy, JavaScript is also pretty speedy. Like most scripting languages, it's interpreted (as opposed to being compiled). When you program using a compiled language, such as C++, you must always reformat, or compile, your code file before you can run it. This interim step can take anywhere from a few seconds to several minutes or more.

The beauty of an interpreted language like JavaScript, on the other hand, is that when you make changes to your code — in this case, to your JavaScript script — you can test those changes immediately; you don't have to compile the script file first. Skipping the compile step saves a great deal of time during the debugging stage of Web page development.

Another great thing about using an interpreted language like JavaScript is that testing an interpreted script isn't an all-or-nothing proposition, the way it is with a compiled language. For example, if line 10 of a 20-line script contains a syntax error, the first half of your script may still run, and you may still get feedback immediately. The same error in a compiled program may prevent the program from running at all.

The downside of an interpreted language is that testing is on the honor system. Because there's no compiler to nag you, you might be tempted to leave your testing to the last minute or — worse yet — skip it altogether. However, remember that whether the Web site you create is for business or pleasure, it's a reflection on you, and testing is essential if you want to look your very best to potential customers, associates, and friends. (A few years ago, visitors to your site might have overlooked a buggy script or two, but frankly, Web site standards are much higher these days.) Fortunately, Chapter 17 is chock-full of helpful debugging tips to help make testing your JavaScript code as painless as possible.

Everybody's doing it! (Okay, almost everybody!)

Two generally available Web browsers currently support JavaScript: Microsoft's Internet Explorer and Netscape/AOL's Navigator. (Beginning with version 4.0, Navigator became synonymous with Communicator, even though technically Netscape Communicator includes more components than just the Navigator Web browser.) Between them, these two browsers have virtually sewn up the browser market; almost everyone who surfs the Web is using one or the other — and thus has the ability to view and create JavaScript-enabled Web pages.

JavaScript and HTML

You can think of JavaScript as an extension to HTML; an add-on, if you will.

Here's how it works. HTML tags create objects; JavaScript lets you manipulate those objects. For example, you use the HTML `<BODY>` and `</BODY>` tags to create a Web page, or document. As shown in Table 1-1, after that document is created, you can interact with it by using JavaScript. For example, you can use a special JavaScript construct called the `onLoad` event handler to trigger an action — play a little welcoming tune, perhaps — when the document is loaded onto a Web browser. (I cover event handlers in Chapter 13.) Examples of other HTML objects that you interact with using JavaScript include windows, text fields, images, and embedded Java applets.

Table 1-1	Creating and Working with Objects	
Object	*HTML Tag*	*JavaScript*
Web page	`<BODY> . . . </BODY>`	`document`
Image	`<IMG NAME="myImage">`	`document.myImage`
HTML form	`<FORM name="myForm">` `. . . </FORM>`	`document.myForm`
Button	`<INPUT TYPE="button"` `NAME="myButton">`	`document.myForm.` `myButton`

To add JavaScript to a Web page, all you have to do is embed JavaScript code in an HTML file. Below the line in which you embed the JavaScript code, you can reference, or call, that JavaScript code in response to an event handler or an HTML link.

You have two choices when it comes to embedding JavaScript code in an HTML file:

> ✔ **You can use the `<SCRIPT>` and `</SCRIPT>` tags to include JavaScript code directly into an HTML file.**
>
> In the example below, a JavaScript function called `processOrder()` is defined at the top of the HTML file. Further down in the HTML file, the JavaScript function is associated with an event handler — specifically, the `processOrder` button's `onClick` event handler. (In other words, the JavaScript code contained in the `processOrder()` function runs when a user clicks the `processOrder` button.)

```
<HTML>
<HEAD>
<SCRIPT LANGUAGE="JavaScript">
    // JavaScript statements go here
    function processOrder() {
        // More JavaScript statements go here
    }
</SCRIPT>
</HEAD>
<BODY>
<FORM NAME="myForm">
<INPUT TYPE="button" NAME="processOrder" VALUE="Click to process your
        order" onClick="processOrder();">
...
</HTML>
```

✔ **You can use the** `<SCRIPT>` **and** `</SCRIPT>` **tags to include a separate, external JavaScript file (a file containing only JavaScript statements and bearing a** `.js` **extension) into an HTML file.**

In the example below, the JavaScript `processOrder()` function is defined in the `myJSfile.js` file. The function is triggered, or called, when the user clicks the Click Here to Process Your Order link.

```
<HTML>
<HEAD>
<SCRIPT LANGUAGE="JavaScript" SRC="myJSfile.js">
</SCRIPT>
</HEAD>
<BODY>
<A HREF="javascript:processOrder();">Click here to process your order.</A>
...
</BODY>
</HTML>
```

Keep in mind that most of the examples in these printed pages focus on the JavaScript portion of the code (naturally!). But I include the HTML that you need to create the examples on the CD-ROM, so you don't have sweat re-creating the Web pages from scratch!

Because Web pages aren't made of HTML alone, however, JavaScript provides access to more than just HTML objects. JavaScript also provides access to browser- and platform-specific objects. Browser plug-ins (such as RealPlayer and Adobe Acrobat), the name and version of a particular viewer's browser, and the current date are all examples of non-HTML objects that you can work with by using JavaScript.

Together, all the objects that make up a Web site — HTML objects, browser- and platform-related objects, and special objects built right into the JavaScript language — are known as the document object model (DOM).

JavaScript and Your Web Browser

You need to use Netscape Navigator 7.1 (or higher) or Microsoft Internet Explorer 6.0 (or higher) to use the latest JavaScript enhancements that I demonstrate in this book.

Not all browsers are created equal: Internet Explorer's support for JavaScript differs significantly from Navigator's, and support for JavaScript varies from browser version to browser version. For details, check out Chapter 5.

Although you can create and view JavaScript scripts with an old version of one of these browsers, I recommend that you install the most current version of Navigator or Internet Explorer. (What the heck — they're both free!) The latest versions of each product boast the very latest JavaScript features and bug fixes; they're also the versions that you see in the figures and examples in this book.

You can use another browser, such as Opera or America Online (or even another Internet protocol, such as FTP) to download the latest version of Navigator or Internet Explorer and try it out. The section "What Do I Need to Get Started?" later in this chapter is devoted to the ins and outs of obtaining and installing a JavaScript-enabled browser. For now, suffice it to say that

- ✔ You need Navigator or Internet Explorer to work with JavaScript, which means that you have to be running one of the client platforms that supports these browsers. (The Macintosh operating system and Windows both support Navigator and Internet Explorer.)

- ✔ You need to be aware that people might use other, non-JavaScript-enabled browsers to view your Web pages — or they might use JavaScript-enabled browsers with JavaScript support turned off. Either way, you have no way to guarantee that everyone who visits your page can view your JavaScript handiwork. (Check out Chapter 5 for more information on this topic.)

JavaScript and browser security

In an era when computer viruses proliferate faster than crab grass, browser security is an important issue. You might be relieved to know that JavaScript poses no special security threats. Because JavaScript can't access any objects other than browser-contained objects (with the exception of cookies, which I discuss in Chapter 6), no one can use JavaScript to open up secret dial-up connections, wipe users' hard drives, or perform other malicious acts, even by accident. In other words, JavaScript is subject to the security controls built into JavaScript-supporting browsers.

What Can I Do with JavaScript That I Can't Do with Web Languages?

HTML. DHTML. XML. JavaScript. Java. Flash. When it comes to Web development, the sheer array of languages and development tools can be confusing — and you might be left wondering which language is best for which task.

The fact is that each language was designed with a particular kind of task in mind, and JavaScript is no exception. Table 1-2 shows you the types of tasks that JavaScript is best (and least) suited to perform. JavaScript is best suited for client-side (browser-based) tasks.

Table 1-2	Using JavaScript for the Right Task	
Task	*Is JavaScript Useful?*	*Are JavaScript and CSS (DHTML) Useful?*
Provide users with helpful feedback	Yes	No
Customize page appearance	Yes	Yes (more sophisticated than JavaScript alone)
Examine or change HTML form data	Yes	No
Create simple animations	Yes	Yes (more sophisticated than JavaScript alone)
Create complex animations	No	No
Perform server-side processing	No	No

JavaScript performs its magic by working together with HTML and cascading style sheets (CSS). Here's how it works: HTML and CSS let you create static Web pages by using tag building blocks, or objects. JavaScript lets you inspect and manipulate the objects to punch up static pages with interactivity and simple animations. (In other words, to use JavaScript, you need to use HTML; to take advantage of dynamic HTML, or DHTML, features, you need to use both HTML and CSS.)

By using JavaScript, you can make a Web site easy to navigate and even customize your page depending on who's viewing it, what browser the visitor is using to view it, and what time of day it is. You can even create simple (but effective) animated effects.

Make your Web site easy for folks to navigate

The most common way to perk up your pages with JavaScript is to make them easier to navigate. For example, you can use JavaScript to

✔ Create expandable site maps.

✔ Add tooltips — helpful bits of text that appear when a user moves a mouse over a particular section of your Web site.

✔ Swap images when a user drags a mouse over a certain area of the screen. (This effect is called a mouse rollover, and it helps users determine at a glance which parts of your Web page are interactive, or clickable.)

✔ Inspect the data that your users enter and pop up helpful suggestions if they make an invalid entry.

✔ Display a thank-you message after a user submits a form.

✔ Load content into multiple frames when a user clicks a button so that the user can view multiple chunks of related information at the same time.

In addition to user-initiated events, such as clicking and dragging a mouse, JavaScript also recognizes automatic events — for example, loading a Web page onto a browser. (Check out Chapter 5 for details, including sample scripts that run in response to automatic events.)

Customize the way your Web site looks on-the-fly

Everyone likes to feel special, and the folks who visit your Web site are no exception. By using JavaScript, you can tailor the way your pages look to different users based on criteria such as

✔ The specific kinds and versions of browser that visitors use to view your page

✔ The current date or time

✔ Your users' behaviors the last time they visited your pages

✔ Your users' stated preferences

✔ Any other criteria you can imagine

Create cool, dynamic animated effects

Many folks assume that you need Java to create animations for the Web, but that's just not so. Although JavaScript certainly won't be mistaken for the most efficient way to create high-density animations, you can use JavaScript with cascading style sheets (the combination is sometimes known as DHTML) to create a variety of really neat animated effects. As a matter of fact, using JavaScript is the easiest way to implement common effects, such as rollovers, as you can see in Chapter 8.

What Do I Need to Get Started?

I hope you're chomping at the bit to get started on your first JavaScript-enabled Web page! First things first, though . . . You have an idea of what JavaScript can do for you, and you might already have something specific in mind for your first attempt. Now's the time to dive into the preliminaries: what you need to get started and how to get what you need if you don't already have it. After you complete the setup, you can go on to the really fun stuff!

Hardware

For the purposes of this book, I assume that you're beginning your JavaScript adventure with a personal computer or a Mac. Your machine (or box, to use the vernacular) should be a Pentium PC or better (unless it's a Power Mac) and should have at least 32MB of RAM and at least 25MB free hard drive space. If none of this makes sense, try asking your local hardware guru; every organization seems to have at least one guru. (I've found, through extensive trial and error, that most hardware gurus are fairly responsive to sugar-based snack foods.)

You also need hardware installed that lets you connect to the Internet. This hardware usually consists of a modem and a phone line, although some folks opt for even faster options such as cable or DSL (digital subscriber line). Depending on your computer, you might have an internal modem installed — many come complete with a built-in modem. If not, you can buy a modem at your local computer discount store. The differentiating factor among modems is line speed: the faster the better. (Most computers these days come with a 56.6 Kbps model preinstalled, but 28.8 works just fine.) If you don't already have a modem, consider buying the fastest modem in your price range; you'll be very glad you did when you try to look at spiffy Web pages with multiple graphics, each of which takes a loooong time to load (because graphics files are typically very large).

Software

For the purposes of this book, I assume that you have a Mac OS 0 or later or a personal computer loaded with Windows 95, Windows NT, Windows 98, Windows 2000, Windows XP, or Linux. (Currently, only Netscape Navigator is available for use with Linux.)

I also assume that you have some way to create text files. (Most operating systems come packaged with a variety of text editors and word processors, any of which work just fine for creating JavaScript scripts.)

On the CD included with this book you can find some great text-editing utilities that are designed specifically for creating JavaScript files.

JavaScript-specific software

You need a Web browser. Navigator (Netscape Communication's commercial Web browser) and Microsoft's Internet Explorer are the only generally available browsers that support JavaScript at the time of this writing. So, the first thing to do is to get a copy of Navigator or Internet Explorer.(The examples that you see in this book are demonstrated by using both Netscape Navigator and Internet Explorer running on Windows XP.)

Most personal computers come with Internet Explorer already installed. To find out if this is the case for your particular computer, choose Start⇨All Programs and look for Internet Explorer.

Netscape Navigator

Netscape Navigator version 7.x bundles the Navigator browser with messaging, Web construction, and other Internet-related goodies.

You can download a copy by visiting the following site (which offers step-by-step installation instructions):

```
http://channels.netscape.com/ns/browsers/default.jsp
```

Of course, I'm assuming that you already have a Web browser installed or that you have access to FTP. (FTP is short for file transfer protocol, which is an Internet application that enables you to download files from other people's machines.)

Internet Explorer

If you're a Microsoft buff, you might want to download a copy of Internet Explorer. Download it for free (or order your copy on CD-ROM for a nominal fee) from the following site, which offers easy-to-follow installation instructions:

```
www.microsoft.com/windows/ie/default.htm
```

Documentation

For the latest Netscape Navigator and Microsoft Internet Explorer documentation and technical support, respectively, check out the following URLs:

```
http://channels.netscape.com/ns/browsers/default.jsp
```

```
www.microsoft.com/windows/ie/default.htm
```

To view or download a copy of the Core JavaScript Reference, the documentation from Netscape that explains JavaScript basics and language concepts, visit the following Web page:

```
http://devedge.netscape.com/central/javascript/
```

Microsoft's documentation for its JavaScript-compatible scripting language, called JScript, can be found at

```
http://msdn.microsoft.com/library/default.asp?url=/library/en-
            us/script56/html/js56jsoriJScript.asp
```

or you can visit `http://msdn.microsoft.com` and search for documents on scripting.

Chapter 2

Writing Your Very First Script

● ●

In This Chapter

▶ Designing your first JavaScript application

▶ Creating an HTML file

▶ Creating and attaching a script

▶ Running the JavaScript application

● ●

*O*ne of the best ways to figure out the particulars of a new scripting language is to dive right in and create a script — and that's just what this
chapter shows you how to do! Actually, this chapter shows you how to do more
than just create a script; it shows you how to create a JavaScript application.
JavaScript isn't much use all by itself. It really needs to work in conjunction
with HTML. So, a JavaScript application includes at least one script and at
least one HTML file.

This chapter covers every single, solitary aspect of JavaScript development
from coming up with a useful idea to implementing, testing, and executing that
idea. I don't assume that you have any previous knowledge at all, so even if
you're new to JavaScript or the Web, you can follow along with the examples
in this chapter. And because the example that I use demonstrates most of the
common JavaScript constructs — including statements, variables, operators,
functions, and event handlers — you can apply the strategies and code shown
here to your very own script creations.

So turn on your computer, roll up those sleeves, and get ready to have
some fun!

From Idea to Working JavaScript Application

Like great art, great software doesn't just happen. Creating either one requires you to do a bit of planning first, and then you have to use a tool — along with some kind of logical process — to translate your plan into something concrete.

In this section, you become familiar with the basic tools that you need to create a JavaScript application: a simple text editor and a JavaScript-supporting Web browser. You also get a good look at the logical process (called the development cycle in programming circles) that you need to follow to create a JavaScript application.

Ideas?! I got a million of 'em!

The first step to creating a knock-out JavaScript application is deciding exactly what you want your application to do. Provide some feedback to your visitors? Perform some calculations? Display requested information in a pop-up window?

 This book describes many of the things that you want to do with JavaScript — from validating user input to creating mouse rollovers. For more ideas, check out ScriptSearch.com's JavaScript section at www.scriptsearch.com/ JavaScript.

When you have a clear idea in mind, take a few minutes to jot your thoughts down on a piece of paper. This phase — clarifying in writing exactly what you want your application to accomplish — has a long history of usefulness in professional software development. Formally dubbed the requirements phase, completing this step gives you the means to test your application at the end of the process. (Hey, you can't test something if you don't know exactly how it's supposed to work!)

Here are the requirements for the first JavaScript proverb application that I describe in this section:

I want to create a Web page that displays the current date and time.

Notice that the requirements can be in your own words. You don't need to fill out a formal requirements document, or (gasp!) labor over a flowchart. A simple, concise description fills the bill nicely.

Part 1: Creating an HTML file

When you have your script requirements in hand, you're ready to hit the coding slopes!

First off, you need to create a Web page. You do that by typing HTML code into a text editor and saving that code as a separate file on your computer's hard drive, which I show you how to do in this section.

Because this book is all about JavaScript — not HTML — I don't go into great detail about the HTML language. Instead, I demonstrate only as much HTML as I need to describe all the wonderful things that you can do with JavaScript. If you need a good introduction to HTML, I suggest *HTML 4 For Dummies*, 4th Edition, by Ed Tittel and Natanya Pitts (Wiley Publishing, Inc.).

Throughout this book, I use the Notepad text editor. Why? Because it comes free with the Windows operating system. (It's also easy to use.) But if you have another text-editing program installed on your machine that you'd rather use to create your scripts, by all means, use that program.

The companion CD contains trial versions of a handful of cool text editors that are optimized for JavaScript, including HELIOS Software Solutions' TextPad, Bare Bones Software's BBEdit, Macromedia Dreamweaver, and Adobe GoLive.

Just make sure that you use a text editor to create your scripts and HTML files rather than using a word processor. The difference is this: When you save a file by using a word processor application, such as Microsoft Word, the application adds special nontext characters to the saved file. Unfortunately, HTML and JavaScript interpreters — the bits of software inside Web browsers that process HTML and JavaScript code, respectively — can interpret only text; they can't interpret word-processing files containing special characters.

One exception exists to the rule about not using word processors to create HTML or JavaScript files. Some word processors allow you to save files in HTML or plain text format. To save a file in plain text format by using Microsoft Windows, for example, you simply choose File⇨Save As and select Text Only from the Save As Type drop-down list. If your word processor offers the ability to save files in HTML or plain text format, you can use that word processor to create HTML and script files. Otherwise, you need to use a text editor, such as Notepad.

Here are the steps you need to follow to create a file by using Notepad:

1. **Choose Start➪All Programs➪Accessories➪Notepad to pull up the Notepad editing window.**

2. **When the Notepad editing window appears, type in your HTML and JavaScript code. (See Figure 2-1.)**

3. **When you're finished typing, save the file by choosing File➪Save.**

   If you're creating an HTML file containing embedded JavaScript statements — such as the one that I describe in this chapter — make sure that the name you give your file contains the .htm or .html extension.

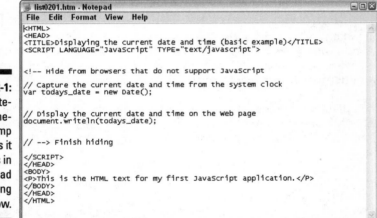

Figure 2-1:
The date-and-time-stamp script as it appears in the Notepad editing window.

```
list0201.htm - Notepad
File  Edit  Format  View  Help
<HTML>
<HEAD>
<TITLE>Displaying the current date and time (basic example)</TITLE>
<SCRIPT LANGUAGE="JavaScript" TYPE="text/javascript">

<!-- Hide from browsers that do not support JavaScript

// Capture the current date and time from the system clock
var todays_date = new Date();

// Display the current date and time on the web page
document.writeln(todays_date);

// --> Finish hiding

</SCRIPT>
</HEAD>
<BODY>
<P>This is the HTML text for my first JavaScript application.</P>
</BODY>
</HEAD>
</HTML>
```

The script that I demonstrate in this chapter is embedded in an HTML file, which is the most common way to implement JavaScript scripts. However, you can also implement a script as a separate file by using the .js extension, and then reference that JavaScript file explicitly from an HTML file. I cover this technique in Chapter 1.

Listing 2-1 shows you what the HTML code for the date-and-time-stamp application looks like in the Notepad editing window.

To see how the code in Listing 2-1 behaves in a Web browser, load the file list0201.htm — which you find on the companion CD — into Netscape Navigator or Internet Explorer.

Listing 2-1:   The HTML Code for the Date-and-Time-Stamp Application

```
<HTML>
<HEAD>
<TITLE>Displaying the current date and time (basic example)</TITLE>
</HEAD>
<BODY>
<P>This is the HTML text for my first JavaScript application.</P>
</BODY>
</HTML>
```

The code in Listing 2-1 displays the following:

- ✔ **A title:** The title text, `Displaying the current date and time (basic example)`, appears in the title bar of the document window.

- ✔ **A bit of text:** The `This is the HTML text for my first JavaScript application` text appears in the body of the Web page.

Figure 2-2 shows how the HTML code in Listing 2-1 appears in Netscape 7.1.

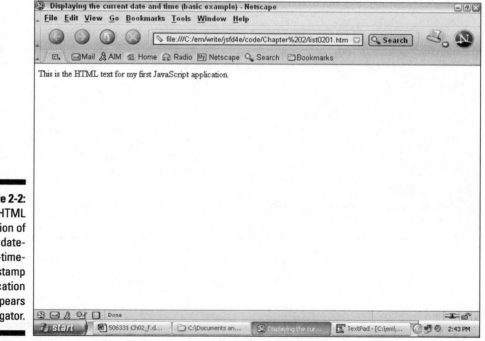

Figure 2-2: The HTML portion of the date-and-time-stamp application as it appears in Navigator.

Number crunching

Some JavaScript programmers set the LAN-GUAGE attribute of the `<SCRIPT>` tag equal to a value of `JavaScript1.1`, `JavaScript1.2`, or `JavaScript1.3` (as opposed to plain old `JavaScript`) if their script takes advantage of version-specific JavaScript code. For example, you can use any of the following three options:

```
<SCRIPT LANGUAGE="JavaScript">
. . . (JavaScript code version 1.0 and
        up)
</SCRIPT>

<SCRIPT LANGUAGE="JavaScript1.2">
. . . (JavaScript code version 1.2 or
        up)
</SCRIPT>

<SCRIPT LANGUAGE="JavaScript1.3">
. . . (JavaScript code version 1.3 or
        up)
</SCRIPT>
```

The trouble with that approach is that keeping track of JavaScript support in the many different versions of Navigator and Internet Explorer is enough to keep a full-time accountant busy! Take a look at the following and you see what I mean:

✔ Navigator 2.0 and Internet Explorer 3.0 support JavaScript 1.0.

✔ Navigator 3.0x and Internet Explorer 3.0x and 4.0x support JavaScript 1.1.

✔ Navigator 4.0 through 4.05 supports Java-Script 1.2.

✔ Navigator 4.06 through 4.5 supports Java-Script 1.3.

✔ Internet Explorer 5.x supports JScript 5.x (which is compatible with JavaScript 1.3, more or less).

✔ Navigator 6.0x and 7.1 and Internet Explorer 6 support JavaScript 1.5.

Whew! Even if you *do* manage to identify which version of JavaScript or JScript first introduced support for which JavaScript constructs you're using, specifying a value of `JavaScript 1.3` (rather than `JavaScript`) for the LANGUAGE attribute doesn't provide any additional Java-Script support. It simply prevents browsers that don't support JavaScript version 1.3 from trying to interpret those JavaScript statements sand-wiched between the `<SCRIPT LANGUAGE="JavaScript1.3">` and `</SCRIPT>` tags.

My advice? Stick with `LANGUAGE="Java Script"`, use cutting-edge JavaScript con-structs sparingly, and test your scripts in as many different browsers (and versions of browsers) as you possibly can.

Even though the Web page in Figure 2-2 looks nice, it's only half done. No date or time stamp appears on the page.

That's where JavaScript comes in! You need a script to capture the current date and time and display it on the page. You find out all you need to know to create a script to do just that — as well as attach that script to an HTML file — in the next two sections.

Part II: Creating your script

When you have a working HTML file, such as the one shown previously in Figure 2-2, you can begin creating your script.

For the date-and-time-stamp application that I describe in "Ideas?! I got a million of 'em!" earlier in this chapter, you need to create a script that

- ✔ Captures the current date and time.
- ✔ Displays the current date and time on the Web page.

The JavaScript code required to do all this, as shown in Listing 2-2, is simpler than you might think. In Chapter 3, you get familiar with each and every line of JavaScript code in detail, including comments, variables, and methods. For now, just take a gander at Listing 2-2.

Listing 2-2: JavaScript Code for the Date-and-Time-Stamp Application

```
// Capture the current date and time from the system clock
var todays_date = new Date();

// Display the current date and time on the Web page
document.writeln(todays_date);
```

As you glance over Listing 2-2, notice that

- ✔ **Lines that begin with // are JavaScript comments.** The JavaScript interpreter doesn't attempt to execute comments. Instead, comments serve to describe in human terms what you, the JavaScript programmer, want the JavaScript code to accomplish. In Listing 2-2, you see two comment lines. (For more about JavaScript comments, flip to Chapter 3.)

- ✔ **The first JavaScript statement** captures the current date and time by creating a new instance of the built-in Date object and assigning the value of that instance to a variable called todays_date.

  ```
  var todays_date = new Date();
  ```

  Note: You can find out more about how variables work by turning to Chapter 3. For the nitty-gritty on the built-in Date object, check out Chapter 4.

- ✔ **The second JavaScript statement** uses the writeln() method of the document object to write the contents of the todays_date variable to the body of the Web page.

  ```
  document.writeln(todays_date);
  ```

  In case you're interested, Chapter 4 describes the document object and the writeln() method in detail.

Part III: Putting it all together by attaching a script to an HTML file

Together, the HTML code that you see in Listing 2-1 and the JavaScript code you see in Listing 2-2 comprise the date-and-time-stamp application. Only one step remains: combining the two into a single HTML file. (This step is often referred to as attaching a script to an HTML file.)

Listing 2-3 shows you how to do just that.

To experiment with the code in Listing 2-3 on your own computer, just load the `list0203.htm` file (located on the companion CD) into your Web browser.

Listing 2-3:   The Whole Enchilada: The HTML and JavaScript Code for the Date-and-Time-Stamp Application

```
<HTML>
<HEAD>
<TITLE>Displaying the current date and time (basic example)</TITLE>
<SCRIPT LANGUAGE="JavaScript" TYPE="text/javascript">
<!-- Hide from browsers that do not support JavaScript

// Capture the current date and time from the system clock
var todays_date = new Date();

// Display the current date and time on the Web page
document.writeln(todays_date);

// --> Finish hiding
</SCRIPT>
</HEAD>
<BODY>
<P>This is the HTML text for my first JavaScript application.</P>
</BODY>
</HTML>
```

The code that you see in Listing 2-3 combines the HTML code shown in Listing 2-1 with the JavaScript code shown in Listing 2-2 — along with four lines of additional code. It's this additional code, shown in bold, that attaches the JavaScript script to the HTML file.

As you scan through Listing 2-3, notice the following:

✔ **The JavaScript code is shoehorned into the HTML file by using the HTML** `<SCRIPT>` **and** `</SCRIPT>` **tags.**

All JavaScript code must appear between beginning `<SCRIPT>` and ending `</SCRIPT>` tags. You can include more than one script per HTML file as long as you surround each script with the `<SCRIPT>` and `</SCRIPT>` tags. Because more than one scripting language exists, the `LANGUAGE` and `TYPE` variables specify JavaScript as the scripting language for this particular script.

✔ **The JavaScript code is placed in the header section of the HTML file (between the HTML** `<HEAD>` **and** `</HEAD>` **tags).**

You can include multiple `<SCRIPT>` and `</SCRIPT>` tags in different places in the HTML file. For example, you can include the `<SCRIPT>` and `</SCRIPT>` tags in the body section of an HTML file between the beginning and ending `<BODY>` and `</BODY>` tags. However, because the browser executes JavaScript code as it encounters that code, from top to bottom, the fact that you include your script at the very top of an HTML file (in the header section, as shown in Listing 2-3) ensures that the JavaScript code is available for execution as soon as the Web page is loaded.

✔ **HTML comments hide the script from browsers that don't support JavaScript.**

Browsers that don't support JavaScript ignore everything between these two lines:

```
<!-- Hide from browsers that do not support JavaScript
// --> Finish hiding
```

Surrounding your JavaScript statements with these two hiding symbols prevents non-JavaScript-enabled browsers from displaying your JavaScript statements as text.

Make sure that you put the beginning and ending hiding symbols (`<!--` and `// -->`, respectively) on their own separate lines. Placing either symbol on the same line as a JavaScript statement could cause a non-JavaScript-enabled browser to display your JavaScript code, just as though the hiding symbols didn't exist.

Following each pair of `<SCRIPT>` and `</SCRIPT>` tags with the HTML `<NOSCRIPT>` and `</NOSCRIPT>` tags allows you to control more precisely what folks using non-JavaScript-enabled browsers see when they visit your Web page. For example, the following code displays a message telling users that they need to use a JavaScript-enabled Web browser to get the most from your Web page:

```
...
</SCRIPT>
<NOSCRIPT>
You must be running a JavaScript-enabled Web browser, such as the latest version
          of Microsoft Internet Explorer or Netscape Navigator, to get the
          most from this Web page.

</NOSCRIPT>
```

Testing Your Script

When you have an HTML file that contains embedded JavaScript code, as shown previously in Listing 2-3, you're ready to test your JavaScript application! (This is the really fun part.)

To test a JavaScript application, all you need to do is load the JavaScript-containing HTML file into a JavaScript-supporting Web browser. Figure 2-3 shows you how the code in Listing 2-3 looks when it's loaded into the Netscape 7.1 browser.

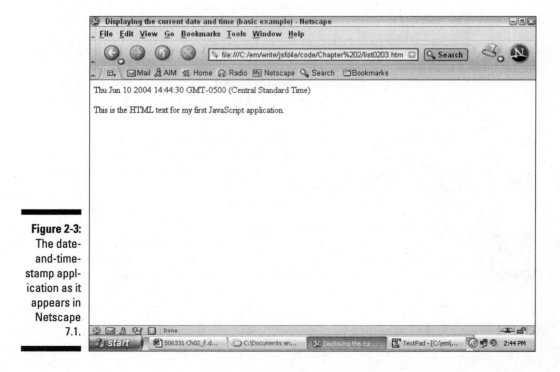

Figure 2-3: The date-and-time-stamp application as it appears in Netscape 7.1.

Note: You can find a fancier version of the date-and-time-stamp application in Chapter 3.

If you load the code in Listing 2-3 in your browser and see a Web page similar to the one shown in Figure 2-3, congratulations! You've just successfully tested your very first JavaScript script.

If you don't see a Web page similar to the one in Figure 2-3, however, don't despair. Chances are good that the problem is due to one of the following situations:

✔ **The correct HTML file isn't loaded.** If you created your HTML file from scratch, you might have inadvertently mistyped a statement or otherwise introduced a bug. No problem; you can fix the bug later. (Chapter 17 is packed with tips for debugging your scripts.) For now, try loading the bug-free `list0203.htm` file from the companion CD.

✔ **You're not using a JavaScript-enabled browser.** Make sure that you're using Microsoft Internet Explorer 6.0 (or higher) or Netscape Navigator 7.1 (or higher).

✔ **JavaScript support is turned off in your browser.** Netscape Navigator and Microsoft Internet Explorer both provide ways to turn off JavaScript support. When you turn off JavaScript support in your browser and then load a JavaScript-containing Web page, your browser ignores all the JavaScript code. It's as if it didn't exist!

To make sure that JavaScript support is turned on, do the following:

✔ **If you're using Netscape Navigator 7.x,** choose Edit➪Preferences and double-click the Advanced menu option to display the Scripts & Plugins menu selection. Click the Scripts & Plugins men selection and make sure that the Enable JavaScript for Navigator check box is selected.

✔ **If you're using Internet Explorer 6.x,** choose Tools➪Internet Options➪Security. Then select the Internet Web Content Zone, click the Custom Level button, and scroll down until you find the Active Scripting category. Finally, ensure that the Enable option (right under the Active Scripting option) is selected.

Chapter 3

JavaScript Language Basics

Although JavaScript is an awfully powerful language, the way you use it can be boiled down to just two major concepts: syntax and the JavaScript object model (also called the document object model).

Syntax refers to the rules that you must follow to write JavaScript code. Not many syntax rules exist, but you do need to understand them — just as you need to understand and follow the rules of English syntax to write a sentence that English-speaking folks can understand.

The document object model (DOM) refers to the Web page components, or objects, that you can access and manipulate by using JavaScript. In the same way that you need to have a vocabulary of English words before you can write a story in English, you need to be somewhat familiar with the DOM before you can write your own JavaScript scripts. (I devote Chapter 4 to the DOM.) This chapter arms you with the syntax knowledge that you need to write your own scripts!

JavaScript Syntax

The rules and regulations that govern how humans can communicate with the JavaScript interpreter — that piece of the Web browser that understands and executes JavaScript code — is called the JavaScript syntax. Although you might feel a little overwhelmed (especially at first!) with all the technicalities of JavaScript syntax, you can focus on just these few things, which are the building blocks of your code:

- **Comments:** Comments are human-readable (as opposed to JavaScript-interpreter-readable) descriptions you can add to your script to make your script easier to understand and maintain.

- **Conditionals:** Conditionals are logical constructs that you can add to your script to decide whether a particular condition is true or false at runtime. The most basic conditional is `if-else`.

- **Functions:** Functions are named groups of statements that you define once, and then reuse to your heart's content.

- **Loops:** Loops are specialized forms of conditionals. You can add a loop to your script that checks a particular condition multiple times, executing whatever JavaScript code you like, until that condition becomes true or false. Common examples of loops include the `for`, `while`, and `do-while` loops.

- **Operators:** Operators are the JavaScript answer to conjunctions. Operators include the commas, periods, and other symbols that you use to compare and assign values to variables.

- **Variables:** Variables are named placeholders that represent the bits of data that you work with in your scripts.

I discuss each of these syntactical building blocks in the following sections.

Don't keep your comments to yourself

The JavaScript interpreter ignores comments. Comments do have value, though; they're very useful for explaining things to human readers of your script. (Include yourself in this category, by the way — after you finish a script and put it aside for a few months, you might appreciate those comments!)

You can write JavaScript comments in two different ways. Either type of comment can appear anywhere in your script and as many times as you like.

The first type of comment is a single-line comment. It begins with two forward slashes, and it's good for only one line. Here's an example of a single-line comment.

```
// Single-line comments don't require an ending slash.
```

The second type of comment is a multiple-line comment. Because it spans multiple lines, you have to tell it where to start (by using a forward slash followed by an asterisk) and where to end (by using an asterisk and then a forward slash). For example:

```
/* This comment can span multiple lines. Always remember
to close it, though; if you forget, you'll get weird errors
when you try to display your script. */
```

Don't overlap or nest multiline comments in your JavaScript code. If you do, the JavaScript interpreter generates an error.

Remember that JavaScript scripts are the lines of code that come between the <SCRIPT> and </SCRIPT> tags in an HTML file. You can't use HTML comment characters (<!-- to begin a comment line and --> to end it) to create JavaScript comments, and you can't use JavaScript comment characters (// and /* */) to create HTML comments.

Mint conditionals

JavaScript offers several conditional expressions that you can use to test the value of a condition at runtime. The two most popular conditionals are the if-else and switch statements.

if-else

The if-else conditional expression is one of the most powerful constructs in JavaScript.

You use if-else to test a condition:

- ✔ If the condition is true, the JavaScript interpreter executes all the statements that follow the if clause.

- ✔ If the condition is false, the JavaScript interpreter executes all the statements that follow the else clause (if the else clause exists).

Here's the generic description of how to use if-else:

```
if (condition) {
    statements
}
[ else {
    statements
}]
```

The curly braces ({ and }) combine statements into one big block. For example, if you follow an if condition with three JavaScript statements, all of which are surrounded by curly braces, the JavaScript interpreter executes all three of those statements when the if condition is true.

The square brackets ([and]) mean that the entire else clause is optional. You don't actually put the square brackets in your JavaScript code; you just add the else clause if you want it or leave it off if you don't.

Suppose that you want to figure out which browser a user is running so that you can tailor your Web page accordingly. (As you see in Chapter 5, differences exist between the JavaScript support provided by Internet Explorer and Netscape Navigator.) Listing 3-1 shows how you can use if-else (and the built-in navigator object) to accomplish this goal.

Listing 3-1: JavaScript if-else Example

```
if (navigator.appName == "Microsoft Internet Explorer") {
    document.write("You're running Microsoft IE")
}
else {
    if (navigator.appName == "Netscape") {
        document.write("You're running Netscape")
    }

    else {
        document.write("You're not running Microsoft IE or Netscape")
    }
}
```

First, the JavaScript code in Listing 3-1 compares the value of the appName property of the built-in navigator object to the text string Microsoft Internet Explorer. (A text string is a group of characters that you manipulate as a single block.)

✔ If this condition is true (the value of appName is indeed Microsoft Internet Explorer), the JavaScript code performs the next statement, which displays You're running Microsoft IE on the Web page.

✔ If the condition is false (the value of appName isn't Microsoft Internet Explorer), the JavaScript code tests to see whether the value of appName is equal to Netscape:

   • If this second condition is true, the JavaScript interpreter displays You're running Netscape on the Web page.

   • If the second condition is false, the JavaScript interpreter displays You're not running Microsoft IE or Netscape on the Web page.

You might notice that Listing 3-1 contains two `if-else` statements, one nested inside the other. Technically speaking, you can nest as many `if-else` statements as you want. If you run across a situation in which you need more than one or two nested `if-else` statements to do the job, however, you might want to consider the `switch` statement (which I describe in the next section) instead. The `switch` statement is much more efficient at testing a condition multiple times.

Some JavaScript programmers end each statement with a semicolon, like this:

```
if (a == b) { // if a is equal to b
    c = d;      // assign the value of d to the c variable,
    e = f;      // assign the value of f to the e variable,
                // and assign the string "American Beauty"
                // to the variable called favoriteMovie
    favoriteMovie = "American Beauty";
}
```

Semicolons are optional in JavaScript, with one exception. If you place more than one JavaScript statement on the same line, you must separate those statements with semicolons. For example:

```
// Wrong!
c = d   e = f   favoriteMovie = "American Beauty"

// Correct (if a bit hard to read)
c = d; e = f; favoriteMovie = "American Beauty";
```

switch

The `switch` statement provides an easy way to check an expression for a bunch of different values without resorting to a string of `if-else` statements.

Here's the syntax:

```
switch (expression) {
        case label :
            statement
            break
        case label :
            statement
            break
        ...
        default : statement
}
```

Suppose you want to examine a value and find out whether it matches one of a number of predefined values. Listing 3-2 shows how you can go about it by using the `switch` statement.

Listing 3-2:   Using the switch Statement to Match Values

```
switch (month) {
    case 0 :
        displayMonth = "January"
        break
    case 1 :
        displayMonth = "February"
        break
    case 2 :
        displayMonth = "March"
        break    case 3 :
        displayMonth = "April"
        break
    case 4 :
        displayMonth = "May"
        break
    case 5 :
        displayMonth = "June"
        break
    case 6 :
        displayMonth = "July"
        break
    case 7 :
        displayMonth = "August"
        break
    case 8 :
        displayMonth = "September"
        break
    case 9 :
        displayMonth = "October"
        break
    case 10 :
        displayMonth = "November"
        break
    case 11 :
        displayMonth = "December"
        break

    default: displayMonth = "INVALID"
}
```

The code shown in Listing 3-2 tests the value of the month variable. If month contains the number 0, the variable displayMonth is set to January. If month contains the number 1, displayMonth is set to February — and so on, all the way through the 12 months of the year.

The companion CD contains a date_and_time_formatted.htm file, a working copy of the script in Listing 3-2.

Note that if you forget to finish each case with a break statement (and it's easy to do), the interpreter falls through, meaning that it performs all the statements that it finds until it either

- Finds a break
- Detects the end of the switch statement

For instance, in Listing 3-2, if you removed all the break statements, a month value of 0 would cause displayMonth to be set not to January, as it should be, but to INVALID instead.

In some cases, you may want to leave out the break statement on purpose to force the JavaScript interpreter to fall through two or more cases. Doing so allows you to group values easily. For example, the following code treats month values of 0, 1, or 2 (which correspond to January, February, and March, respectively) the same, by assigning the value Q1 to the displayQuarter variable. Months 3, 4, and 5 (April, May, and June, respectively) are treated the same, by assigning the value Q2 to the displayQuarter variable; and so on.

```
switch (monthId) {
  case 0:
  case 1:
  case 2:
    displayQuarter = "Q1";
    break;
  case 3:
  case 4:
  case 5:
    displayQuarter = "Q2";
    break;
  case 6:
  case 7:
  case 8:
    displayQuarter = "Q3";
    break;
  case 9:
  case 10:
  case 11:
    displayQuarter = "Q4";
    break;
}
```

Fully functioning

A function is a named group of JavaScript statements that you can declare once, near the top of your script, and call over and over again. Adding a reusable function to your script — instead of adding several slightly different versions of the same code — cuts down on the amount of typing that you need to do (yay!), as well as the number of potential bugs in your script (double yay!).

Organizing your script into functions, like organizing your closet, might seem like loads of up-front work for nothing — after all, you don't have to do it. Your script and your closet can be functional even if they're messy. The payoff comes when you have to quickly find a problem (or the perfect brown leather belt) hiding somewhere in all that confusion!

Declaring a function

Here's the syntax for a function declaration:

```
function name([parameter] [, parameter] [..., parameter]) {
    statements
    return value
}
```

And here's an example:

```
function calculateTotal(numberOrdered, itemPrice) {
    var totalPrice = (numberOrdered * itemPrice) + salesTax
    return totalPrice
}
```

This code snippet declares a `calculateTotal` function that accepts two arguments: `numberOrdered` and `itemPrice`. The function uses these two arguments (plus an additional variable called `salesTax`) to calculate the `totalPrice` variable, which it then returns to the JavaScript code that originally called it.

Your function can take as many arguments as you want it to (including none at all), separated by commas. You generally refer to these argument values in the body of the function (otherwise, why bother to use them at all?), so be sure to name them something meaningful. In other words, I could have substituted `x` and `y` for `numberOrdered` and `itemPrice`, and the code would work just as well. It just wouldn't be very easy to read or maintain!

Because the optional `return` statement is so important, I devote a whole section to its use. (See the section "Returning a value from a function.")

Calling a function

After you declare a function, which I describe in the preceding section, you can call that function. You call a function by specifying the name of the function, followed by an open parenthesis, comma-delimited parameters, and a closing parenthesis. For example:

```
alert("Total purchases come to " +
     calculateTotal(10, 19.95))
```

Notice that you can embed a function call within another expression. In this example, calculateTotal(10, 19.95) is actually part of the expression being sent to the alert() method. (You find out all about methods in Chapter 4, but for now, you can think of them as special kinds of functions.)

Returning a value from a function

You use the return statement to return a value from a function. To understand why you might want to return a value from a function, imagine yourself asking a friend to look up some information for you. If your friend went ahead and did the research but neglected to pass it along to you, you'd be pretty disappointed. Well, in this case, you're just like a bit of JavaScript code calling a function, and your friend is the function that you're calling. Basically, no matter how many useful things a function does, if it doesn't return some sort of result to the piece of code that needs it, it hasn't finished its job.

The syntax for the return keyword is simple:

```
return expression
```

Here's how it looks in action:

```
function calculateTotal(numberOrdered, itemPrice) {

    var totalPrice = (numberOrdered * itemPrice) + salesTax
    return totalPrice
} // Now the function is defined, so it can be called

...
document.write("The total amount to remit to us is " + calculateTotal(3, 4.99))
```

In this example code, the document.write() method calls the calculate Total() function. The calculateTotal() function returns the value of the totalPrice variable, which the document.write() method then displays on the Web page.

Loop-the-loop

Loops are powerful constructs that you can use to reiterate a series of JavaScript statements over and over again. JavaScript supports a number of loops you can choose from, including the `for` loop and `for-in` loops, the `while` loop, and the `do-while` loop. As you see in the following section, each loop is tailored for specific kinds of situations.

The for loop

The `for` loop lets you step through, or traverse, a number of items quickly and easily. As an example, suppose that you want to find out whether users have a particular plug-in installed in their Web browsers. You can use the `for` loop to step through each of the plug-ins one by one.

First, take a peek at the generic form of the `for` loop.

```
for ([initial expression]; [condition]; [update expression]) {
statements
}
```

The `for` loop introduces three terms that might be new to you: the initial expression, the condition, and the update expression. Here's how it all works:

1. The JavaScript interpreter looks at the initial expression.

   The initial expression is almost always a number (usually 0 because that's the number JavaScript arrays begin with) assigned to a variable, such as `var i=0`.

2. The JavaScript interpreter looks at the condition to see whether it's true.

   The condition compares the variable in Step 1 to some programmer-defined constant; for example, `i<10`. If the value of `i` is indeed less than 10, for instance, the `i<10` statement is true.

3. If the value of the condition is `true`, the JavaScript interpreter performs all the statements in the body of the `for` loop, and then it evaluates the update expression.

   The update expression typically increments the initial expression by 1; for example, `i++` or `eachOne++`. (Although ++ looks kind of funny, it's not a typo. It's an operator that adds 1 to the variable that it's next to. Think of `eachOne++` as a shorthand way of typing `eachOne = eachOne + 1`.)

4. Now that the variable has been bumped up, the JavaScript interpreter goes back to Step 2 to see whether value of the condition is `true`, and if it is, the whole thing starts over again. (That's why it's called a loop!)

   Of course, at some point the condition's value is no longer `true`. When that happens, the JavaScript interpreter hops out of the `for` loop and picks up again at the first statement after the loop.

It's possible to create a `for` loop condition that always has a `true` value. The easiest way to make this mistake is to specify an update condition that doesn't actually update the initial expression (for example, leaving off the ++ in the example code preceding steps.) Creating a loop condition that is always `true` and can never be changed or set to `false` is known as creating an endless or infinite loop because the JavaScript interpreter evaluates and performs the same statements in the body of the loop endlessly! (Okay, never is a long time. In practice, the interpreter keeps evaluating it until you kill the Web browser session. I've found that turning off the machine works nicely.)

Here's an example of the `for` loop in action.

```
for (var i = 1; i <= 10; i++) {
    document.writeln(i)
}
```

The file detecting_embedded_objects.htm, which you find on the companion CD, contains an example of the for loop in action.

Here's what's going on in the preceding code snippet:

1. `var i = 1` creates a variable called i and sets it to equal 1.

2. `i <= 10` tests to see whether the i variable is less than or equal to 10.

3. The first time through, i is 1, and 1 is less than or equal to 10, so the statement in the body of the `for` loop (`document.writeln(i)`) is performed. (The value of i appears on the Web page.)

4. `i++` adds one to i.

5. `i <= 10` tests to see whether i is still less than or equal to 10.

6. The second time through, i is 2, and 2 is less than 10, so the statement in the body of the `for` loop (`document.writeln(i)`) is performed. (The value of i appears.)

7. Now the whole thing repeats from Step 3. The JavaScript interpreter adds one to i, tests the variable to see whether it's still less than or equal to 10, and so on, for as many times as i satisfies the condition.

Nothing is magical about the i variable name. You could just as easily have named your variable `numberOfTimesToPrint`, `numberOfPigsOrdered`, or `Fred`. The i variable name in `for` loops just happens to be a convention, nothing more.

As you might expect, the following appears on-screen when the `for` loop is executed:

```
1 2 3 4 5 6 7 8 9 10
```

The for-in loop

If you like `for`, you'll love the `for-in` loop. You use the `for-in` loop for loop-ing, or iterating, through all properties of an object, like so:

```
for (var in object) {
    statements
}
```

As an example, here's a function that you can use to loop through all pro-perties of a given object and display each property's name and associated value:

```
function displayProperties(inputObject, inputObjectName){

    var result = ""

    for (var eachProperty in inputObject) {

        result += inputObjectName + "." + eachProperty +
    " = " + inputObject[eachProperty] + "<BR>"
    }

    return result
}
```

This code might appear confusing at first, but it's pretty straightforward when you understand what the `for-in` loop does:

1. The code declares a function called `displayProperties()` that accepts two arguments: `inputObject` and `inputObjectName`. Here's one way to call this function:

   ```
   document.writeln(displayProperties(document, "document"))
   ```

2. The JavaScript interpreter hops up to the `displayProperties()` defini-tion, only this time it substitutes the `document` object for the argument `inputObject` and substitutes the `"document"` string for the argument `inputObjectName`.

3. Inside the `for-in` loop, the JavaScript interpreter loops through all prop-erties of the `document` object. Each time it comes to a new property, the interpreter assigns the new property to the `eachProperty` variable. Then the interpreter constructs a string and adds the string to the end of the `result` variable.

   After the `for-in` loop has looped through all properties of the `document` object, the `result` variable holds a nice long string containing the names and values of all properties in the `document` object. (For the skinny on objects, flip to Chapter 4.)

Displaying (or dumping, as it's called in programmerese) the property values of an object can be useful when you're trying to track down an error in your script. A method like `document.writeln()` enables you to know exactly what the interpreter thinks objects look like (which is sometimes quite different from the way you think they look).

Take a look at the `ch3_forin.htm` file to see an example of the `for-in` loop.

The while loop

The `while` loop's job is to do something — that is, to execute one or more JavaScript statements — while some programmer-defined condition is true.

Obviously, then, you want to make sure that one of the statements in the body of your `while` loop changes the `while` condition in some way so that at some point it becomes false.

Here's the generic version of the `while` loop.

```
while (condition) {
    statements
}
```

In the following code, you see an actual JavaScript example of the `while` loop in action.

```
var totalInventory=700
var numberPurchased=200
var numberSales=0

while (totalInventory > numberPurchased) {
    totalInventory = totalInventory - numberPurchased
    numberSales++
}
document.writeln("Our stock supply will support " +
numberSales + " of these bulk sales")
```

Step into the JavaScript interpreter's virtual shoes for a minute and take a look at how this all works! (Remember, you're the JavaScript interpreter now, so be serious.)

> While the total inventory is more than the number purchased. . . . Well, 700 is greater than 200. Okay. Subtract the number purchased from the total inventory and bump up the number of sales by 1. Number of sales is now 1. That's one loop down.

> While the total inventory is more than the number purchased. . . . Hmm. Total inventory is 500 now, and that's still greater than 200, so I need to subtract the number purchased from the total inventory and add another 1 to the number of sales. Number of sales is now 2. Two loops down.

While the total inventory is more than the number purchased. . . . Okay, total inventory is 300 now, which is still greater than 200. Subtract number purchased from total inventory, add 1 to the number of sales. Number of sales is now 3. Three loops down.

While the total inventory is more than the number purchased. . . . Hey! It's not! Total inventory is 100, and the number purchased is 200. I'm outta here.

Here's what I'll write to the screen: Our stock supply will support 3 of these bulk sales.

Nice to know how the other half thinks, isn't it?

The do-while loop

The do-while loop is mighty close to the while loop that I describe in the preceding section. The main difference between the two loops is that unlike while, which might never be executed depending on whether the value of the while condition is true when the loop begins to execute, the do-while loop always executes at least once.

Take a look at the syntax for the do-while loop:

```
do {
    statements
}
while (condition)
```

Here's a real-life example:

```
var article = "a"

do {
    var answer = prompt("Would you like to purchase "
+ article
            + " t-shirt? If so, enter the size.", "L")
    article = "ANOTHER"
}
while (answer != null)
```

The first time this JavaScript code executes, the user sees a dialog box containing this message: Would you like to order a t-shirt? If so, enter the size. The second time through the do-while loop (and for each time thereafter that the user clicks the OK button on the dialog box) this message appears: Would you like to order ANOTHER t-shirt? If so, enter the size.

Load up the data_gathering.htm file to see a working example of the do-while code shown here.

Never mind! Changing your mind with continue and break

The `continue` and `break` statements are both used inside loops to change how the loops behave. (The `break` statement can be used also inside a `switch` statement, as the example earlier in this chapter demonstrates.) The `continue` and `break` statements do slightly different things and can be used in the same loop (although they don't have to be).

When the JavaScript interpreter encounters a `break` statement, the interpreter breaks out of the loop that it's currently processing and starts interpreting again at the first line following the loop.

In contrast, the `continue` statement also tells the JavaScript interpreter to stop what it's doing, but on a somewhat smaller scale. The `continue` statement tells the interpreter to stop the loop it's currently processing and hop back up to the beginning of the loop again, to continue as normal.

The `continue` and `break` statements are useful for exceptions to the rule. For example, you might want to process all items the same way except for two special cases. Just remember that `break` breaks out of a loop altogether, and `continue` stops iteration execution, but then continues the loop.

Here is an example of the `break` statement used inside a `while` loop:

```
var totalInventory=700, numberPurchased=200, numberSales=0
while (totalInventory > numberPurchased) {
    totalInventory=totalInventory - numberPurchased
    numberSales++
    if (numberSales > 2) {
        break
    }
}
```

When the number of sales is greater than 2 (in other words, when the number of sales reaches 3), the `break` statement causes the JavaScript interpreter to hop out of the `while` loop altogether.

And here's an example of `continue` used inside a `for` loop:

```
for (var i = 1; i <= 20; i++) {
    if (i == 13) {  // superstitious; don't print number 13
        continue
    }
    document.writeln(i)
}
```

In this code snippet, when the `i` variable contains the value 13, the JavaScript interpreter stops what it's doing. It does not execute the `writeln()` method but continues on with the next iteration of the `for` loop (that is, the interpreter sets the `i` variable equal to 14 and keeps going).

You can test this scrap of code for yourself. It should produce the following result:

```
1 2 3 4 5 6 7 8 9 10 11 12 14 15 16 17 18 19 20
```

Operators are standing by

Operators are like conjunctions. Remember fifth-grade English? (Or if you were a cartoon connoisseur, maybe you remember "Conjunction Junction." "And, but, and or, get you pretty far. . . .") Ahem.

Operators, like conjunctions, enable you to join multiple phrases together to form expressions. If you're familiar with addition and subtraction, you're familiar with operators. Two categories of operators exist:

- **Binary:** Two items (or operands) must be sandwiched on either side of the operator.

- **Unary:** Only one operand is required.

Table 3-1 gives you a rundown of the basic operators. The JavaScript interpreter always evaluates the expression to the right of the equal sign first, and only then does it assign the evaluated value to the variable. (**Note:** The two exceptions to this rule include the unary decrement operator (--), and the unary increment operator (++). In these cases, if you place the operand after the operator — as in the expression --1 — the JavaScript interpreter evaluates the expression before evaluating anything else in the statement, including any assignment. Check out Table 3-1 for more information about the decrement and increment operators.)

Table 3-1		JavaScript Operators		
In all these examples, x is initially set to 11.				
Operator	*Meaning*	*Example*	*Result*	*How Come?*
%	modulus	x = x % 5	x = 1	11 / 5 = 2 with 1 remainder, so modulus returns 1 in this case
++	increment	x = x++	x = 11	++ is applied after assignment when you put it after x
		x = ++x	x = 12	++ is applied before assignment when you put it *before* x
--	decrement	x = x--	x = 11	-- is applied after assignment when you put it after the var
		x = --x	x = 10	-- is applied before assignment when you put it before the var

In all these examples, x is initially set to 11.				
Operator	**Meaning**	**Example**	**Result**	**How Come?**
-	negation	x = -x	x = -11	Turns positive numbers negative and vice versa
+	addition	x = x + x	x = 22	11 + 11 is 22

Some of the operators are pretty normal (addition and negation, for example). The increment and decrement operators are a little weird, though, because not only are they a new thing (you never see ++ or -- outside a computer program listing), but depending on whether you put them before or after the variable, they behave differently, as I describe in Table 3-1.

Operator precedence

Just as in math, an order of evaluation is applied to a statement that contains multiple operators. Unless you set phrases off with parentheses, the JavaScript interpreter observes the precedence order shown in Table 3-2 (from the semicolon, which has the lowest order of precedence, to the parentheses, which has the highest).

Table 3-2	**JavaScript Operator Precedence (From Lowest to Highest)**
Operator	**Syntax**
semicolon	; (separates JavaScript statements that appear on the same line)
comma	,
assignment	=, +=, -=, *=, /=, %=
conditional	? :
logical "or"	||
logical "and"	&&
equality	==, !=
relational	<, <=, >, <=
mathematical	+, -, *, /, %
unary	!, -, ++, -- (negation, increment, and decrement operators)
call	( )

So, how exactly does operator precedence work? Well, suppose the JavaScript interpreter runs into the following statement in your script:

```
alert("Grand total: " + getTotal() + (3 * 4 / 10) + tax++)
```

The interpreter knows that its job is to evaluate the statement, so the first thing that it does is scan everything between the alert() parentheses. When it finds the next set of parentheses, it knows that's where it needs to start. It thinks to itself, "Okay, first I'll get the return value from getTotal(). Then I'll evaluate (3 * 4 / 10). Within (3 * 4 / 10), I'll do the division first, and then the multiplication. Now I'll add one to the tax variable. Okay, the last thing I have to do is add the whole thing to come up with a string to display."

Frankly, it's okay if you can't remember the precedence order. Just group expressions in parentheses like you did back in high school algebra class. Because parentheses outrank all the other operators, you can force JavaScript to override its default precedence order and evaluate expressions the way that makes the most sense to you!

Assignment operators

Assignment operators enable you to assign values to variables. Besides being able to make a straight one-to-one assignment, though, you can also use some assignment operators as a kind of shorthand to bump up a value based on another value. Table 3-3 describes how this process works.

Table 3-3	JavaScript Assignment Operators (From Lowest to Highest Precedence)	
Assignment	**Alternate Approach**	**Description**
x = y	(none)	(assignment)
x += y	x = x + y	(addition)
x -= y	x = x - y	(subtraction)
x *= y	x = x * y	(multiplication)
x /= y	x = x / y	(division)
x %= y	x = x % y	(modulus)

The order of precedence in Table 3-3 is from lowest to highest, so the JavaScript interpreter first evaluates any modulus operations first, then division, then multiplication, and so on.

Comparison operators

When comparing two values or expressions, you can compare for equality, as shown in Table 3-4.

Table 3-4	JavaScript Comparison Operators	
Operator	*Example*	*Meaning*
==	x == y	x is equal to y
!=	x != y	x is not equal to y
<	x < y	x is less than y
>	x > y	x is greater than y
<=	x <= y	x is less than or equal to y
>=	x >= y	x is greater than or equal to y
?:	x = (y < 0) ? -y : y	if y is less than zero, assign -y to x; otherwise, assign y to x

Logical operators

Logical operators take logical (also called Boolean) operands, and they also return Boolean values. A Boolean value can be just one of two possibilities: `true` or `false`. When you see two expressions separated by a logical operator, the JavaScript interpreter first resolves the expressions to see whether each is `true` or `false`, and then resolves the entire statement:

- ✔ If an expression equates to a nonzero value, that expression is considered to be `true`.

- ✔ If an expression equates to zero, that expression is considered to be `false`.

Table 3-5 describes the logical operators available in JavaScript.

Table 3-5	JavaScript Logical Operators	
Operator	*Meaning*	*Example*
&&	and	if (x == y && a != b)
||	or	if (x < y || a < b)
!	not	if (!x)

The new and this operators

Two operators are designed especially to work with objects: new and this.

The new operator allows you to create your very own objects in JavaScript. (For a list of built-in objects, check out Chapter 4.)

When you use the new operator with a function that defines a type of object, you can create an instance (or a dozen instances) of that type of object.

The best way to explain this is by an example. Suppose that you want to write a script that lets users input information about multiple people — family members, say, or employees. You can create a generic function called person and then use the new and this operators to allow users to create multiple instances of the person function and customize each instance. Here's an example of a simple, generic person function:

```
function person(inputName, inputAge, inputSex, inputOccupation) {
    this.name = inputName
    this.age = inputAge
    this.sex = inputSex
    this.occupation = inputOccupation
}
```

The person() function that you see here takes four parameters, one each for inputName, inputAge, inputSex, and inputOccupation. Then the person() function immediately assigns these input values to its own instance attributes. (The this.name variable is set to the inputName variable, the this.age variable to the inputAge variable, and so on.)

Watch out!

A common mistake, even (especially?) among seasoned programmers, is to use a single equal sign (=, an *assignment* operator) in place of a double equal sign (==, a *comparison* operator) or vice versa. The statement x = 6 *assigns* the value of 6 to x. The x == 6 statement, on the other hand, *compares* 6 to x but doesn't assign any value at all! Mistakenly typing == when you mean = (or vice versa) is a very common programming bug.

```
if (x = 6) { // At first glance, this looks like it compares 6 to x, but it doesn't. It
        assigns 6 to x!
    document.writeln("x is 6, all right.")
}
```

In this example, the `this` keyword is shorthand for the `person` function. The JavaScript interpreter knows that you're inside a function called `person()`, so it automatically substitutes the function name for the `this` keyword so that you don't have to spell out the whole function name.

Now, whenever you want to create a specific, concrete instance of the `person` function, here's what you do:

```
var jennifer = new person("Jennifer McLaughlan", 33, "F", "lion tamer")
```

This code snippet uses the `new` operator in conjunction with the predefined, generic `person()` function to create a specific instance of person whose name is Jennifer McLaughlan, age is 33, sex is F, and occupation is lion tamer.

After the preceding statement is performed, you can use the `jennifer` object as you would any built-in object in JavaScript.

If you think that objects with properties but no methods are kind of boring, you're right. Here's how you add your own methods to the objects that you create:

```
function ftalk(kindOfPet){
    if (kindOfPet == "dog") {
        document.writeln("bow-wow!")
  }
  else {
        if (kindOfPet == "cat") {
            document.writeln("meow-meow-meow")
        }
    }
}
function pet(inputName, inputKind, inputColor) {
    this.name = inputName
    this.kind = inputKind
    this.color = inputColor
    this.talk = ftalk(inputKind)
}
```

Bear with me here; it all makes sense when you see it in action!

The following code first creates an instance of `pet` and names that instance `Boots`, and then it calls the `talk()` method associated with `Boots`.

```
Boots = new pet("Boots", "cat", "orange striped");
Boots.talk;
```

Here's how the JavaScript interpreter executes these two JavaScript statements:

1. The first statement passes three variables to the pet() constructor function and assigns the resulting object to the Boots variable.

   When this first statement finishes processing, the Boots variable contains an object associated with the following three properties:

   • Boots.name = "Boots"

   • Boots.kind = "cat"

   • Boots.color = "orange striped"

2. The second statement (Boots.talk) passes the value of Boots.kind, which is "cat", to the ftalk() function.

3. The ftalk() function contains an if statement that says, "If the input variable is cat, print meow-meow-meow to the screen."

   So, because the string "cat" was passed to the ftalk() function, you see meow-meow-meow on the screen.

If creating your own objects and methods isn't clear to you right now, it will be after you've had a chance to load and play with the ch2_new_this.htm file, located on the companion CD.

Working with variables

A variable is a named placeholder for a value. You use the var keyword to construct an expression that first declares a variable and then (optionally) initializes its value. To declare a variable, you type something like this:

```
var myCat;
```

This tells the JavaScript interpreter "Yo, here comes a variable, and name it myCat, will you?"

Initializing a variable means setting a variable equal to some value, which you typically do at the same time you declare the variable. Here's how you might initialize the variable myCat:

```
var myCat = "Fluffy"
```

Technically, you can declare a variable in JavaScript without using the var keyword, like so: myCat = "Fluffy". However, using the var keyword to declare all your variables is a good idea because it helps the JavaScript interpreter properly scope variables with the same name.

As of this writing, the next version of JavaScript, version 2.0 — due to be finalized later this year and (with luck) supported by upcoming browser versions — provides for the strongly typed variables with which C and C++ programmers are familiar. What this means to you is that when browsers support JavaScript 2.0, you may use variable descriptors such as integer and number to declare upfront precisely what kind of value you want each variable to contain. Until then, however, no variable descriptors are necessary.

After you declare a variable — whether you use the var keyword or not — you can reset its value later in the script by using the assignment operator (=). The name of the variable can be any legal identifier (you want to use letters and numbers, not special characters), and the value can be any legal expression. (A legal expression is any properly punctuated expression that you see represented in this chapter: an if-else expression, an assignment expression, and so on.)

A variable is valid only when it's in scope. When a variable is in scope, it's been declared between the same curly brace boundaries as the statement that's trying to access it. For example, if you define a variable named firstName inside a function called displayReport(), you can refer to the variable only inside the displayReport() function's curly braces. If you try to access firstName inside another function, you get an error. If you want to reuse a variable among functions (shudder — that way lies madness), you can declare that variable near the top of your script before any functions are declared. That way, the variable's scope is the entire script, and all the functions get to see it. Take a look at the following code example:

```
...
function displayReport() {
    var firstName = document.myForm.givenName.value
    ...
    alert("Click OK to see the report for " + firstName)
    // Using firstName here is fine; it was declared
    // inside the same set of curly braces.
    ...
}
function displayGraph() {
    alert("Here's the graph for " + firstName) // Error!
    // firstName wasn't defined inside this
    // function's curly braces!
    ...
}
```

As you can see from the comments in the this code fragment, it's perfectly okay to use the firstName variable inside the displayReport() function because the firstName variable is in scope anywhere inside the displayReport() function. It's not okay, however, to use firstName inside displayGraph(). As far as displayGraph() is concerned, no such animal as firstName has been declared inside its scope!

Literally speaking

Sometimes you want to use a number, a string, or some other value that you know for a fact will never change. For example, suppose that you want to write a script that uses pi in some calculation. Instead of creating a pi variable and assigning it the value of 1.31415, you can use the number 1.31415 directly in your calculations. Values that aren't stored in variables are called *literals*.

Here are a few examples of using literals in JavaScript:

```
alert("Sorry, you entered your e-mail address incorrectly.")//string literal
x = 1.31415 * someVariable // floating-point literal
if (theAnswer == true) // boolean literal
document.write("The total number of users is " + 1234)//integer literal
```

Putting It All Together: Building JavaScript Expressions and Statements

In "JavaScript Syntax," earlier in this chapter, you get familiar with the nuts and bolts of the JavaScript language. In this section, I demonstrate how to string these components together to create JavaScript expressions and statements.

JavaScript scripts are made up of JavaScript statements, which in turn are made up of JavaScript expressions. A JavaScript expression is any combination of variables, operators, literals (nonvarying values), and keywords that can be evaluated by the JavaScript interpreter.

For example, the following are all valid JavaScript expressions:

```
new Date()

numberSold * salesPrice

"Thanks for visiting my site, " + document.myForm.yourName.value
```

These three examples are each slightly different, but they all have one thing in common: They can all be evaluated to something. The first example evaluates to the current date; the second, to a number; the third, to a string. (A string is a group of characters that you manipulate as a single block.)

To create a JavaScript statement, all you need to do is put together one or more JavaScript expressions (shown in bold in the following code). For example:

```
var todays_date = new Date();

calculateTotal(numberSold * salesPrice);

alert("Thanks for visiting my site, " + document.myForm.yourName.value);
```

In the first statement shown here, the current date is assigned to a variable called `todays_date`. In the second statement, the number produced by multiplying the `numberSold` and `salesPrice` variables is passed to the `calculateTotal()` function. And in the third example statement, the `"Thanks for visiting my site "` string appears in a dialog box.

The difference between a JavaScript expression and a JavaScript statement might seem esoteric at first, but understanding this difference pays big dividends in the long run. It might help if you think of a JavaScript expression as a sentence fragment and a JavaScript statement as a complete sentence. Although an interoffice memo composed entirely of sentence fragments might not cause you any problems (unless your vocation happens to be teaching English), a JavaScript script composed of expressions does cause problems — in the form of runtime errors.

To prevent these errors (and to save the time you'd spend debugging them), you need to construct complete JavaScript statements. In the following sections, I use three useful scripts to demonstrate how to do just that.

The browser-detection script

Back in the old days, before the Web came along, developers knew exactly what hardware and software their audience would use to run their applications before they wrote a lick of code. (In other words, these developers knew their applications' target platforms in advance.) Using this information, developers could implement their applications with confidence, secure in the knowledge that their application code would behave in the field just as it did in their testing labs.

Not so on the Web. Users can choose to view Web pages with whatever target platform they choose. They might, for instance, use a Mac, a PC, a UNIX box, or a hand-held device running some version of Netscape Navigator, Internet Explorer, or any of the other dozens of Web browsers that are available on the market. Unfortunately, your users' choices affect their ability to run your JavaScript-enabled Web pages, as you see in this chapter.

Can't we all just get along? The ECMA standard

Netscape (with some help from Sun Microsystems) invented JavaScript clear back in the early 1990s, so it's no surprise that JavaScript support first appeared in Netscape's browser (Netscape Navigator 2.0, if you're a history buff).

Soon after, Microsoft released version 3.0 of Internet Explorer, which featured support for their own JavaScript-compatible scripting language — called *JScript*. Minor differences existed between these two browsers' scripting implementations, however, and as each successive version appeared, those differences continued to grow.

In 1998, Netscape decided to hand over the task of creating a formal JavaScript standard to the ECMA, an international standards body comprising companies from all over the world. (Both Netscape and Microsoft are ECMA members.) In theory, this was a great thing. It allowed a relatively impartial group of folks to decide the best, most efficient way to implement a cross-browser Web scripting language. Unfortunately — in software as in life — the reality of real-world implementation hasn't quite yet achieved the perfection promised by the standard.

The ECMAScript language specification, called ECMA-262, describes how a scripting language *should* be implemented in an ECMA-compliant browser, not how it *is* implemented. So even though ECMAScript has the potential to unify JavaScript implementations and guarantee developers a consistent, cross-browser JavaScript execution platform, the differences in JavaScript support still exist between the latest Navigator and Internet Explorer browsers. One reason for these differences is the inevitable lag time between creating a standard and then scurrying to implement and release it. Another reason is the inherent tendency of software companies to embellish standards with additional, proprietary features. (The same tendency that led to the need for a standard in the first place!)

The bottom line is this: Although ECMAScript offers the potential for increased consistency across browsers, the final word on JavaScript implementation comes from the browsers themselves — *not* the specification.

The two latest versions of the most popular Web browsers — Internet Explorer and Netscape Navigator — do support JavaScript. But despite their creators' claims of support for something called the ECMA standard (created by the European Computer Manufacturers Association) both browsers support slightly different versions of the following elements:

- ✔ The JavaScript language
- ✔ The document object model that the JavaScript language was designed to access

Unfortunately, no single up-to-date source exists that describes which JavaScript features are supported in which version of which browser. Your best bet is to visit Netscape's and Microsoft's JavaScript documentation pages for the latest in feature support:

- http://channels.netscape.com/ns/browsers/default.jsp
- www.microsoft.com/windows/ie/default.htm

What this means is that if you want to use a JavaScript feature that Internet Explorer supports (but that Netscape Navigator doesn't), you face three choices:

- **Assume that everyone who visits your Web site is running Internet Explorer.** This assumption might be correct if you're creating an intranet application (an application targeted for use on a company's private network); in this case, you might know that all the company's employees have Internet Explorer installed. However, if you want to make your pages available on the World Wide Web, this assumption isn't a good one. When you make it, you risk alienating the visitors who surf to your page with Netscape or some other non-Microsoft browser.

- **Don't use the feature.** You can choose to use only those JavaScript features that are truly cross-platform; that is, JavaScript features that work the same way in both Internet Explorer and Netscape Navigator. (In most cases, this is the easiest approach, assuming that you can keep up with the rapidly changing JavaScript support provided in each new browser version.) In some cases, however, avoiding a feature might not be an option (for example, if you're creating a page for your boss or a client).

- **Create a script that detects which browser your visitors are running and tailor your pages on-the-fly accordingly.** This option gives you the best of both worlds: You get to use the specialized browser features that you want, and yet you don't alienate users running different browsers. (You do, however, have to create multiple pages to support multiple browsers, which increases your workload.)

In Listing 3-3, I demonstrate the final option in the preceding list: a script that recognizes whether a user is running Internet Explorer, Netscape Navigator, or some other browser. The script then displays an appropriate Web page. Figure 3-1 shows you how the script appears when loaded into Netscape 7.1, and Figure 3-2 shows you how it appears when it's loaded into Internet Explorer 6.0.

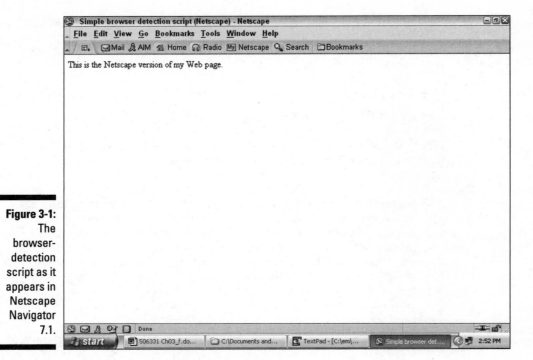

Figure 3-1:
The browser-detection script as it appears in Netscape Navigator 7.1.

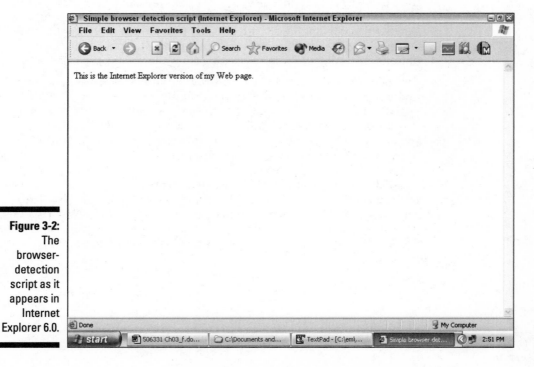

Figure 3-2:
The browser-detection script as it appears in Internet Explorer 6.0.

You can experiment with the code shown in Listing 3-3: Just load the file
`list0302.htm`, which you find on the companion CD.

Listing 3-3:   The Browser-Detection Script

```
<HTML>
<HEAD><TITLE>Simple browser detection script</TITLE>
<SCRIPT LANGUAGE="JavaScript" "TYPE="text/javascript">
<!-- Hide from browsers that do not support JavaScript

// If the user is running IE, automatically load the
// HTML file ie_version.htm
// Beginning of an if/else statement:
// "Microsoft Internet Explorer" is a string literal
// == is a comparison operator
if (navigator.appName == "Microsoft Internet Explorer") {
    // "ie_version.htm" is a string literal
    window.location = "ie_version.htm"
    // = is a comparison operator

}

// Otherwise, if the user is running Netscape, load the
// HTML file netscape_version.htm
else {
    Nested if/else statement:
    if (navigator.appName == "Netscape") {
    // == is a comparison operator
        window.location = "netscape_version.htm"
        // = is a comparison operator
    }

// If the user is running some other browser,
// display a message and continue loading this generic
// Web page.
    else {
        document.write("You're not running Microsoft IE or Netscape.")
    }
}

// --> Finish hiding
</SCRIPT>
</HEAD>
<BODY>
This is the generic version of my Web page.
</BODY>
</HTML>
```

The code that you see in Listing 3-3 combines comments, conditionals, and
operators to create two complete JavaScript statements.

As you read through the code, notice the following:

- The `appName` property of the built-in `navigator` object is preloaded with one of two text strings: "Microsoft Internet Explorer" (if the loading browser is Internet Explorer) or "Netscape" (if the loading browser is Netscape Navigator).

- Setting the `window` property of the `location` object equal to a new Web page causes that new Web page to load automatically.

Determining which brand of browser a user runs is relatively easy, as you can see by the code in Listing 3-3. However, determining the browser version is much trickier — and beyond the scope of this book. (Although the built-in `navigator` object does indeed contain useful properties such as `appCodeName`, `appName`, `appVersion`, `userAgent`, `language`, and `platform` — all of which you can display on-screen by using the `alert()` method — the contents of these properties are neither intuitive nor consistent between browsers.) For more information on browser-version detection, visit `http://developer.netscape.com/docs/examples/javascript/browser_type_oo.html`.

The date-formatting script

In Chapter 2, I introduce a simple date-and-time-stamp script that captures the current date and time and displays it on a Web page, like so:

```
Sat May 22 19:46:47 CDT 2004
```

In this section, I demonstrate how to combine comments, conditionals, operators, and variables into JavaScript statements that not only capture the current date and time but format the date and time so that they appear in a more human-friendly format, like the following:

```
Good evening! It's May 22, 2004 - 8:24 p.m.
```

To see how, take a look at the code in Listing 3-4.

You can find the code shown in Listing 3-4 on the companion CD by loading up the `list0303.htm` file.

Listing 3-4: The Date-Formatting Script

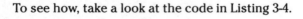

```
<HTML>
<HEAD>
<TITLE>Displaying the current date and time (formatted example)</TITLE>
```

```
<SCRIPT LANGUAGE="JavaScript" TYPE="text/javascript">

<!-- Hide from browsers that do not support JavaScript

// Comments begin with //
// Get the current date
// The following statements declare variables
var today = new Date();

// Get the current month
var month = today.getMonth();

// Declare a variable called displayMonth
var displayMonth="";

// The following is a switch statement
// Attach a display name to each of 12 possible month numbers
switch (month) {
    case 0 :
        displayMonth = "January"
        break
    case 1 :
        displayMonth = "February"
        break
    case 2 :
        displayMonth = "March"
        break
    case 3 :
        displayMonth = "April"
        break
    case 4 :
        displayMonth = "May"
        break
    case 5 :
        displayMonth = "June"
        break
    case 6 :
        displayMonth = "July"
        break
    case 7 :
        displayMonth = "August"
        break
    case 8 :
        displayMonth = "September"
        break
    case 9 :
        displayMonth = "October"
        break
```

(continued)

Listing 3-4 *(continued)*

```
    case 10 :
        displayMonth = "November"
        break
    case 11 :
        displayMonth = "December"
        break

    default: displayMonth = "INVALID"
}

// Set some more variables to make the JavaScript code
// easier to read

    var hours = today.getHours();
    var minutes = today.getMinutes();
    var greeting;
    var ampm;

    // We consider anything up until 11 a.m. "morning"

    if (hours <= 11) {
        greeting = "Good morning!";
        ampm="a.m.";

        // JavaScript reports midnight as 0, which is just
        // plain crazy; so we want to change 0 to 12.

        if (hours == 0) {
            hours = 12;
        }
    }

    // We consider anything after 11:00 a.m. and before
    // 6 p.m. (in military time, 18) to be "afternoon"

    else if (hours > 11 && hours < 18) {
        greeting = "Good afternoon!";
        ampm = "p.m.";

        // We don't want to see military time, so subtract 12
        if (hours > 12) {
            hours -= 12;
        }
    }
```

```
    // We consider anything after five p.m. (17 military) but
    // before nine p.m. (21 in military time) "evening"
    else if (hours > 17 && hours < 21) {
        greeting = "Good evening!";
        ampm = "p.m.";
        hours -= 12;
    }

    // We consider nine o'clock until midnight "night"
    else if (hours > 20) {
        greeting = "Good night!";
        ampm = "p.m.";
        hours -= 12;
    }

    // We want the minutes to display with "0" in front
    // of them if they're single-digit. For example,
    // rather than 1:4 p.m., we want to see 1:04 p.m.

    if (minutes < 10) {
        minutes = "0" + minutes;
    }

// + is a concatenation operator
var displayGreeting = displayMonth + " "
        + today.getDate() + ", "
        + today.getYear()
        + " - " + hours + ":" + minutes + " " + ampm

document.writeln(displayGreeting)

// --> Finish hiding
</SCRIPT>
</HEAD>
</HTML>
```

The code that you see in Listing 3-4 is a bit long, but understandable when you break it down bit by bit.

First off, the code captures the current date and time in the today variable. Then the code calls the getMonth() method associated with the Date object to capture the current month (a number between 0 and 11).

The switch statement examines the contents of the month variable and assigns an appropriate text string ("January", "February", and so on, up through "December") to the displayMonth variable.

Several `if-then` statements examine the `hours` variable to determine the appropriate time of day (`"a.m."` or `"p.m."`) and the appropriate greeting (`"Good morning!"`, `"Good afternoon!"`, `"Good evening!"`, or `"Good night!"`).

The second-to-last statement composes a message called `displayGreeting` and finally, the very last statement writes `displayGreeting` to the Web page.

The data-gathering script

Gathering information from the folks who visit your Web site is one of the more useful things that you can do with JavaScript. In Listing 3-5, I show you how to combine comments, conditionals, functions, loops, operators, and variables into JavaScript statements that capture user input. The statements then make calculations based on that input.

Figure 3-3, Figure 3-4, and Figure 3-5 show you the data-gathering script in action.

Figure 3-3:
The data-gathering script allows users to specify t-shirt size.

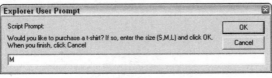

Figure 3-4:
The script allows users to specify as many different t-shirt sizes as they want.

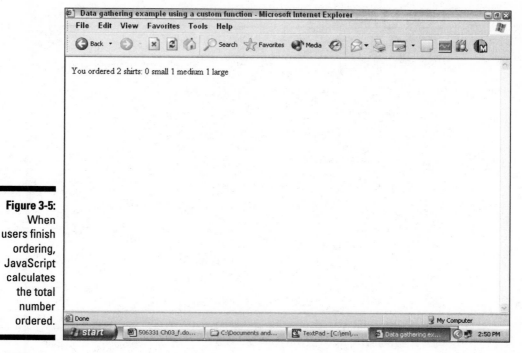

You ordered 2 shirts: 0 small 1 medium 1 large

Figure 3-5:
When
users finish
ordering,
JavaScript
calculates
the total
number
ordered.

You can find the code shown in Listing 3-5 on the companion CD. Just load up the list0304.htm file.

Listing 3-5:   The Data-Gathering Script

```
<HTML>
<HEAD>
<TITLE>Data gathering example using a custom function</TITLE>
<SCRIPT LANGUAGE="JavaScript">
<!-- Hide from browsers that do not support JavaScript

// The following statements declare variables.
// = is an assignment operator.
var article = "a";
var numShirts = 0;
var smallShirts = 0;
var medShirts = 0;
var largeShirts = 0;
```

(continued)

Listing 3-5 *(continued)*

```javascript
// The following is a function declaration.
function calc_shirts(sizeShirt) {

    // Add 1 to the number of sized shirts ordered, as well
    // as to the number of total shirts ordered

    if (sizeShirt == "S" || sizeShirt == "s") {
        // ++ is a unary increment operator.
        smallShirts++;
        numShirts++;
    }
    // == is a comparison operator.
    else if (sizeShirt == "M" || sizeShirt == "m") {
        medShirts++;
        numShirts++;
    }

    else if (sizeShirt == "L" || sizeShirt == "l") {
        largeShirts++;
        numShirts++;
    }
}

// The following is a do-while loop.
do {
    // The following line of code pops up a JavaScript
    // prompt.
    // The 'answer' variable is set to null if the user
    // clicks 'Cancel'

    var answer = prompt("Would you like to purchase "
            + article
            + " t-shirt? If so, enter the size (S,M,L) and click OK. When you
                finish, click Cancel", "M")

    // Change 'a' to 'ANOTHER' to make the display message
    // grammatically correct the second (and subsequent)
    // time around.
    article = "ANOTHER"

    if (answer != null) {
        calc_shirts(answer);
    }

}
while (answer != null)
```

```
document.writeln("You ordered " + numShirts + " shirts: "
    + smallShirts + " small "
    + medShirts +   " medium "
    + largeShirts + " large");

// --> Finish hiding
</SCRIPT>
</HEAD>
</HTML>
```

The heart of the script you see in Listing 3-5 is the do-while loop — the code you see in bold. The first line inside the do-while loop calls the prompt() method, which displays the user prompt shown in Figure 3-3. If the user clicks Cancel, the answer variable receives a value of null, and the JavaScript interpreter exits the do-while loop.

If the user enters a t-shirt size and clicks OK, however, the answer variable receives a non-null value and the do-while loop calls the calc_shirts() function.

The calc_shirts() function uses conditional if-then statements to calculate the number of sized shirts (as well as the number of total shirts) ordered. Then calc_shirts() returns control to the do-while loop, and the process begins all over again, with a call to the prompt() method. Each time the user clicks OK, the do-while loop calls the calc_shirts() function.

When at last the user clicks Cancel, the answer variable receives a value of null, and code execution drops out of the do-while loop and passes to the final JavaScript statement, which constructs a message and writes to the Web page by using the writeln() method associated with the document object.

Chapter 4

JavaScript-Accessible Data: Getting Acquainted with the Document Object Model

. . . .

In This Chapter

▶ Understanding how object models work

▶ Exploring properties and methods

▶ Adding text to a Web page dynamically

▶ Positioning text on a Web page

▶ Changing Web page appearance on-the-fly

▶ Getting familiar with Netscape Navigator's object model

▶ Getting familiar with Internet Explorer's object model

. . . .

*T*o create powerful scripts, you need to be familiar with two things: JavaScript syntax (which I discuss in Chapter 3) and the document object model.

The document object model, or DOM, refers to the Web page components, or objects, that you can access and manipulate by using JavaScript. Examples of objects that you can work with in JavaScript include the window that a Web page appears in, the Web page itself, embedded images and text, and much, much more.

In this chapter, I demonstrate how to find out which objects you can access in JavaScript, including those objects' properties and methods. First, I discuss the nuts and bolts of the DOM; then, I present three scripts that use document objects to change the appearance of a Web page on-the-fly.

Object Models Always Pose Nude

Because JavaScript is object-based, when you program in JavaScript you get to take advantage of a predefined object model. Object-based programming languages package, or encapsulate, data and functionality into useful units called objects. (Collectively, the objects that you work with in an object-based programming language are called the object model.) Encapsulation is a good thing because it hides nitty-gritty programming details — allowing you, the programmer, to write code with the least amount of hassle possible.

Human beings tend to think in terms of object models naturally, so object-based languages like JavaScript are typically much easier to handle than their procedural counterparts. (Examples of procedural languages include BASIC, C, and COBOL.)

Here's a real-world example of an object model. If I tell you my friend Ralph works in an office, you might reasonably assume that Ralph has a boss, a few co-workers, sits at a desk, and does some kind of work. How do you know all this without me telling you? Because you've seen or heard of other offices; perhaps you've even worked in one yourself. In other words, you're familiar with the office model — so even though you don't know anything about Ralph's particular office just yet, you can correctly guess a great deal. In fact, all I have to do is fill in a few specific details (the names of Ralph's co-workers, what kind of work he does, and so on) for you to have a complete picture of how Ralph spends his day.

The beauty of an object model is that it helps people communicate clearly and efficiently.

JavaScript's object model (called the document object model, or DOM) is no exception. Specifically, it helps you clearly and efficiently communicate what you want your script to do to the JavaScript interpreter. (The JavaScript interpreter is the part of a Web browser that executes a script. You can see the JavaScript interpreter in action in Chapter 2.)

The DOM performs this oh-so-useful task by describing

- All the **objects** that go into making up a Web page, such as forms, links, images, buttons, and text.

- The descriptive **properties** associated with each of the DOM objects. For example, an image object can be associated with specific properties describing its height and width.

- The behaviors, or **methods,** associated with each of the DOM objects. For example, the `window` object supports a method called `alert()` that allows you to display an alert message on a Web page.

> ✔ The special built-in methods, called **event handlers,** associated with automatic and user-initiated events. For instance, loading a Web page into a browser is considered an event; so is clicking a button. The event handlers that you use to trigger some JavaScript code when these events occur are called `onLoad` and `onClick`, respectively.

In the following sections, I give you an in-depth look at each of these four categories and how you can use them to create your own powerful JavaScript scripts!

Conceptually, the DOM is the same whether you're viewing a Web page in Internet Explorer, Netscape Navigator, or another browser entirely. In practice, however, the versions of the DOM implemented for Internet Explorer and Netscape Navigator differ — and you must pay attention to these differences or risk creating scripts that some users can't view. See "Browser Object Models" later in this chapter for details.

Object-ivity

In nerd-talk, an object is a software representation of a real-world thing. Theoretically, any person, place, thing, or can be represented as an object.

In practice, however, most of the objects that you work with in JavaScript fall into the first three of the following four categories:

> ✔ **Objects defined by using HTML tags.** This category includes documents, links, applets, text fields, windows, and so on. For the purposes of this book, JavaScript scripts are always attached to HTML documents. By using JavaScript, you can access any object defined in the HTML document to which a script is attached. (To see an example of a script accessing HTML objects, check out Listing 4-3 later in this chapter.)

> ✔ **Objects defined automatically by Web browsers.** One example is the `navigator` object, which, despite its name, holds configuration and version information about whichever browser is currently in use, even if that browser happens to be Internet Explorer. (To see an example of a script accessing a browser object, check out Chapter 3.)

> ✔ **Objects that are built into JavaScript, such as** `Date` **and** `Number`. (To see an example of a script accessing built-in JavaScript objects, take a look at Chapter 3.)

> ✔ **Objects you yourself have created by using the JavaScript** new **operator.** (To see an example of how you can create and access your own objects using JavaScript, check out Chapter 3.)

Just like their real-world counterparts, software objects are typically associated with specific characteristics and behaviors. Because this is a computer topic, though, programmers can't call these bits of information characteristics and behaviors. No, that would take all the fun out of it. Programmers call characteristics properties (or attributes), and they call behaviors methods — except for certain event-related behaviors whose names begin with on, such as onLoad, onResize, and onSubmit. Programmers call these special on methods event handlers.

Properties and attributes are really the same thing, but some JavaScript programmers tend to differentiate between the following:

- ✔ Properties (which belong to JavaScript objects)
- ✔ Attributes (which are associated with HTML objects)

Because most of the JavaScript code that you write involves objects, properties, methods, and event handlers, understanding what these object-oriented terms mean is essential for folks planning to write their own scripts.

You can think of it this way:

- ✔ Objects are always nouns.
- ✔ Properties are adjectives.
- ✔ Methods are verbs.
- ✔ Event handlers are verbs with on tacked to their fronts.

Got it? Take a look at Table 4-1 to see examples of some common object definitions.

Table 4-1		Sample Object Definitions		
Kind of Object	**Object (Noun)**	**Property (Adjective)**	**Method (Verb)**	**Event Handler ("on" + Verb)**
HTML	button	Such as name, type, and value	click()	onClick
HTML	link	Such as href, port, protocol, and so on	(none)	Such as onClick, onMouseOver, onKeyPress, and so on
HTML	form	Such as action, elements, length, and so on	Such as reset() and submit()	Such as onReset and onSubmit

Kind of Object	Object (Noun)	Property (Adjective)	Method (Verb)	Event Handler ("on" + Verb)
Browser	Navigator	Such as `appVersion`, `appName`, `language`, and `platform`	`javaEnabled()`	(none)
JavaScript	Number	Such as `MAX_VALUE` and `MIN_VALUE`	`toString()`	(none)
Programmer-defined	customer	Such as `name`, `address`, and `credit-History`	Such as `change-Address()`, `changeName()`, and `placeOrder()`	(none)

For sale by owner: Object properties

Properties are attributes that describe an object. Most of the objects available in JavaScript have their own set of properties. (Appendix C contains a listing of JavaScript properties arranged alphabetically.)

An image object, for example, is usually associated with the properties shown in Table 4-2.

Table 4-2	Properties Associated with the Image Object
Image Property	**Description**
`border`	The thickness of the border to display around the image, in pixels
`complete`	Whether or not the image loaded successfully (true or false)
`height`	The height of the image, in pixels
`hspace`	The number of pixels to pad the sides of the image with
`lowsrc`	The filename of a small image to load first
`name`	The internal name of the image (the one you reference by using JavaScript code)
`src`	The filename of the image to embed in an HTML document
`vspace`	The number of pixels to pad the top and bottom of the image with
`width`	The width of the image, in pixels

At runtime, all object properties have a corresponding value, whether it's explicitly defined or filled in by the Web browser. For example, consider an image object created with the HTML code in Listing 4-1.

Listing 4-1:   Creating an Image Object with the HTML <IMG> Tag

```
<BODY>
...
<IMG SRC="myPicture.jpg" NAME="companyLogo" HEIGHT="200" WIDTH="500" BORDER="1">
...
</BODY>
```

Assuming that you have a file on your computer named myPicture.jpg, at runtime, when you load the HTML snippet into your Web browser and query the Image properties, the corresponding values appear as shown in Table 4-3.

You can query the properties by calling the alert() method; for example, alert(document.companyLogo.src).

Table 4-3	Accessing Image Properties
Property Name	*Value*
document.companyLogo.**src**	file:///C:/myPicture.jpg
document.companyLogo.**name**	companyLogo
document.companyLogo.**height**	200
document.companyLogo.**width**	500
document.companyLogo.**border**	1
document.companyLogo.**complete**	true

To see an example of this HTML and JavaScript code in action, take a look at the ch4_properties.htm file located on the companion CD.

In the code snippets shown in Table 4-3, the name of each object property is fully qualified. If you've ever given a friend from another state driving directions to your house, you're familiar with fully qualifying names — even if you've haven't heard it called that before now. It's the old narrow-it-down approach:

"Okay, as soon as you hit Texas, start looking for the signs for Austin. On the south side of Austin, you'll find our suburb, called Travis Heights. When you hit Travis Heights, start looking for Sledgehammer Street. As soon as you turn onto Sledgehammer, you can start looking for 111 Sledgehammer. That's our house."

The JavaScript interpreter is like that out-of-state friend. It can locate and provide you with access to any property — but only if you describe that property by beginning with the most basic description (in most cases, the document object) and narrowing it down from there.

In Listing 4-1, the document object (which you create by using the HTML `<BODY>` and `</BODY>` tags) contains the image called `companyLogo`. The `companyLogo` image, in turn, contains the properties `src`, `name`, `height`, `width`, `border`, and `complete`. That's why you type **document.company Logo.src** to identify the `src` property of the image named `companyLogo`; or type **document.companyLogo.width** to identify the `width` property; and so on.

Note, too, that in the HTML code in Listing 4-1, the values for `src`, `name`, `height`, `width`, and `border` are taken directly from the HTML definition for this object. The value of `true` that appears for the `complete` property, however, appears courtesy of your Web browser. If your browser couldn't find and successfully load the `myPicture.jpg` file, the value of the complete property associated with this object would have been automatically set to `false`.

In JavaScript as in other programming languages, success is represented by `true` or 1; failure is represented by `false` or 0.

There's a method to this madness!

A method by any other name (some programmers call them behaviors or member functions) is a function that defines a particular behavior that an object can exhibit.

Take, for example, your soon-to-be-old friend the HTML button. Because you can click an HTML button, the button object has an associated method called the `click()` method. When you invoke a button's `click()` method by using JavaScript, the result is the same as though a user clicked that button.

Unlike objects, properties, and event handlers, methods in JavaScript are always followed by parentheses, like this: `click()`. This convention helps remind programmers that methods often (but not always) require parameters. A parameter is any tidbit of information that a method needs in order to do its job. For example, the `alert()` method associated with the `window` object allows you to create a special kind of pop-up window (an alert window) to display some information on the screen. Because creating a blank pop-up window is pretty useless, the `alert()` method requires you to pass it a parameter containing the text that you want to display:

```
function checkTheEmailAddress () {
    ...
    window.alert("Sorry, the e-mail address you entered is not complete.  Please
            try again.")
}
```

Some objects, like the built-in `window` object, are associated with scads of methods. You can open a window by using the `open()` method; display some text on a window by using the `write()` and `writeln()` methods; scroll a window up or down by using the `scroll()`, `scrollBy()`, and `scrollTo()` methods; and so on.

Just as you do when referring to an object, a property, or an event handler, when you refer to a method in JavaScript you must preface that method with the specific name of the object to which it belongs. Table 4-4 shows you examples of how to call an object's methods.

Table 4-4	Calling Object Methods
JavaScript Code Snippet	*What It Does*
`annoyingText.blink()`	Calls the `blink()` method associated with the `string` object. Specifically, it causes the string object called `annoyingText` to blink on and off.
`self.frame1.focus()`	Calls the `focus()` method associated with the `frame` object. Specifically, it sets the input focus to a frame called `frame1` (which itself is associated with the primary document window).
`document.infoForm.request ForFreeInfoButton.click()`	Calls the `click()` method associated with the button object. Specifically, this code clicks the button named `requestForFree InfoButton`, which is contained in the form called `infoForm`. (The `infoForm` form is contained in the primary HTML document.)

Why use methods?

Many of the methods defined in JavaScript's DOM are things that users can do simply by clicking a mouse: for example, stopping a window from loading (the `stop()` method); focusing on a particular input field (the `focus()` method); printing the contents of a window (the `print()` method); and so on. Why go to the trouble of including method calls in your script?

In a word, *automation.* Say you want to create a Web page that does several things in response to a single event. For example, when a user loads your Web page, you might want to set focus to a particular input field, open a small What's New window, and display today's date automatically. By using methods, you can do all this — and the user doesn't have to do a thing!

To see an example of a method call in JavaScript, take a look at the `ch3_methods.htm` file located on the companion CD.

You see another example of methods in action in Chapter 2, and Appendix C lists the methods that are available to you in JavaScript's DOM.

How do you handle a hungry event? With event handlers!

An event handler is a special kind of method that a JavaScript-enabled Web browser triggers automatically when a specific event occurs. Event handlers give you, the JavaScript programmer, the ability to perform whatever instructions you like — from performing calculations to displaying messages — based on events such as

- ✔ A user loading a Web page into a browser
- ✔ A user stopping a Web page from loading
- ✔ A user entering or changing some information in an input field
- ✔ A user clicking an image, button, or link
- ✔ A user submitting or resetting a form

For example, when a user loads a Web page into a browser, the `onLoad` event handler associated with that page (or document) executes; when a user clicks an HTML button, that HTML button's `onClick` event handler executes; and so on.

Here's an example of how you call a built-in event handler:

```
<BODY
    onLoad="window.alert('Hello!');"
    onUnload="window.alert('Goodbye!');"
>
...
</BODY>
```

To see an example of calling event handlers in JavaScript, check out the `ch3_events.htm` file located on the companion CD.

Take a look at the code snippet in this section. Two event handlers are associated with the `document` object. (The document object is defined in HTML using the `<BODY>` and `</BODY>` tags.) One of the event handlers is named `onLoad`; the other, `onUnload`.

As you might guess, loading this code into a Web page causes a `Hello!` message to appear. Loading another page, or closing the browser altogether, causes a Goodbye! message to appear. Event handling is a wonderful thing. With it you can figure out when and precisely how a user interacts with any part of your Web page, and you can respond to that action as you see fit.

Appendix C contains a list of all the event handlers that JavaScript supports. To see additional examples of JavaScript event handlers in action, check out Chapter 2.

Company functions

Like methods, functions are behaviors — but that's where the similarity ends.

- ✔ Functions are standalone bits of JavaScript code that can be reused over and over again.
- ✔ Unlike methods, functions aren't associated with a particular object.

The JavaScript language provides a handful of built-in functions, but you can create your own, as well — as many as you need.

Here's an example. Say you want to create an HTML form that asks the user to enter her age and the number of pets she owns. You could create a JavaScript function that examines a number and makes sure that it's between certain reasonable parameters — say, 0 and 100. After you create such a function, you can call it twice: once to validate the age that the user types in and once to validate the number of pets the user owns. This ability to create reusable functions can save you quite a bit of time if you plan to create a lot of JavaScript-enhanced Web sites.

Listing 4-2 shows you how you define and use a function in JavaScript.

Listing 4-2:   Defining and Calling a Custom Function in JavaScript

```
<SCRIPT LANGUAGE="JavaScript">

function checkNumber(aNumber) {

    if (aNumber > 0 && aNumber < 100) {

        ////////////////////////////////////////////////////
        // If the number is greater than 0 and less than
        // 100, pop up a "congratulations" message and return
        // a value indicating success.
        ////////////////////////////////////////////////////

        alert("The number you specified is valid (it is between 0 and 100).")
        return true

    }
```

```
//////////////////////////////////////////////////////////
// Otherwise, the number is negative or over 100,
// so return a value indicating failure.
//////////////////////////////////////////////////////////

    else {
        alert("The number you specified is invalid (not between 0 and 100).
            \nPlease try again.")
        return false
    }
}


...
<FORM NAME="myForm">


...
Please type in a number: <INPUT TYPE="text" SIZE="5" NAME="inputNumber">
...
<INPUT TYPE="button" VALUE="Push to validate number"
    onClick="checkNumber(document.myForm.inputNumber.value);">

</FORM>
```

Don't worry if you see some unfamiliar symbols inside the `checkNumber()` function definition, like > and &&; you find out what these symbols mean in Chapter 3.

To see the `checkNumber()` function example in action, check out the file `ch3_functions.htm` located on the companion CD.

For now, take a look at the penultimate line in the code snippet, the one where the `checkNumber()` function is being called:

```
<INPUT TYPE="button" VALUE="Push to validate number"
    onClick="checkNumber(document.myForm.inputNumber.value);">
```

Notice that `checkNumber()` is being called with a single argument (`document.myForm.inputNumber.value`)? That single argument represents the number that a user typed into the HTML form. ("For sale by owner: Object properties," earlier in this chapter, explains why you must fully qualify a property this way.) When a user clicks the Push to Validate Number button, the `checkNumber()` function then

1. Springs into action

2. Takes a look at the input number passed to it

3. Pops up a message telling the user whether the number is valid (that is, whether the number falls inside the range of 0 to 100)

Because functions are so useful in JavaScript, you see lots of examples of them in this book. For now, just remember that

✔ You define a function inside the `<SCRIPT>` and `</SCRIPT>` tags, which I explain in detail in Chapter 2.

✔ You let the JavaScript interpreter know a function declaration is coming by starting it with the special JavaScript keyword `function`, followed by a pair of curly braces `{}`.

✔ Between the curly braces you put any JavaScript statements you like.

Appendix C lists a handful of built-in JavaScript functions. For additional examples of creating and calling your own functions, see Chapter 2.

Anatomy of an Object: Properties, Methods, Event Handlers, and Functions in Action

In this section, I demonstrate how to work with the most commonly used objects in JavaScript to perform three cool interactive effects:

✔ Adding text to a Web page dynamically

✔ Positioning text on a Web page dynamically

✔ Changing other aspects of Web page's appearance (background, text color, and so on) on-the-fly

Because these particular examples use cascading style sheets, or CSS, to perform their magic — a common (and highly useful) approach referred to as dynamic HTML, or DHTML — I first describe cascading style sheets and how you use them in JavaScript.

Dynamic objects: The least you need to know about CSS and DHTML

If you've ever tried to make the text on your Web page look spiffy by using plain old HTML, you might have been sorely disappointed. Why? Because HTML was designed to allow you to add content to your Web page — not to control precisely how that content is represented.

Recognizing the need for a way to control Web page layout, the good folks at the World Wide Web Consortium came up with a standard called cascading style sheets, or CSS. And fortunately, browser makers took heed: Both Navigator and Internet Explorer support CSS.

CSS allows you to describe how you want the text elements on your Web page to appear. For example, you might decide you want all level-one headings to appear in blue, all level-two headings to appear in red, and every other paragraph to be italicized. To accomplish this goal, you simply

> ✔ Add special CSS descriptors to your HTML code.
> ✔ Reference your special CSS descriptors by using JavaScript.

The combination of CSS and a scripting language is often referred to as DHTML.

CSS is a fairly broad topic. This book is devoted to JavaScript, so I don't go into the nitty-gritty details of CSS here. Instead, in the following sections I give you the nuts-and-bolts information that you need to create CSS objects and access those objects by using JavaScript. For an in-depth look at CSS, I suggest a book such as Cascading Style Sheets by Example, by Steve Callihan (Que). Or check out the World Wide Web Consortium's cascading style sheets specification by pointing your browser to www.w3.org/Style/CSS.

Defining CSS objects

When it comes to defining CSS objects, you have two choices:

> ✔ **Associate a style with an HTML tag by using the HTML** `<STYLE>` **tags.**
> Here's an example:
>
> ```
> <HTML>
> <HEAD>
> <STYLE TYPE="text/css">
> H1 {color: red;}
> </STYLE>
> </HEAD>
> ...
> <BODY>
> <H1>This heading is red!</H1>
> <H2>This heading is plain old black</H2>
> </BODY>
> </HTML>
> ```
>
> This code associates the color red with every occurrence of the `<H1>` tag that appears in the body of the document.

> ✔ **Define a custom-named CSS object by using the ID property of another HTML tag.** For example:
>
> ```
> <HTML>
> <HEAD>
> <STYLE TYPE="text/css">
> ```

```
#blueHeading {color: blue;}
</STYLE>
</HEAD>
<BODY>
<H1 ID="blueHeading">My blue heading<H1>
```

In this case, the name of the CSS object is blueHeading — and you can easily use this name to access the CSS object using JavaScript. This is the approach I demonstrate in the example scripts that you find in this chapter.

No matter how you define CSS objects, you can access those objects by using JavaScript and the DOM. To minimize the amount of CSS expertise you need — this is a book on JavaScript, after all — I demonstrate the second approach.

Accessing CSS objects by using JavaScript

After you define a CSS object, you can access that object by using JavaScript. The following code shows you how:

```
document.getElementById("blueheading").style.fontStyle="italic";
```

The JavaScript code you see here uses the getElementById() method to set the fontStyle property of the blueheading element to italic — effectively displaying the heading in italics.

In addition to the fontStyle property, you can access a variety of CSS properties (such as background-color, background-image, font-weight, font-size, text-align, text-indent, and much more) using a variety of methods.

In the example scripts that you find in the next three sections, I introduce you to several different CSS properties and methods. For an ultracomplete list, however, consult your favorite browser's DOM reference. (One good online reference is http://msdn.microsoft.com/library/default. asp?url=/workshop/author/dhtml/reference/objects.asp.)

Example DHTML script: Adding text dynamically

Using plain HTML, what you see is what you get: When the text for a page is loaded, that's the text the user sees. Not so when you add JavaScript and CSS to the mix! Using this powerful combination, you can create a script that adds or changes the appearance of text on a Web page after that page has been loaded.

To see what I mean, take a look at Figures 4-1, 4-2, and 4-3.

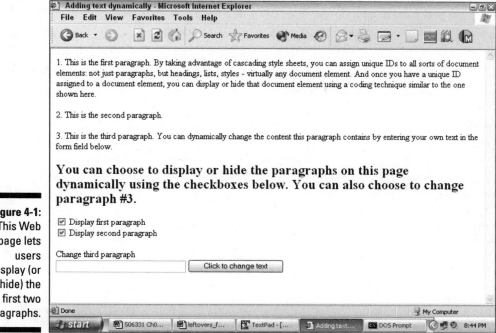

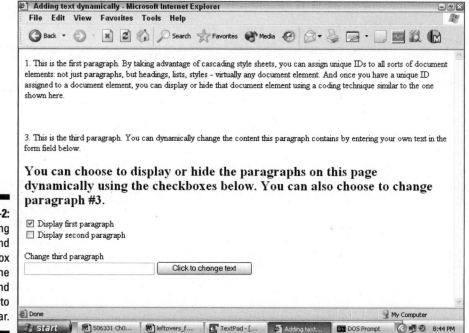

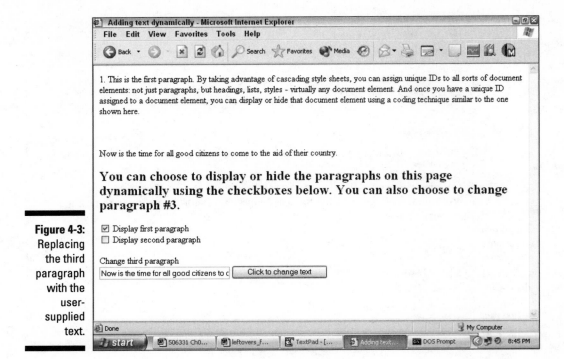

1. This is the first paragraph. By taking advantage of cascading style sheets, you can assign unique IDs to all sorts of document elements: not just paragraphs, but headings, lists, styles - virtually any document element. And once you have a unique ID assigned to a document element, you can display or hide that document element using a coding technique similar to the one shown here.

Now is the time for all good citizens to come to the aid of their country.

You can choose to display or hide the paragraphs on this page dynamically using the checkboxes below. You can also choose to change paragraph #3.

☑ Display first paragraph
☐ Display second paragraph

Change third paragraph
Now is the time for all good citizens to c   [Click to change text]

Figure 4-3:
Replacing
the third
paragraph
with the
user-
supplied
text.

To see the code responsible for Figures 4-1, 4-2, and 4-3, take a look at Listing 4-3.

You can experiment with the example script you find in Listing 4-3 by loading the file list0403.htm which you find on the companion CD.

Listing 4-3:   Allowing a User to Add or Change Text Dynamically on a Web Page

```
<HTML>
<HEAD>
<TITLE>Adding text dynamically</TITLE>
<SCRIPT LANGUAGE="JavaScript" TYPE="text/javascript">
<!-- Hide from browsers that do not support JavaScript

function displayText() {

    // Store the heading elements in local variables
    // so we can work with them easily
    var firstGraf = document.getElementById("graf1");
    var secondGraf = document.getElementById("graf2");
```

```
        // If graf1 is selected, change visibility to visible;
        // if graf1 is NOT selected, change visibility to hidden
   firstGraf.style.visibility=(document.myForm.graf1box.checked) ? "visible" :
            "hidden";

        // if graf2 is selected, change visibility to visible;
        // if graf2 is NOT selected, change visibility to hidden
   secondGraf.style.visibility=(document.myForm.graf2box.checked) ? "visible" :
            "hidden";

}

function changeText() {

        // Store the new text in a variable called newText
        var newText = document.myForm.changeableText.value;

        // Get the existing element text and store it in
        // "oldText"
        var oldText = document.getElementById("graf3");

        // Swap old text with new text.
        // Replace oldText with newText
        oldText.firstChild.nodeValue = newText;

}

// --> Finish hiding
</SCRIPT>
</HEAD>
<BODY>

// Defining three named paragraphs
<P ID="graf1">1. This is the first paragraph.  By taking advantage of cascading
style sheets, you can assign unique IDs to all sorts of document elements: not
just paragraphs, but headings, lists, styles - virtually any document element.
And once you have a unique ID assigned to a document element, you can display or
hide that document element using a coding technique similar to the one shown
here.</P>
<P ID="graf2">2. This is the second paragraph.</P>
<P ID="graf3">3. This is the third paragraph. You can dynamically change the
content this paragraph contains by entering your own text in the form field
below.</P>

<H2>You can choose to display or hide the paragraphs on this page dynamically
using the checkboxes below. You can also choose to change paragraph #3.</H2>
```

(continued)

Listing 4-3 *(continued)*

```
<FORM name="myForm">
// The displayText() function is called when the user checks or unchecks the
// checkbox.

 <INPUT TYPE="checkbox" NAME="graf1box" CHECKED onClick="displayText();">
Display first paragraph
<br>
<INPUT TYPE="checkbox" NAME="graf2box" CHECKED onClick="displayText();">
Display second paragraph
<br><br>
Change third paragraph
<br>
<INPUT TYPE="text" NAME="changeableText" defaultValue="Type here" SIZE="35">

// The changeText() function is called when the user clicks the "Click to change
// text" button.
<INPUT TYPE="button" VALUE="Click to change text" onClick="changeText();">

</FORM>

</BODY>
</HTML>
```

The code in Listing 4-3 defines three CSS paragraphs named graf1, graf2, and graf3, respectively. When a user selects one of the HTML check boxes, the displayText() function is called. The displayText() function changes the visibility property associated with graf1 and graf2 to display (or hide) each paragraph according to the user's selection.

When the user enters text in the text field and clicks the Click to Change Text button, the JavaScript interpreter calls the changeText() function. The changeText() function uses DOM methods to access paragraph text and replace that text with the user-supplied text.

Example DHTML script: Positioning text dynamically

You can change the way Web page elements are positioned at runtime by using a combination of JavaScript and CSS.

To accomplish this task, you first create named elements by using CSS; then, you access and move those elements by using JavaScript. Figures 4-4 and 4-5 show you an example of a text element that can be moved in response to a user's clicking a button.

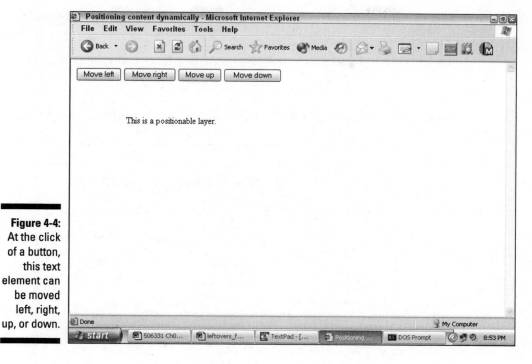

Figure 4-4:
At the click
of a button,
this text
element can
be moved
left, right,
up, or down.

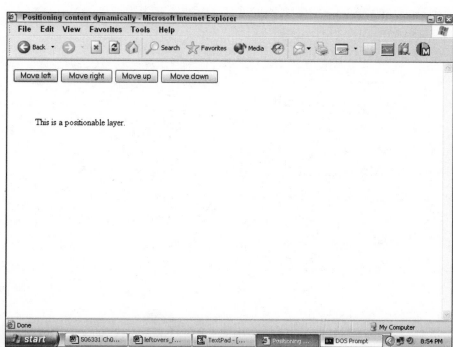

Figure 4-5:
Clicking the
Move Left
button
moves the
text element
to the left.

You can experiment with the example script you find in Listing 4-4 by loading the file `list0404.htm` you find on the companion CD.

As you skim through the code in Listing 4-4, pay particular attention to the HTML `<DIV>` tag and the JavaScript `move()` function.

Listing 4-4: Allowing a User to Change the Position of a Web Page Element

```
<HTML>
<HEAD>
<TITLE>Positioning content dynamically</TITLE>
<SCRIPT LANGUAGE="JavaScript" TYPE="text/javascript">
<!-- Hide from browsers that do not support JavaScript

function move(direction) {

    var layerText = document.getElementById("myLayer");

    switch(direction) {
        // If move() is called with an argument of "left," reposition text
        // layer so that it is now 50 pixels from the left-hand side of the
        // window.

        case "left":
            layerText.style.left = 50;
            break;

        case "right":
            layerText.style.left = 150;
            break;

        case "up":
            layerText.style.top = 50;
            break;

        case "down":
            layerText.style.top = 150;
            break;
    }
}

// --> Finish hiding
</SCRIPT>
</HEAD>
```

```
<BODY>
// Creating a CSS layer object named myLayer and positioning it 100 pixels from
// the top of the window and 100 pixels from the left-hand side of the window.

<DIV ID="myLayer" STYLE="position:absolute; left:100; top:100;">
<P>This is a positionable layer.</P>
</DIV>


<FORM>
// Clicking any of the four buttons calls the move() function with a different
// argument.
<INPUT TYPE="button" NAME="moveLayer" VALUE="Move left" onClick="move('left');">
<INPUT TYPE="button" NAME="moveLayer" VALUE="Move right"
               onClick="move('right');">
<INPUT TYPE="button" NAME="moveLayer" VALUE="Move up" onClick="move('up');">
<INPUT TYPE="button" NAME="moveLayer" VALUE="Move down" onClick="move('down');">

</FORM>

</BODY>
</HTML>
```

In the example code you see in Listing 4-4, a positionable layer is created and displayed on-screen by using the HTML `<DIV>` tag. When a user clicks one of the buttons — say, the Move Left button — the JavaScript interpreter calls the `move()` function, passing in the value `left`.

Inside the `move()` function, the JavaScript interpreter first identifies the positionable layer by name, and then it uses the `switch` conditional statement to determine which direction to move the layer.

Example DHTML script: Changing page appearance on-the-fly

Here you find out how to change overall Web page characteristics such as background and text color. First, take a look at Figures 4-6 and 4-7; then, take a peek at the code in Listing 4-5.

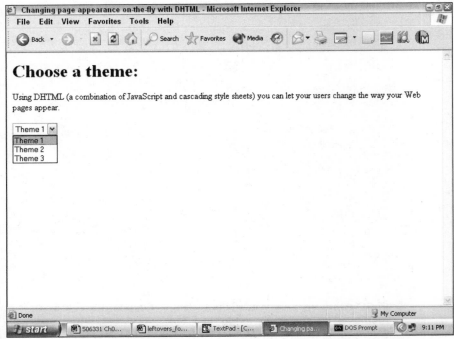

Figure 4-6:
This Web
page offers
users a
choice of
themes.

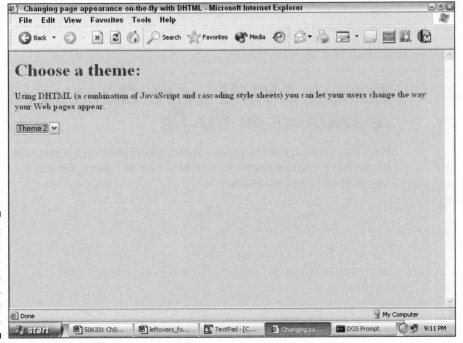

Figure 4-7:
Choosing
a theme
background,
paragraph,
and heading
text color.

You can experiment with the example script that you find in Listing 4-5 by loading up the file `list0405.htm` you find on the companion CD.

Listing 4-5:   Using DHTML to Change Page Appearance on-the-Fly

```
<HTML>
<HEAD>
<TITLE>Changing page appearance on-the-fly with DHTML</TITLE>
<SCRIPT LANGUAGE="JavaScript" TYPE="text/javascript">
<!-- Hide from browsers that do not support JavaScript

function changeTheme() {

     switch(document.myForm.themes.selectedIndex) {

         case 0:
             // Changing the background and foreground (text) color.
             document.bgColor = "blue";
             document.fgColor = "yellow";

// Changing the heading color.
  document.getElementById("heading1").style.color="pink";
             break;

         case 1:
             document.bgColor = "pink";
             document.fgColor = "green";
             document.getElementById("heading1").style.color="red";
             break;

         case 2:
             document.bgColor = "green";
             document.fgColor = "red";

                  document.getElementById("heading1").style.color="pink";
             document.getElementById("graf1").style.fontWeight="bold";
             break;
     }
}

// --> Finish hiding
</SCRIPT>
</HEAD>
<BODY>
// Creating a named heading element.
<H1 ID="heading1">Choose a theme:</H1>
// Creating a named paragraph element.
<P ID="graf1">Using DHTML (a combination of JavaScript and cascading style
                sheets) you can
let your users change the way your Web pages appear.</P>
```

(continued)

Listing 4-5 *(continued)*

```
<FORM NAME="myForm" >
// When a user selects a new theme, the changeTheme() function is called.
<select name="themes" onChange="changeTheme();">
  <option value="theme1">Theme 1</option>
  <option value="theme2">Theme 2</option>
  <option value="theme3">Theme 3</option>
</select>
</FORM>

</BODY>
</HTML>
```

As you glance over the code in Listing 4-5, notice that two CSS objects are created in the body of the document: `heading1` and `graf1`. When a user selects a theme, the JavaScript interpreter calls the `changeTheme()` function, which uses the `switch` conditional statement to determine which theme the user selected.

The appearance of the page — the background color, foreground color, heading color, and font weight of the paragraph text — is set based on which theme the user selected.

Browser Object Models

Conceptually, Web pages are all the same: They're displayed in browser windows, contain text and images, and so on. And, in fact, the World Wide Web Consortium (the W3C), an industry group responsible for many Web-related standards, has hammered out a standard document object model — a blueprint, if you will, that browser manufacturers can follow. (You can find a copy of the W3C's DOM specification at `www.w3.org/DOM`.)

In reality, however, each browser manufacturer performs slightly different behind-the-scenes magic when it comes to implementing the DOM (and providing JavaScript support). What this means is that the browser models you work with in JavaScript — Microsoft's Internet Explorer DOM and Netscape's DOM — are similar but not identical.

Netscape Navigator

Netscape Navigator's DOM describes all the objects you can access in JavaScript to create cool scripts that execute flawlessly in Netscape Navigator.

When you want to reference any of the following objects in your script, you use that object's fully qualified name, as shown in the Syntax column of the following list. The `window` object is the only exception to this rule. By default, every Web page contains one all-encompassing, granddaddy window, no matter how many additional windows you choose to include. Because this overall window is a given, you don't have to mention it specifically when you refer to one of the objects that it contains.

For example, the following two JavaScript code snippets both set the `src` property of an `Image` object named `myImage` equal to `"happycat.jpg"`:

```
window.document.myForm.myImage.src="happycat.jpg"
```

```
document.myForm.myImage.src="happycat.jpg"
```

The following is a short list of the basic objects that you work with in Netscape Navigator. You can find a list of all the objects in the DOM implementation for Navigator 7.1, including associated properties, methods, and event handlers, in Appendix C. Or check out Netscape's exhaustive DOM reference at `www.mozilla.org/docs/dom/domref/dom_shortTOC.html`.

Object	Syntax
window	window (optional)
document	document
applet	document.applets[0]
anchor	document.*someAnchor*
area	document.*someArea*
classes	document.classes
form	document.*someForm*
button	document.*someForm.someButton*
checkbox	document.*someForm.someCheckbox*
fileUpload	document.*someForm.someFileElement*
hidden	document.*someForm.someHidden*
image	document.*someForm.someImage*
password	document.*someForm.somePassword*
radio	document.*someForm.someRadio*
reset	document.*someForm.someReset*
select	document.*someForm.someSelect*
submit	document.*someForm.someSubmit*
text	document.*someForm.someText*
textarea	document.*someForm.someTextarea*
ids	document.ids
layers	document.layers
link	document.*someLink*

(continued)

Object	Syntax
object	document.*someObject*
plugin	docment.embeds[0]
tags	document.tags
frame, parent, self, top	(all of these are also synonyms for window)
history	history
location	location
locationbar	locationbar
menubar	menubar
navigator	navigator
personalbar	personalbar
scrollbar	scrollbar
statusbar	statusbar
toolbar	toolbar

JavaScript data types

Much of what you want to do with a JavaScript script involves programmer-defined objects, such as the values that a user types into your HTML form, some calculations that you make based on those values, and so on.

Most programming languages require you to declare special placeholders, called variables, to hold each piece of data you want to work with. Not only that, but most programming languages require you to specify — up front — what type of data you expect those variables to contain. (This requirement makes it easy for those languages' compilers but tough on us programmers!)

JavaScript expects you to declare variables to represent bits of data, too. But because JavaScript is a loosely typed language, you don't necessarily have to declare the type of a variable up front, nor do you have to perform cumbersome type conversions the way you do in languages like C and C++. Here's an example:

```
var visitor           // Defines a variable called "visitor" of
                      // no particular type
var visitor = "george" // Resets "visitor" to a text string

var visitor = 3       // Resets "visitor" to a numeric value

var visitor = null    // Resets "visitor" to null
```

You can get away without specifying string or numeric data types explicitly, as shown in this code snippet, because the JavaScript interpreter takes care of figuring out what type of value is associated with any given variable at runtime.

There are two data types that JavaScript requires you to explicitly specify: the `Array` and `Date` data types. You must declare variables of type `Array` and `Date` explicitly because the JavaScript interpreter needs to know certain extra details about these types of values in order to store them properly.

JavaScript supports the following data types:

✔ `Array` **An ordered collection. For example:**

```
var animals = new Array("cat", "dog", "mouse") //
load array
```

```
var firstAnimal = animals[0] // access first array
element
```

```
var secondAnimal = animals[1] // access second element
```

```
var thirdAnimal = animals[2] // access third element
```

✔ `Boolean` **True/false data type (values of** `true` **or** `false` **only). For example:**

```
var cookieDetected = false
```

```
var repeatVisitor = true
```

✔ `Date` **Time and date data type. For example:**

```
var today = new Date() // current time/date via
system clock
```

```
var newYearsDay = new Date(2001, 01, 01) // specific
date
```

✔ `null` **A special data type denoting nonexistence. For example:**

```
if (emailAddress == null) { // check for null

  alert("Please enter an e-mail address")

}
```

Null is not the same as 0 (zero).

✔ `Number` **Numerical data type. For example:**

```
var numberHits = 1234 // implied numeric data type
```

```
var numberHits = new Number(1234) // explicit
```

✔ `String` **String (text) data type. For example:**

```
alert("This is a string") // implied string with
double quotes
```

```
alert('So is this') // implied string with single
quotes
```

```
var myString = new String("Yet another string") //
explicit
```

TIP

JavaScript supports additional data types, including the Function and RegExp data types. Because these data types aren't often used, I don't describe them here. For details on how to use these data types, check out `http://devedge.` `netscape.com/library/manuals/2000/javascript/1.5/guide`.

Leftovers: The Math object

JavaScript provides a utility object for you to use in your script endeavors. This object — the Math object — isn't part of the DOM proper (that is, it doesn't represent a conceptual component of a Web page). It isn't a data type, either. It's simply a standalone object provided for you to use whenever you need mathematical constants or functions. Here are a few examples:

```
var x = Math.PI // assigns "x" the value of pi
```

```
var y = Math.round(158.32) // assigns "y" the result of rounding 158.32
```

```
var z = Math.sqrt(49) // assigns "z" the square root of 49
```

Check out Appendix C for a full list of all the properties and methods associated with the Math object.

Microsoft Internet Explorer

Microsoft's document object model is often referred to as the DHTML DOM, which is alphabet-soup-ese for dynamic Hypertext Markup Language document object model. Although Microsoft's DHTML DOM is based on the same standard that Netscape Navigator's is based on — the World Wide Web Consortium's DOM specification — it varies a bit from Netscape's implementation. This variation is important to keep in mind because if your script references objects that exist in one DOM and not another, your script will run in just that one object-supporting browser. (Flip to Chapter 5 to find tips for creating cross-platform scripts that work in both browsers.)

Microsoft's DHTML DOM describes all the objects you can access with JavaScript to create cool scripts that execute flawlessly in Internet Explorer. The following is a short list of the basic objects that you work with in Internet Explorer.

Object	Syntax
window	window (optional)
document	document
applet	document.applets[0]
anchor	document.*someAnchor*
area	document.*someArea*

Object	Syntax
form	document.*someForm*
button	document.*someForm.someButton*
checkbox	document.*someForm.someCheckbox*
file	document.*someForm.someFileElement*
hidden	document.*someForm.someHidden*
image	document.*someForm.someImage*
password	document.*someForm.somePassword*
radio	document.*someForm.someRadio*
reset	document.*someForm.someReset*
select	document.*someForm.someSelect*
submit	document.*someForm.someSubmit*
text	document.*someForm.someText*
textarea	document.*someForm.someTextarea*
link	document.*someLink*
object	document.*someObject*
plugin	document.embeds[0] (no, this isn't a typo!)
embed	document.embeds[0]
frame	*someFrame*
frameset	*someFrameset*
history	history
location	location
navigator	navigator
clientInformation	clientInformation

 You can find a list of the objects in the DOM implementation for Internet Explorer 6.0, including associated properties, methods, and event handlers, in Appendix C. Or check out Microsoft's own exhaustive DHTML DOM reference at

```
http://msdn.microsoft.com/workshop/author/dhtml/reference/objects.asp
```

Part II
Creating Dynamic Web Pages

The 5th Wave   By Rich Tennant

"OH, I'LL GET US IN — I USED TO RUN TECH SUPPORT AT AN INTERNET ACCESS COMPANY."

In this part . . .

In this part, you find practical ways to create Web pages that appear differently to different users. Chapter 5 shows you how to modify the way your pages appear automatically based on which browser your users are running. Chapter 6 describes how you can create Web pages that remember visitors, and Chapter 7 demonstrates how to manipulate browser frames and windows to create sophisticated navigational schemes.

Best of all, you see real working examples of all the techniques presented in Part II. (The examples are also included on the CD-ROM at the back of this book, so you don't even have to type the code.)

Chapter 5

Detecting Your Users' Browser Environments

. . . .

In This Chapter

▶ Understanding how (and why) JavaScript support differs among browsers

▶ Applying strategies for cross-platform script creation

▶ Taking advantage of advanced JavaScript features with a browser-detection script

. . . .

*T*he biggest challenge facing Web developers today isn't hardware- or software-based: It's wetware-based. (Wetware — a term that refers to the supposed squishiness of the human brain — is geek-speak for human beings.) And that challenge is trying to get the companies that create Web browsers to agree on a single, standard implementation of browser-supported technologies like JavaScript!

With the current situation, the brand of browser that someone has installed, the browser's version, and the underlying operating system all affect that person's ability to view your JavaScript-enabled Web pages. As a JavaScript developer, you need to be aware of the differences in JavaScript implementations among browsers and write your scripts accordingly. If you don't, you might end up creating a whiz-bang script that runs only on your computer.

Whacking Your Way through the Browser Maze

From the latest reports, both Microsoft and Netscape have promised to support the ECMAScript standard (which I discuss in detail in Chapter 3) in future versions of their respective browsers.

Even if Internet Explorer and Netscape Navigator were fully ECMAScript-compliant (and offered no additional features), the same JavaScript script still might not execute identically in both browsers. Why? For JavaScript to be a true cross-browser language, both the syntax and the document object model (DOM) would have to be consistent.

ECMA-262 takes JavaScript halfway to cross-browser nirvana by defining a standard language specification, but it doesn't define the DOM. As you see in Chapter 4, the DOMs for the two browsers are far from identical, despite the efforts of the World Wide Web Consortium to define a unified standard.

Fortunately, as you see in the next section, you don't have to depend on differences between JavaScript implementation and object models to write great cross-browser scripts. All you need to do is identify the differences at runtime and display customized Web pages accordingly.

Detecting Features

By using JavaScript, you can detect what make and version of Web browser a user is using to view your pages — useful information that lets you customize Web pages on-the-fly to provide your users with the best possible viewing experience. But make and version aren't the only bits of browser-related information that you can detect by using JavaScript. You can also determine which Java applets and browser plug-ins a user has installed, which Web page your user visited directly before surfing to yours (called the referring page), and even user preferences. Read on to find out how!

Browser make and version

The most reliable way to figure out which browsers are loading your script is to ask. You ask programmatically, using JavaScript, by adding a bit of code to the beginning of your script, querying the DOM for browser-specific details. When you determine which make, model, and version of browser is attempting to load your JavaScript-enabled Web page, you can display your page accordingly.

The easiest way to implement this functionality is to use the <MARQUEE> tag, which is an HTML tag (and corresponding scripting object) supported by Internet Explorer (beginning with version 3.x). The trouble is that some versions of Navigator don't support the <MARQUEE> tag. When a non-marquee-supporting browser loads a Web page containing the <MARQUEE> tag, it might do one of three things:

✔ Display the scrolling text statically or not at all

✔ Ignore your marquee-related JavaScript code

✔ Generate a JavaScript error

One way to ensure that your viewers see what you want them to see is to use JavaScript to see whether the browser loading your script is Internet Explorer.

✔ If it is, you can use the `<MARQUEE>` tag with confidence.

✔ If the browser isn't Internet Explorer, you can display the scrolled information in an alternate eye-catching fashion — for example, as a bolded, centered heading.

Listing 5-1 shows the code for a "sniffer" script that examines (sniffs out) browser settings and displays a string of text as either a scrolling marquee or as a bolded, centered heading, depending on whether the browser loading the script is Internet Explorer.

A custom fit, every time

Creating different versions of each of your Web pages for each and every different browser version in existence ensures an optimum experience for all of your users. It also represents a maintenance nightmare!

A good design approach to follow is this:

1. Provide absolutely essential information (such as contact information) in the form of plain old, every-browser-supports-it text — rather than, say, a scrolling JavaScript marquee.

2. Provide additional information and effects by using cross-browser techniques wherever possible. For example, layers aren't implemented in all browsers, but depending on the effect that you want to achieve, you might be able to make do by using an image-swapping technique (like the one you see in

Chapter 8) or an animated GIF file instead. (GIF stands for *graphics interchange format*.) You can find more information on animated GIFs, including links to free animation software, at `http://animation.about.com/arts/animation/msubgif.htm`.

3. If you want to take advantage of the latest and greatest Web effects (and who doesn't, from time to time?), implement them in conjunction with a browser sniffer script — a script that "sniffs" out which browser a user is running — like the one shown in this chapter. For example, you can create a JavaScript-enabled Web page that draws a viewer's attention by scrolling a line of text, and you can allow the user to stop (and restart) the scrolling action.

Take a quick peek at Listing 5-1, and then check out Figures 5-1 and 5-2, which show how this script appears in Netscape Navigator 7.0. Also see Figures 5-3 and 5-4, which show how the same script appears in Microsoft Internet Explorer 6.0. I spend the remainder of this section describing exactly how the script in Listing 5-1 works, step by step, so you can apply the principles you see here to your own browser-sniffing scripts.

You can find the code shown in Listing 5-1 in the file list0501.htm, which is located on the companion CD. Check it out in your own browser!

Listing 5-1:   Sniffing Out Browser Versions

```
<SCRIPT LANGUAGE="JavaScript" TYPE="javascript/text">
<!-- Hide from browsers that do not support JavaScript

if (navigator.appName == "Microsoft Internet Explorer") {

    // Create a MSIE-specific Web page
    document.write("You're running Microsoft IE, which supports MARQUEE
            scrolling.")
    var builtInScroll = '<FORM NAME="myForm"><MARQUEE ID=abc DIRECTION=LEFT
            BEHAVIOR=SCROLL SCROLLAMOUNT=4>JavaScript For
            Dummies...</MARQUEE><INPUT TYPE="button" VALUE="Start scrolling"
            NAME="startscroll" onClick="document.all.abc.start()"><INPUT
            TYPE="button" VALUE="Stop scrolling" NAME="stopScroll"
            onClick="document.all.abc.stop()"></FORM>';
}
else {

    // Create a Web page that doesn't use MSIE-specific features
    var builtInScroll = '<CENTER><H1>JavaScript For Dummies...</H1></CENTER>'

    if (navigator.appName == "Netscape") {
        document.write("You're running Netscape, which doesn't provide
            consistent support for MARQUEE scrolling.")
    }

    else {
        document.write("You're not running Microsoft IE or Netscape")
    }
}

// Display the contents of two important navigator properties
alert("navigator.appName is: " + navigator.appName
        + "\navigator.appVersion is: " + navigator.appVersion)

// Display the appropriate Web page
document.write(builtInScroll)

// --> Finish hiding
</SCRIPT>
```

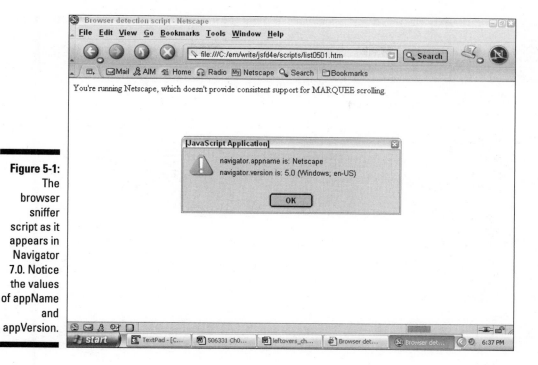

Figure 5-1:
The browser sniffer script as it appears in Navigator 7.0. Notice the values of appName and appVersion.

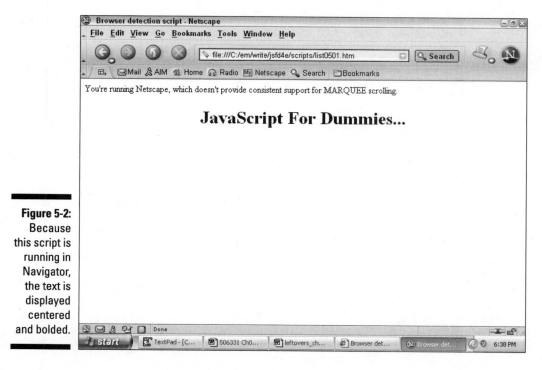

Figure 5-2:
Because this script is running in Navigator, the text is displayed centered and bolded.

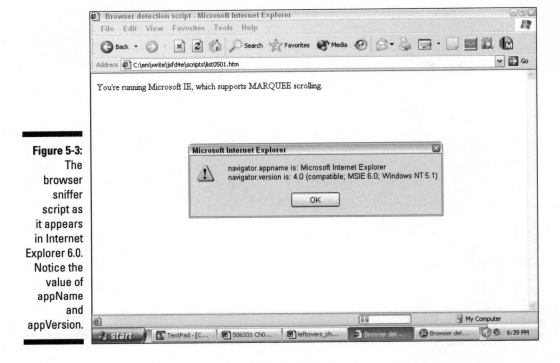

Figure 5-3:
The
browser
sniffer
script as
it appears
in Internet
Explorer 6.0.
Notice the
value of
appName
and
appVersion.

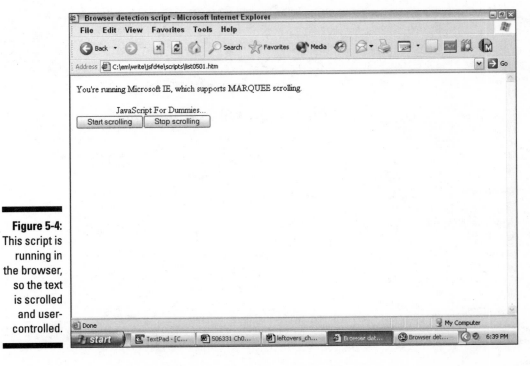

Figure 5-4:
This script is
running in
the browser,
so the text
is scrolled
and user-
controlled.

The code that you see in Listing 5-1 uses the `if-else` statement to examine the contents of the built-in `navigator.appName` property and determine whether the user is running Internet Explorer. (A `navigator.appName` value of `"Microsoft Internet Explorer"` means that the user is running Internet Explorer.)

✔ If the user is running Internet Explorer, the JavaScript code

- Writes a message to the screen, which you see in Figure 5-1. (`You're running Microsoft IE, which supports MARQUEE scrolling.`)

- Creates a variable named `builtInScroll` that contains all the HTML code necessary to display scrolling text — along with buttons that a user can use to turn scrolling on and off.

✔ If the user is not running Internet Explorer, the JavaScript code

- Creates a variable called `builtInScroll` that contains all the HTML necessary to display centered, bolded text.

- Examines the `navigator.appName` property again to determine whether the user is running Netscape Navigator or another browser.

- Displays an appropriate message based on the value of the `navigator.appName` property.

Regardless of the make of browser the user is running, the JavaScript code

✔ Displays a pop-up message describing the contents of the `navigator.appName` and `navigator.appVersion` properties.

✔ Writes the contents of the `builtInScroll` variable to the screen.

The built-in `navigator` object stores many different browser details. You can examine the contents of the `navigator.appVersion` property to determine which version of a particular make of browser a user is running (for example, 6.0 or 7.0). Unfortunately, however, no standard approach to version naming exists. For example, notice in Figure 5-1, the value of `appVersion` is 5.0 — even though the actual version of Navigator running is 7.0. Notice also that in Figure 5-3, the value of `appVersion` is listed as 4.0, not 6.0 as you might expect (although the string `MSIE 6.0`, the actual version of Internet Explorer running, also appears as part of the `appVersion` value.) The upshot is that to determine the correct version of browser running, you need to perform the following two steps:

1. **Check with each browser manufacturer to find out what** `appVersion` **value to expect for each browser version.** For example,

- You can find out all about the `navigator` object that Internet Explorer supports (including the `appVersion` property) by visiting `http://msdn.microsoft.com/library/default.asp?url=/workshop/author/dhtml/reference/objects.asp`.

- To see how Netscape describes the built-in navigator object, check http://devedge.netscape.com/library/manuals/2000/javascript/1.5/reference/ix.html.

2. **If necessary, use a String method, such as** indexOf(), **to extract the value of the** appVersion **property.** The indexOf() method returns one of two values: -1 if a given string isn't found, or the position of a string if that string is found. (Note: JavaScript begins counting string positions at 0, not 1.) For example, the following JavaScript code searches the contents of the appVersion property to determine whether it contains the string "6.0":

```
if (navigator.appVersion.indexOf("6.0") == -1) {
    alert("The string '6.0' was not found in the value for appVersion)
}
else {
    alert("The string '6.0' was found in the value for appVersion")
}
```

Embedded objects

Netscape Navigator and Internet Explorer both support embedded objects — specialized applications that run inside Web pages.

Embedded objects allow users to view non-HTML content. For example, a Flash embedded object allows Navigator users to load Web pages containing animations created with Macromedia Flash, a RealPlayer embedded object allows Navigator users to load Web pages containing RealAudio clips, and so on.

By using JavaScript, you can determine at runtime whether a user has a specific embedded object installed and display your Web page accordingly. For example, you might want to begin playing a QuickTime movie as soon as a user loads your page — but only if that user has QuickTime capability already installed.

Internet Explorer supports embedded objects through Microsoft's ActiveX components. Netscape Navigator supports embedded objects through a technology called plug-ins. Both browsers support specialized embedded objects called Java applets.

How do you determine whether a user has specific plugged-in content? JavaScript offers two different ways:

- **Both Navigator and Internet Explorer:** The `document.embeds[]` array contains a list of all the objects embedded in a document via the `<OBJECT>` tag (Internet Explorer) and the `<EMBED>` tag (Netscape Navigator). The `document.applets[]` array contains a list of all the applets embedded in a document via the `<APPLET>` tag.

- **Navigator:** The `navigator.plugins[]` array contains a list of all the plug-ins that Navigator supports. (Popular plug-ins include Adobe Acrobat and Apple QuickTime.) The `navigator.mimeTypes[]` array contains a list of all of the MIME types supported by Navigator. (MIME, or Multipurpose Internet Mail Extension, refers to the file types that Navigator can understand and display. Examples of popular MIME types include Adobe's portable document framework (`.pdf`) and RealNetworks' RealAudio (`.ram`).

The `<APPLET>` tag was deprecated in HTML 4.0, which means that programmers are encouraged to use the `<OBJECT>` or `<EMBED>` tag (instead of the `<APPLET>` tag) to embed Java applets in Web pages. Future browsers might not support the `<APPLET>` tag. I demonstrate detecting Java applets via the `document.applets[]` array, however, because many `<APPLET>`-tag-containing Web pages still exist.

In IE, the `navigator.plugins[]` and `navigator.mimeTypes[]` arrays are always null because IE implements embedded ActiveX objects in place of plug-ins. To detect embedded content in documents viewed in Internet Explorer, access the `document.embeds[]` array.

Detecting plugged-in content can be a little tricky. Fortunately, the code that you see in Listing 5-2 helps you understand the differences between embedded objects and plug-ins.

Before scanning the code listing, though, take a look at Figures 5-5 through 5-8, which show the code in Listing 5-2 loaded in Netscape Navigator. Then see Figures 5-9 through 5-12, which show the same code loaded in IE.

You can experiment with the code in Listing 5-2 by loading the file `list0502.htm` from the companion CD into your own Web browser. To duplicate the example shown in this chapter, you can download a copy of Apple QuickTime at `www.apple.com/quicktime/download`.

Figure 5-6 shows how clicking the Detect Embedded Objects button displays the total number of `<EMBED>` and `<OBJECT>` tags in this document. Clicking the Detect Plug-Ins button, as shown in Figure 5-7, displays the number of downloaded and installed browser plug-ins; clicking the Detect Applets button, as shown in Figure 5-8, displays the number of Java applets embedded in the document using the `<APPLET>` tag.

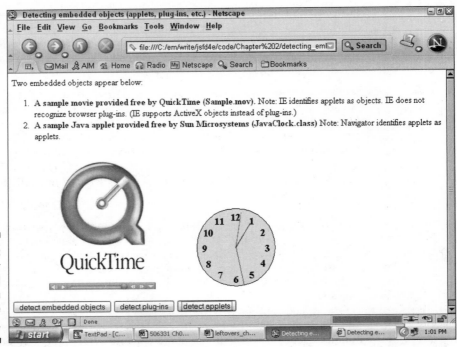

Two embedded objects appear below:

1. A sample movie provided free by QuickTime (Sample.mov). Note: IE identifies applets as objects. IE does not recognize browser plug-ins. (IE supports ActiveX objects instead of plug-ins.)
2. A sample Java applet provided free by Sun Microsystems (JavaClock.class) Note: Navigator identifies applets as applets.

Figure 5-5:
Checking for embedded objects in Netscape Navigator.

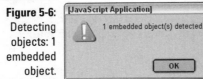

Figure 5-6:
Detecting objects: 1 embedded object.

[JavaScript Application]

1 embedded object(s) detected.

OK

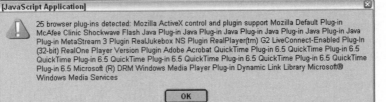

Figure 5-7:
Detecting plug-ins: 25 browser plug-ins.

[JavaScript Application]

25 browser plug-ins detected: Mozilla ActiveX control and plugin support Mozilla Default Plug-in McAfee Clinic Shockwave Flash Java Plug-in Java Plug-in Java Plug-in Java Plug-in Java Plug-in MetaStream 3 Plugin RealJukebox NS Plugin RealPlayer(tm) G2 LiveConnect-Enabled Plug-In (32-bit) RealOne Player Version Plugin Adobe Acrobat QuickTime Plug-in 6.5 QuickTime Plug-in 6.5 QuickTime Plug-in 6.5 QuickTime Plug-in 6.5 QuickTime Plug-in 6.5 QuickTime Plug-in 6.5 QuickTime Plug-in 6.5 Microsoft (R) DRM Windows Media Player Plug-in Dynamic Link Library Microsoft® Windows Media Services

OK

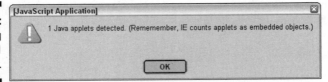

Figure 5-8:
Detecting applets: 1 Java applet.

[JavaScript Application]

1 Java applets detected. (Rememember, IE counts applets as embedded objects.)

OK

The same code — Listing 5-2 — executed in Internet Explorer behaves a bit differently, as you can see in Figures 5-9, 5-10, 5-11, 5-12, and 5-13. When you click the Detect Plug-Ins button, the number of plug-ins detected is always none because Internet Explorer doesn't recognize or implement plug-ins.

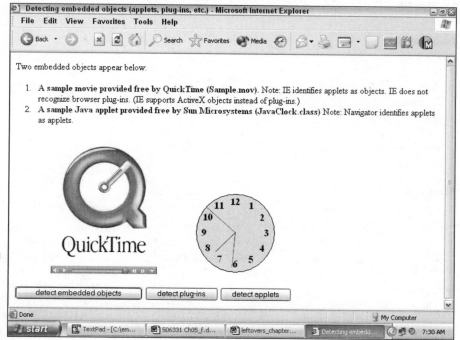

Figure 5-9: Checking for embedded objects in IE.

Figure 5-10: Detecting an embedded QuickTime object . . .

Figure 5-11: . . . and a Java applet.

Figure 5-12:
IE doesn't
support
plug-ins.

Figure 5-13:
In IE,
applets
aren't
differenti-
ated from
any other
embedded
objects.

Take a look at Listing 5-2. As you skim through the code, notice the similari-
ties in detecting different kinds of embedded content. In each case, you examine the `length` property associated with a built-in array (the `navigator.`
`plugins.length`, `document.embeds.length`, and `document.applets.`
`length` properties detect plug-ins, embedded objects, and embedded applets,
respectively).

Listing 5-2:   Detecting Embedded Objects

```html
<HTML>
<HEAD><TITLE>Detecting embedded objects (applets, plug-ins, etc.)</TITLE>

<SCRIPT LANGUAGE="JavaScript" TYPE="text/javascript">
<!-- Hide from browsers that do not support JavaScript

//////////////////////////////////////////////////
// The detectPlugins() function detects
// Navigator browser plug-ins (software "cartridges"
// that have previously been downloaded and
// installed in the Netscape Navigator browser).
//////////////////////////////////////////////////
function detectPlugins() {
    if (navigator.plugins.length > 0) {
        var pluginDescription = "";
```

```
        for (var numPlugins = 0; numPlugins < navigator.plugins.length;
            numPlugins++) {
          pluginDescription = pluginDescription + " " +
            navigator.plugins[numPlugins].name
        }

        alert(navigator.plugins.length + " browser plug-ins detected: "
            + pluginDescription);

    }
    else {
      alert("No browser plug-ins detected. (Remember, IE doesn't support
            plug-ins.)")
    }

}

//////////////////////////////////////////////////
// The detectApplets() function detects Java
// applets embedded in a Web page via the
// APPLET tag - but for Netscape Navigator only.
// To detect applets in a page running in
// Microsoft Internet Explorer, you need to have
// knowledge of the applet: for example,
// document.applets['nameOfApplet'].someMethod();
//
// The length of the document.applets array
// represents the number of objects embedded
// in a Web page.
//
// The existence of additional applets[]
// properties and methods depends on the
// implementation of each individual applet.
//////////////////////////////////////////////////
function detectApplets() {
    if (document.applets.length > 0) {
        alert(document.applets.length + " Java applets detected. (Rememember, IE
                counts applets as embedded objects.)")

    }
    else {
      alert("No Java applets detected.")
    }
}
```

(continued)

Listing 5-2 *(continued)*

```
/////////////////////////////////////////////////
// The detectEmbeds() function detects content
// embedded in a Web page via the EMBED
// or OBJECT tag.
//
// The length of the document.embeds array
// represents the number of objects embedded
// in a Web page.
//
// The existence of additional embeds[]
// properties depends on the implementation
// of each embedded object.
/////////////////////////////////////////////////
function detectEmbeds() {

    if (navigator.appName == "Microsoft Internet Explorer") {
        // The user is running IE, so check for objects
        // embedded using the OBJECT tag.
        //
        // The readyState property of an object embedded
                // using the OBJECT property can contain one of 3
                // values:
                // 0 = uninitialized
                // 1 = loading
                // 4 = finished loading and ready to go

                if (document.QTsample.readyState == 4) {
                    alert("Detected the QTsample embedded object");
        }

                if (document.clock.readyState == 4) {
                    alert("Detected the clock embedded object");
        }

    }
    else {
        if (navigator.appName == "Netscape") {
            // The user is running Navigator, so check
            // for objects
            // embedded using the EMBED tag.

        if (document.embeds.length > 0) {
            alert(document.embeds.length
                    + " embedded object(s) detected.")
```

```
            }
        else {
            alert("No embedded objects detected.");
        }
    }
    }
}


// --> Finish hiding
</SCRIPT>

</HEAD>
<BODY>
Two embedded objects appear below:
<OL>
<LI><b>A sample movie provided free by QuickTime (Sample.mov).</b>
Note: IE identifies applets as objects. IE does not recognize browser plug-ins.
            (IE supports
ActiveX objects instead of plug-ins.)
<LI><b>A sample Java applet provided free by Sun Microsystems
            (JavaClock.class)</b>
Note: Navigator identifies applets as applets.
</OL>

<!--
You use the OBJECT tag to embed an ActiveX component into a
page meant for MSIE; you use the EMBED tag to embed a plug-in into a page meant
for Navigator.
Notice the difference between the way the value of the SRC
variable must be specified.
// -->

<OBJECT CLASSID="clsid:02BF25D5-8C17-4B23-BC80-D3488ABDDC6B"
            WIDTH="320"HEIGHT="250"
ID="QTsample"
CODEBASE="http://www.apple.com/qtactivex/qtplugin.cab">
<PARAM name="SRC" VALUE="c:\Program Files\QuickTime\Sample.mov">
<PARAM name="AUTOPLAY" VALUE="true">
<PARAM name="CONTROLLER" VALUE="true">

<EMBED SRC="file://c:\Program Files\QuickTime\Sample.mov" WIDTH="320"
            HEIGHT="250" AUTOPLAY="true" CONTROLLER="true"
            PLUGINSPAGE="http://www.apple.com/quicktime/download/">
</EMBED>

</OBJECT>
```

(continued)

Listing 5-2 *(continued)*

```
<!--

This Java applet is freely available from Sun Microsystems.
For more info,
visit http://java.sun.com/openstudio/applets/clock.html

Note: The APPLET tag was deprecated in HTML 4.0, which
means that programmers are encouraged to use the OBJECT tag
(instead of the APPLET tag) to embed Java applets
in Web pages. Future browsers might not support the APPLET tag.
// -->

<APPLET ID="clock" CODEBASE="classes" CODE="JavaClock.class" WIDTH="150"
            HEIGHT="150">
<PARAM    NAME="bgcolor"    VALUE="FFFFFF">
<PARAM    NAME="border"     VALUE="5">
<PARAM    NAME="ccolor"     VALUE="dddddd">
<PARAM    NAME="cfont"      VALUE="TimesRoman|BOLD|18">
<PARAM    NAME="delay"      VALUE="100">
<PARAM    NAME="hhcolor"    VALUE="0000FF">
<PARAM    NAME="link"       VALUE="http://java.sun.com/">
<PARAM    NAME="mhcolor"    VALUE="00FF00">
<PARAM    NAME="ncolor"     VALUE="000000">
<PARAM    NAME="nradius"    VALUE="80">
<PARAM    NAME="shcolor"    VALUE="FF0000">
</APPLET>

<P>
<FORM>
<INPUT TYPE="button" VALUE="detect embedded objects" onClick="detectEmbeds()">

<INPUT TYPE="button" VALUE="detect plug-ins" onClick="detectPlugins()">

<INPUT TYPE="button" VALUE="detect applets" onClick="detectApplets()">
</FORM>
</BODY>
</HTML>
```

Keep in mind that you can use two ways to detect Netscape Navigator plug-ins: by examining the `navigator.plugins[]` array and by examining the `navigator.mimeTypes[]` array, as shown in Listing 5-2. Because Internet Explorer doesn't support plug-ins, however, these two arrays are always empty in Internet Explorer.

Objects embedded by using either the `<EMBED>` or `<OBJECT>` tag are added to the `document.embeds[]` array.

The `document.plugins[]` array is a synonym for the `document.embeds[]` array, but because the `document.plugins[]` array appears so similar to the `navigator.plugins[]` array — an array that holds an entirely different kind of object — I suggest sticking with the `document.embeds[]` array when you want to determine the number of embedded `<OBJECT>` and `<EMBED>` tags in a document.

The referrer page

A referrer page is the Web page that a user loaded directly before loading your Web page. You can use JavaScript to determine the referring page at runtime — which is useful if you're keeping track of statistics. (Some programmers enjoy knowing precisely what links users follow to get to their Web pages.)

To identify the referring page, you examine the `referrer` property of the `document` object, as shown in the following JavaScript code:

```
if (document.referrer == "") {
    document.writeln("You pulled this page up fresh in a browser.");
}

else {
    document.writeln("You were referred to this page by " + document.referrer);
}
```

The above code snippet determines the following:

✔ If the value of `document.referrer` is blank (blank is denoted by `" "` in the code snippet), the user typed the name of the Web page directly into the browser address field.

✔ If the value of `document.referrer` isn't blank, `document.referrer` contains the name of the referring page.

The files `detecting_referrer_base.htm` and `detecting_referrer.htm`, which you find on the companion CD, allow you to test the code that I describe in this section. To use these files, upload them to a Web server, load the file `detecting_referrer_base.htm` in your Web browser, and click the link that appears.

You must upload your HTML files to a Web server in order to test the code that you see in this section; the value of `document.referrer` is always blank when tested locally.

User preferences

Wouldn't it be great if your users could choose they way they'd prefer to see your Web pages? Well, if you use JavaScript, they can! You can use JavaScript to present your users with a series of options right away, before your Web page loads — and then use that feedback to display your page the way your users want to see it.

In Figures 5-14 and 5-15, for example, you see prompts asking users which color they prefer for background and text color, respectively. Figure 5-16 shows the result: a Web page containing the user's preferred color scheme.

Figure 5-14:
Asking
users
for their
preferences.

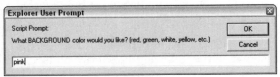

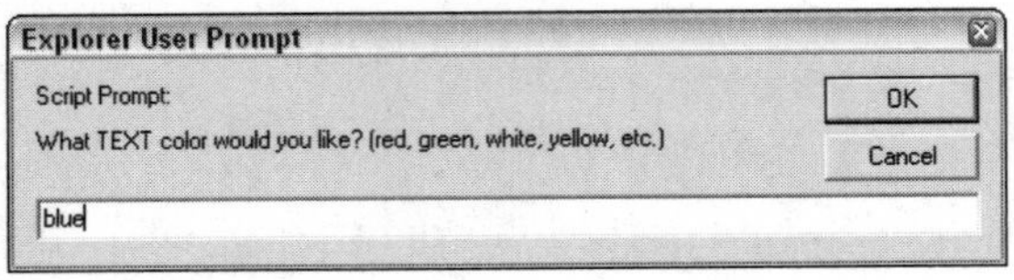

Figure 5-15:
Your users
can enter
the text
color.

The code in Listing 5-3 is available on the companion CD: just load the file `list0503.htm`.

Listing 5-3:   Detecting User Preferences

```
<HTML>
<HEAD>
<TITLE>Detecting user preferences (and customizing display)</TITLE>
<SCRIPT LANGUAGE="JavaScript" TYPE="text/javascript">
<!-- Hide from browsers that do not support JavaScript

// Ask the user for color preferences
var displayColor = prompt("What BACKGROUND color would you like? (red, green,
            white, yellow, etc.)", "pink");
```

```
var textColor = prompt("What TEXT color would you like? (red, green, white,
          yellow, etc.)", "blue");

// Display page content
document.writeln("<BODY BGCOLOR=" + displayColor + " TEXT=" + textColor + ">You
          chose " + textColor + " text on a " + displayColor + "
          background.</BODY>")

// --> Finish hiding
</SCRIPT>
</HEAD>
</HTML>
```

As you skim through the JavaScript code in Figure 5-3, notice that it defines
two variables:

- ✔ displayColor, containing the user's choice of background color
- ✔ textColor, containing the user's choice of text color

After these two variables are defined, the JavaScript code uses them — along
with the writeln() method — to define and display the <BODY> section of
the Web page.

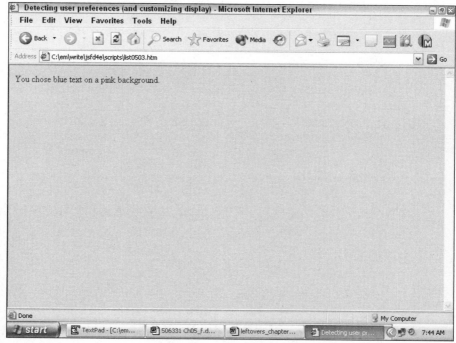

Figure 5-16:
A cus-
tomized
display
based
on user
preferences.

Chapter 6

That's How the Cookie Crumbles

*U*nlike a traditional client/server configuration, in which the client and the server have to agree to begin and end every conversation, the Web is stateless. Stateless means that, by default, neither Web browsers nor Web servers keep track of their conversations for later use. Like two ships that pass in the night, browsers and servers interact only when a user downloads a Web page, and then they immediately forget the other ever existed!

Cookies — tiny text files that a Web server can store on a client's computer via a Web browser — were designed to change all that. By using cookies to keep track of browser-to-server interactions, Web developers can create intelligent Web sites that remember details about each and every user who visits them. You can even create cookies with built-in expiration dates so that information stored as cookies is maintained for only a limited period of time — say, a week or a month.

Cookie Basics

You can use JavaScript, Perl, VBScript, or any other Web-savvy language to store small text files called cookies on your site visitor's computer. Because the whole point of using cookies is for server-side applications to keep track of client information, however, cookies are typically created and set by CGI programs rather than by JavaScript scripts. (CGI stands for Common Gateway Interface. CGI programs, which are usually written in Perl or C/C++, live on

Web servers; their job in life is to transmit data back and forth between a Web server and a Web client.) But because this book is devoted to JavaScript, later in this chapter I show you how to create and interact with cookies by using JavaScript instead of C/C++, Perl, or some other, more traditional cookie-manipulation language.

Before I dive into the code, however, I explain exactly what cookies are and how they work.

Why use cookies?

Cookies allow you to store information about a user's visit on that user's computer and retrieve it when the user revisits your site. Two of the most common reasons Web developers use cookies are

- ✔ **To identify visitors:** You can detect when a user has previously visited your site and customize what that user sees on subsequent visits. For example, you can greet visitors by name, tell them what's changed on your site since their last visits, display customized pages based on their previous purchasing, their site navigation habits, and so on.

- ✔ **To save transaction state:** You can store the status of any lengthy trans-actions between your site and your visitors' browsers to safeguard against interruptions. For example, imagine that I'm filling out a lengthy form on your Web site when all of a sudden my dog chases my cat under my desk. They scuffle, and before I know what's happening, my computer plug comes sailing out of the wall socket! If your site uses cookies, I can throw my beasts out in the backyard, plug my machine back in, reload your Web page, and pick up right where I left off. If your site doesn't use cookies, I have to start filling out the form from the beginning.

Cookie security issues

Cookies have been used safely for a few years now, and because their use is strictly governed by Web browsers, they rank mighty low on the list of poten-tial security threats. Still, they are highly controversial in some programmer circles for two reasons:

- ✔ **Cookies jump the traditional bounds of a Web browser by storing information directly on users' hard drives.** Some folks fear that cookies can damage their computers by infecting their computers with viruses or by storing such huge amounts of data on their hard drives that their computers no longer work properly.

Fortunately, cookies come with built-in safeguards against both these threats. No matter whether you use JavaScript or some other language, you can't get past the following common-sense limits that Web browsers impose:

- **Where cookies are placed:** Internet Explorer 6.x running on Windows XP, for example, stores cookies as individual text files and places them in the following directory:

```
C:\Documents and Settings\Owner\Cookies
```

  Netscape Navigator 7.0 running on Windows XP bunches cookies together in a single file, called `cookies.txt`, and places that file in a random-generated directory name similar to the following:

```
C:\Documents and Settings\Owner\Application Data\Mozilla\profiles\default\
        klambsdn.slt
```

- **How large cookie files can be:** Both Internet Explorer and Netscape Navigator limit cookie files to 4K.

- **How many cookies any given Web site can place on a user's hard drive:** Both Internet Explorer and Netscape Navigator set the limit at 20 cookies per site and set an overall total of 300 cookies per browser.

- **Which sites have access to cookies:** Cookie visibility is configurable. (You see how to configure cookie access in the "Configuring cookie support" section in this chapter.)

✔ **Cookies enable Web developers to gather detailed marketing information about users without those users' knowledge or consent.** Using cookies in conjunction with client-side applications like CGI programs and Java applets, Web developers can save, examine, and interpret virtually every interaction between a user and a Web site. Every click, every keystroke, every credit card purchase can be used to customize what a user sees the next time he visits a cookie-enabled Web site.

Fortunately, users who feel uncomfortable with the Big Brother–like aspect of cookies have a choice: They can configure their browsers to limit cookie support or turn it off altogether. (You see an example of configuring cookies in the very next section.)

Looking at cookies from a user's perspective

One of the best ways to understand how cookies work is to take a look at them from a user's perspective. In this section, I show you how to configure cookie support in your browser, visit a cookie-enabled site, and examine an actual cookie file. When you finish, you have all the background you need to be able to jump right into making cookies with JavaScript code.

Configuring cookie support

Netscape Navigator and Internet Explorer both allow users to specify a level of cookie support.

In Netscape Navigator 7.x, you configure cookie support by following these steps:

1. **Choose Edit⇨Preferences⇨Privacy & Security⇨Cookies.**

2. **Select one of the following options in the Cookies dialog box that appears, as shown in Figure 6-1:**

   - Disable Cookies.

   - Enable Cookies for the Originating Web Site Only (as opposed to any server in the originating domain).

   - Enable Cookies Based on Customizable Privacy Settings. (Click the View button to set privacy settings based on the published privacy policies of cookie-setting sites.)

   - Enable All Cookies.

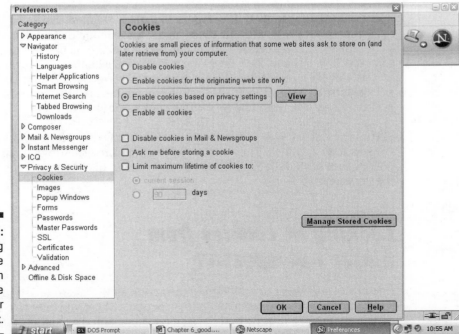

Figure 6-1: Configuring cookie support in Netscape Navigator 7.x.

Click the Manage Stored Cookies button in the Cookies dialog box to view the cookies stored on your computer.

As you might guess, users who disable cookie support can't benefit from the cookie-accessing scripts that you create with JavaScript. One way to alert users that they need to turn on cookie support to get the most out of your site is to tell them! Just include the following sentence at the top of your cookie-enabled Web pages: `This Web site requires you to turn on cookie support.`

To configure cookie support in Internet Explorer, follow these steps:

1. **Choose Tools⇨Internet Options.**

2. **In the Internet Options dialog box that appears, click the Privacy tab.**

3. **Move the slider on the left side of the Privacy tab from all the way up (the Block All Cookies option, as shown in Figure 6-2) to all the way down (the Accept All Cookies option).**

   The interim options are High, Medium High, Medium, and Low. You can customize any option by clicking the Advanced button.

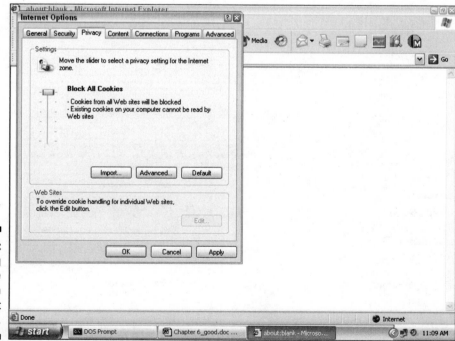

Figure 6-2:
Configuring cookie support in Internet Explorer.

Visiting a cookie-enabled site

When your browser is configured to accept cookies, you can surf to cookie-enabled sites with impunity. Figure 6-3 shows how a cookie can be used to recognize visitors and present them with custom greetings and options. (You find out how to create a similar custom greeting later in this chapter, in "Displaying content based on cookie contents: The repeat-visitor script.")

Exploring a cookie file

This section shows you what goes on underneath the covers when you visit a cookie-enabled site.

In Netscape Navigator 7.1, you can examine the cookie file by choosing Edit⇨Preferences⇨Privacy & Security⇨Cookies and clicking the Manage Stored Cookies button. The resulting Cookie Manager dialog box appears, as shown in Figure 6-4.

You can get your hands on the raw cookie file that Netscape Navigator generates by loading the file `C:\Documents and Settings\Owner\Application Data\Mozilla\profiles\defalt\klambsdn.slt\cookies.txt` (which is the text file in which Netscape Navigator 7.1 stores cookies) into your favorite editor.

Figure 6-3: The results of a cookie: a customized greeting from the folks at Amazon.com.

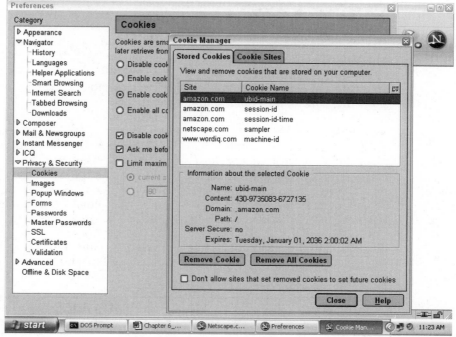

Figure 6-4:
Taking a
look inside
one of the
cookies set
by the www.
amazon.
com
domain.

Internet Explorer stores individually generated cookie files in the following directory: `C:\Documents and Settings\userName\Cookies`. Cookie file-names take the form of `userName@domain[timesAccessed].txt`. For example, on my machine, the following file exists after a visit to Amazon.com:

```
C:\Documents and Settings\Owner\Cookies\owner@amazon[1].txt
```

You can also type **JavaScript:alert(document.cookie);** in the Address bar of Internet Explorer or Netscape Navigator after you load a Web page. When you click Go, you see a pop-up window containing all the cookies associated with that page.

Saving and Retrieving User Information

Working with cookies involves two distinct operations: creating, or setting, a cookie; and accessing the created cookie. Typically, you create a cookie only once, the first time a user visits your site. After that, you can access the cookie every time the user revisits your site or as often as you like. The following sections show you how.

Setting a cookie

The `cookie` property of the `document` object holds all the cookies associated with a document.

To create and set a cookie, you must define a variable/value pair that represents the name of the cookie and the cookie's content (*name=value*). Because cookie values can't contain semicolons, commas, or white space, I recommend using the built-in JavaScript `escape()` function when storing a cookie's value and using the built-in JavaScript `unescape()` function when retrieving a cookie's value. (The `escape()` function encodes any semicolons, commas, and white space that exist in a string, and the `unescape()` function reconstitutes them.) Other than this restriction, a cookie value can contain just about anything you like! (Some programmers come up with fancy encryption schemes, but others stick with simple text-based strings.)

In addition to the mandatory name and value, you might define optional, semicolon-delimited attributes for a cookie (see Table 6-1).

Table 6-1	JavaScript Cookie Attributes
Attribute	*Description*
`expires=expirationDate;`	The date, in milliseconds, after which the cookie expires (and is deleted by the Web browser). Expiration dates are normally stored in the standard Greenwich Mean Time format. (You format a date in GMT by using the `toGMTString()` method of the `Date` object.)
`path=path;`	The path of the CGI program to which the cookie contents can be transmitted. The default is the root path of the originating server.
`domain=domain;`	The domain (for example, `www.acme.com`) to which a cookie can be transmitted. Restricted by default. (See the "Cookie security issues" section for details.)
`secure`	Specifies that this cookie can be transmitted only by a secure protocol such as `https`.

To create a cookie and store it on the user's hard drive, all you need to do is set the `document.cookie` property equal to a string containing the required name/value pair and any optional, semicolon-delimited cookie attributes, as shown in the following code snippet (taken from Listing 6-1, which appears later in this chapter):

```
document.cookie = name + "=" + escape(value) +
    ((expires == null) ? "" : ("; expires=" + expires.toGMTString())) +
    ((path == null) ? "" : ("; path=" + path)) +
    ((domain == null) ? "" : ("; domain=" + domain)) +
    ((secure == true) ? "; secure" : "");
```

The cryptic, odd-looking syntax — `(condition) ? something : somethingElse` — is JavaScript shorthand for "if this condition is true, then add something. Otherwise, add somethingElse."

For example, here's how the JavaScript interpreter sees the JavaScript phrase:

```
((expires == null) ? "" : ("; expires=" + expires.toGMTString()))
```

It thinks to itself "If the value for `expires` is `null`, add `""` to the `document.cookie` property. Otherwise, add the string `expires=someGMTFormattedDate` to the `document.cookie` property."

You can find out more about the conditional `?:` operator in Chapter 3.

Accessing a cookie

You can set attributes for a cookie by using JavaScript (specifically, the `expires`, `path`, `domain`, and `secure` attributes, as I describe in the section "Setting a cookie"), but you can't access those attributes by using JavaScript. In contrast, you can access a cookie's value.

This seemingly odd state of affairs — being able to set attributes that you can't retrieve — actually makes sense when you think about it. All these attributes are security-related, and preventing them from being altered helps maintain cookies' integrity and safety. After you give out your cookies, only the Web browser is privy to cookie attributes.

To access a cookie's value, you query the `cookie` property associated with the `document` object. (You see how to set the `cookie` property in "Setting a cookie," earlier in this chapter.)

Check out the following JavaScript code snippet:

```
var endstr = document.cookie.indexOf(";", offset);
...

return unescape(document.cookie.substring(offset, endstr));
```

This code contains two statements:

- ✔ **The first statement** uses the `indexOf()` method to identify the portion of the `myCookie=userName;` string between the = and the ; (in other words, to identify the stored value of the `userName` string).

- ✔ **The second statement** unescapes the stored value of the userName string. (Unescaping is computerese for decoding any special characters encoded when the cookie was set.)

You can find a working copy of this code snippet in Listing 6-1, later in this chapter.

Displaying content based on cookie contents: The repeat-visitor script

You can create a script that registers a user by saving the user's name to the user's hard drive by using a cookie. On subsequent visits to the site, the script accesses the cookie from the user's hard drive, recognizes the user's name, and uses the information to display a custom greeting. Figure 6-5 shows stage one of the repeat-visitor script where users must first register their names.

In many real-life applications, you want to create and access cookies by using a server-side technology, such as a CGI script. Because CGI scripting is beyond the scope of this book, in this chapter I show you how to create and access cookies with JavaScript instead. (The syntax between CGI scripting languages and JavaScript differs, but the basic ways that you interact with cookies are the same.)

After users register their names, as shown in Figure 6-5, they never see the registration form again. Users can close their browsers, turn off their machines, and go away on vacation for a week. When they return and attempt to access the registration page again, the script recognizes that they've already registered and loads the For Registered Users Only page with a customized greeting (see Figure 6-6).

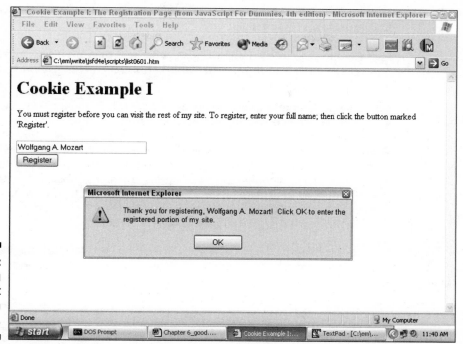

Figure 6-5:
Registering
user input
with
cookies.

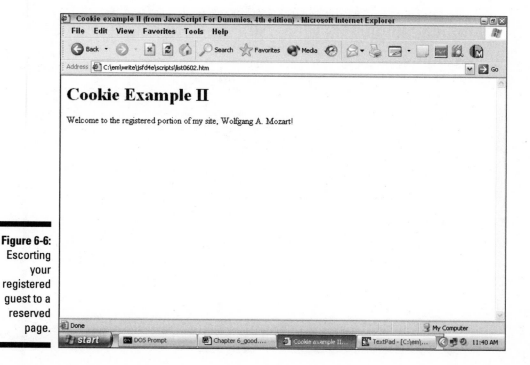

Figure 6-6:
Escorting
your
registered
guest to a
reserved
page.

I implemented the repeat-visitor script in two parts based on the two actions in Figure 6-5 and Figure 6-6:

- **Cookie Example I (For Unregistered Users page):** This script registers a user's name, stores a cookie on that user's machine, and loads the For Registered Users Only page.

- **Cookie Example II (For Registered Users Only page):** This script accesses the cookie and displays a custom greeting.

When you create a cookie, you specify an expiration date. After the specified expiration date, the cookie can no longer be accessed. An expiration of the null value marks a cookie as transient. (Transient cookies stay around in memory only as long as the user's browser session lasts; they aren't saved to the user's hard drive.) In the example in Listing 6-1, you see an expiration date of one year from the time the cookie is created.

The Cookie Example I and Cookie Example II scripts are shown in Listings 6-1 and 6-2, respectively. You can find them in the list0601.htm and list0602.htm files on the companion CD-ROM.

Listing 6-1: Cookie Example I: The Registration Form

```html
<HTML>
<HEAD><TITLE>Cookie Example I: The Registration Page (From JavaScript For
            Dummies, 4th Edition)</TITLE>

<SCRIPT LANGUAGE="JavaScript" TYPE="text/javascript">

<!-- Begin hiding

function getCookieVal (offset) {

    // This function returns the portion of the
    // "myCookie=userName" string
    // between the = and the ;
    var endstr = document.cookie.indexOf (";", offset);

    if (endstr == -1) {
        endstr = document.cookie.length;
    }

    return unescape(document.cookie.substring(offset, endstr));
}

function getCookie (cookieName)  {

    // You have to pick apart the cookie text. To do this,
    // You start by figuring out how many characters are
    // in the string "myCookie="
```

```
    var arg = cookieName + "=";
    var argLength = arg.length;

    // Now find out how long the entire cookie string is
    var cookieLength = document.cookie.length;

    // If cookies were stored as objects,
    // life would be much easier!
    // As it is, you must step through the contents
    // of a cookie character
    // by character to retrieve what is stored there.

    var i = 0;

    // While the "i" counter is less than the number
    // of characters in the cookie . . .
    while (i < cookieLength) {

        // Offset the "j" counter by the number of characters
        // in "myCookie=".
        var j = i + argLength;

        // If you find "myCookie=" in the cookie contents
        if (document.cookie.substring(i, j) == arg) {
            // return the value associated with "myCookie="
            return getCookieVal(j)
        }
        if (i == 0) {
            break
        }
    }
    return null;
}
function setCookie(name, value) {

    // Capture all the arguments passed to the
    // setCookie() function.

    var argv = setCookie.arguments;

    // Determine the number of arguments passed into
    // this function
    var argc = setCookie.arguments.length;

    // You expect the third argument passed in to
    // be the expiration date.
    // If there isn't a third argument, set the expires
    // variable to null.
    // (An expiration date of null marks a cookie as
    // transient. Transient cookies are not saved to the
    // user's hard drive.)
    var expires = (argc > 2) ? argv[2] : null;
```

(continued)

Listing 6-1 *(continued)*

```javascript
    // You expect the fourth argument passed in to be
    // the path.
    // If there isn't a fourth argument, set the
    // path variable to null.
    var path = (argc > 3) ? argv[3] : null;

    // You expect the fifth argument passed in to be
    // the domain.
    // If there isn't a fifth argument, set the
    // domain variable to null.
    var domain = (argc > 4) ? argv[4] : null;

    // You expect the sixth argument passed in to be
    // true or false,
    // depending on whether this cookie is secure
    // (can be transmitted
    // only to a secure server via https) or not.
    // If there isn't a sixth argument, set the
    // secure variable to false.
    var secure = (argc > 5) ? argv[5] : false;

    // Set the cookie.
    document.cookie = name + "=" + escape(value) +
        ((expires == null) ? "" : ("; expires=" + expires.toGMTString())) +
        ((path == null) ? "" : ("; path=" + path)) +
        ((domain == null) ? "" : ("; domain=" + domain)) +
        ((secure == true) ? "; secure" : "");
}

function register(userName, value) {

    if (userName == "" || userName == null) {
        // The name is missing, so register this user as "Unknown User."
        userName = "Unknown User"
    }

    // If no cookie called 'MyCookie' exists . . .
    if(getCookie('myCookie') == null) {

        // Set the expiration date to today.
        var expdate = new Date()

        // Set the expiration date (which JavaScript
        // stores as milliseconds)
        // to a date exactly one year in the future.
        expdate.setTime(expdate.getTime() + (1000 * 60 * 60 * 24 * 365));

        setCookie('myCookie', userName, expdate);
        alert ("Thank you for registering, " + userName + "! Click OK to enter
                the registered portion of my site.");
```

```
        // Whisk the user to the page reserved
        // for registered users.
        location.href = "list0602.htm"


    }
}


/////////////////////////////////////////////////////////////
// This code checks to see whether a cookie named 'myCookie'
// exists on the user's machine.
//
// If it does, the user has already registered, so whisk
// the user to registered-users-only portion of the site.
//
// If no cookie called 'myCookie' exists on the user's
// machine, ask the user to register.
/////////////////////////////////////////////////////////////

// If the "myCookie" cookie exists . . .

if(getCookie('myCookie') != null) {

    // Then redirect the user's browser to the
    // password-protected page called "list0602.htm"

    location.href="list0602.htm"
}

// End hiding -->
</SCRIPT>
</HEAD>

<BODY>
//#2 (from here to the closing </BODY> tag)
<H1>Cookie Example I</H1>

<FORM NAME="loginForm">
You must register before you can visit the rest of my site. To register, enter
            your full name; then click the Register button.
<P>
<INPUT TYPE="text" NAME="fullName" SIZE=35>
<BR>
<INPUT TYPE="button" VALUE="Register"
            onClick="register(loginForm.fullName.value)">
</FORM>
</BODY>
</HTML>
```

Here's a quick run-down on how the JavaScript interpreter handles the code in Listing 6-1:

1. The interpreter first checks to see whether a cookie named myCookie exists. If such a cookie does exist, the interpreter — understanding that this user has previously registered — loads list0602.htm.

2. If no such cookie exists, the interpreter loads the registration page, complete with an input text box and a Register button.

3. When a user clicks the Register button, the interpreter begins executing the register() function, which in turn invokes the setCookie() method to store a cookie on the user's machine. The cookie contains the user's name and an expiration date.

4. After the register() function stores the cookie, the register() function loads the For Registered Users Only page.

Check out Listing 6-2 to see an example of how to access a cookie to create and display a custom greeting.

Listing 6-2: Cookie Example II: Displaying the Custom Greeting

```
<HTML>
<HEAD><TITLE>Cookie Example II: The Custom Greeting (From JavaScript For
               Dummies, 4th Edition)</TITLE>

<SCRIPT LANGUAGE="JavaScript">

<!-- Begin hiding

function getCookieVal (offset) {
    var endstr = document.cookie.indexOf (";", offset);
    if (endstr == -1) {
        endstr = document.cookie.length;
    }

    return unescape(document.cookie.substring(offset, endstr));
}

function getCookie (name)  {

    var arg = name + "=";

    var argLength = arg.length;
    var cookieLength = document.cookie.length;
```

```
        var i = 0;
        while (i < cookieLength) {
            var j = i + argLength;
            if (document.cookie.substring(i, j) == arg) {
                return getCookieVal(j)
            }
            if (i == 0) {
                break
            }
        }
    return null;
}


/////////////////////////////////////////////////////////////
// This code checks to see whether a cookie named
// 'myCookie' exists on the user's machine.
//
// If it does, the user has already logged in with a valid
// userID and password, so display the site; otherwise,
// display an error.
/////////////////////////////////////////////////////////////

// If the "myCookie" cookie exists . . .

// #1 (down to document.write(documentText)

var nameOfVisitor = getCookie('myCookie')

insert // #2 (down to closing brace associated with if statement)
if(nameOfVisitor != null) {

    var documentText = "<BODY><H1>Cookie Example II</H1>Welcome to the
                registered portion of my site, "
    documentText += nameOfVisitor
    documentText += "!</BODY>"
}

insert // #3 (down to closing brace associated with else statement)
else {
    var documentText = "<BODY><H1>Cookie Example II</H1>Sorry! Only registered
                users can access this page.</BODY>"
}

document.write(documentText)

// End hiding -->
</SCRIPT>
</HEAD>
</HTML>
```

You can't expire me . . . I quit!

You can't delete a cookie directly by using JavaScript for the simple reason that only browsers can actually write to the visitor's hard drive. (It's this security measure that prevents cookies from being able to wreak havoc on users' hard drives.)

What you *can* do in JavaScript is to alter a cookie's expiration date to a date far in the past. Doing so causes the Web browser to delete the newly expired cookie automatically.

```
function deleteCookie () {
    var expired = new Date();
    // You can't delete a cookie file directly from the user's
    // machine using JavaScript, so mark it as expired by
    // setting the expiration date to a date in the past.

    // First, set the exp variable to a date in the past . . .
    expired.setTime (expired.getTime() - 1000000000);

    // Then, get the cookie
    var cookieValue = getCookie ('myCookie');

    // Finally, set the cookie's expiration date to the long-past date.
    document.cookie = 'myCookie' + "=" + cookieValue + ";
                    expires=" + expired.toGMTString();
}
```

In Listing 6-2, here's what's going on:

1. The JavaScript interpreter looks for a cookie named `myCookie` on the user's machine.

2. If a cookie named `myCookie` exists, the JavaScript interpreter constructs and displays a custom greeting with the registered user's name.

3. If no such cookie exists, the JavaScript interpreter constructs an error message.

Chapter 7

Working with Browser Windows and Frames

*B*rowser windows and frames are the lenses through which your users view your Web page content.

As a Web page designer, you can choose to create Web pages that open in a single browser window, which is the standard approach. But with JavaScript, you can do much more. You can display content in separate windows and close those windows automatically. You can even display multiple HTML documents inside a single browser window by using frames, and then share information between those frames by using JavaScript.

By using JavaScript, you can create all kinds of sophisticated window and frame effects. This chapter shows you how.

Whether to include HTML frames in your Web site is a personal design decision. Some folks love frames because they not only allow you to create effective navigation structures, they also allow you to provide hyperlinks to other sites while discouraging users from surfing away to those hyperlinked sites and abandoning your site. The downside? Frames can be complicated to implement, and some people dislike the fact that they hide URL information. (Basically, the URL for a link that's open in a frame doesn't appear in the Address bar of the browser.) To see the URL for a link opened in a frame, for example, you can't just click the link; you must right-click and select Properties (Internet Explorer) or This Frame⇨View Page Info (Navigator). If you do decide to implement frames, however, JavaScript can help you make the most effective use of them.

Working with Browser Windows

One browser window per Web page is the basic, bare-bones approach to Web development — and for many applications, this approach works just fine. But sometimes you want to display more than one window. For example, imagine you're a teacher creating a language-arts Web site. You might want to include hyperlinks to vocabulary words so that when your visitors click one of the hyperlinks, the dictionary definition of the hyperlinked word appears in a separate pop-up window.

If you do decide to create a Web page that displays more than one browser window, you need to know how to manipulate the extra windows. For example, you need to know how to position content within the extra windows and close the extra windows. In this section, I show you how to open and manipulate multiple windows from a single Web page.

Displaying new windows — called pop-up windows or just plain pop-ups — can be annoying to your users, so use this skill very sparingly. Also, keep in mind that many users purchase or download free third-party pop-up-blocker software (such as the Google utility that you can find for free at `http://toolbar.google.com`) or turn off JavaScript support in their browsers to avoid pop-ups. When they surf to your site, these users don't see your handiwork.

Opening and closing new browser windows

One popular school of thought when it comes to Web design is to do everything you can (within reason, of course) to keep visitors at your site after they find it. For example, adding hypertext links that lead to other sites — although useful — might backfire by scooting your visitors off to other people's Web sites before they've really looked at yours. After all, who knows when (or whether) your visitors will return?

One remedy for this situation is to make your page's HTML links open the next site in a new browser window. Visitors get to surf freely from your site to others, as appropriate, but without ever leaving your site. It's a win-win situation! Take a look at Figures 7-1 and 7-2 to see what I mean.

In Figure 7-2, you see how creating a new window leaves the original browser window intact. (Clicking the Close the Window button causes the newly opened window to disappear.)

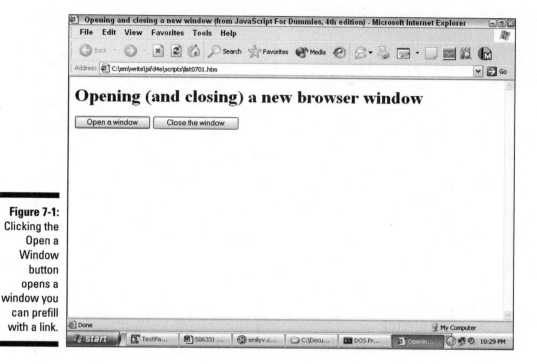

Figure 7-1:
Clicking the Open a Window button opens a window you can prefill with a link.

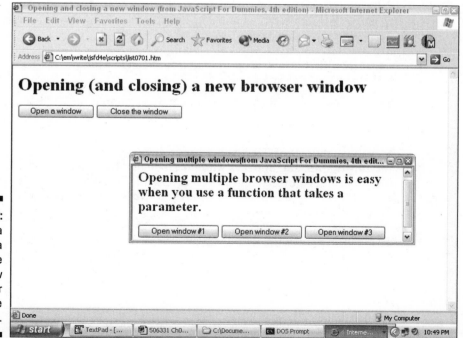

Figure 7-2:
Loading a URL into a separate window keeps your visitor close to home.

Creating such a new window is mighty easy in JavaScript. Listing 7-1 shows you how.

To experiment with the code in Listing 7-1 in your own browser, open the list0701.htm file that you find on the companion CD.

Listing 7-1: Creating (And Destroying) a New Browser Window

```
<SCRIPT LANGUAGE="JavaScript">

var newWindow = null;

function popItUp() {
    newWindow = open("list0702.htm", "secondWindow",
            "scrollbars,resizable,width=500,height=400");
}

function shutItDown() {
    if (newWindow && !newWindow.closed) {
        newWindow.close();
    }
}

</SCRIPT>
```

To create a new browser window and load it with a new document automatically, you need to use the open() method associated with the window object, as shown in Listing 7-1. As you can see, the open() method accepts three parameters:

- ✔ The URL that you want to load into the new window (in this case, list0702.htm)
- ✔ The name for this new window (in this example, secondWindow)
- ✔ A string of configuration options

In this example, the window that you create has scroll bars, has a user-resizing option, and appears with initial dimensions of 500 x 400 pixels. (A quick peek at Figure 7-1 shows you the visible scroll bars. You can verify the other characteristics by loading the file list0701.htm from the companion CD in your own browser.)

To close an open window, all you need to do is invoke the window.close() method by using the name of the open window, like so: newWindow.close();.

To see a full description of the open( ) method, check out the following Web site:

```
http://msdn.microsoft.com/library/default.asp?url=/workshop/author/dhtml/
                    reference/methods/open_0.asp
```

Controlling the appearance of browser windows

In this section, I show you how to customize the windows that you create — specifically, how to create multiple windows and how to position new windows with respect to existing windows.

Creating multiple windows

Creating multiple windows by using JavaScript is almost as easy as creating a single window. The only difference? To create multiple windows, you want to create a custom function that allows you to "rubber-stamp" as many windows as you want. The code in Listing 7-2 shows you how.

Listing 7-2:   Using a Custom Function to Create Multiple Browser Windows

```
<SCRIPT LANGUAGE="JavaScript">

var newWindow = null;

function popItUp(win) {
    var windowFile = win + ".htm"
    newWindow = open(windowFile, win,
             "scrollbars,resizable,width=500,height=400");
}

</SCRIPT>

</HEAD>
<BODY>

<H2>Opening multiple browser windows is easy when you use a function that takes
             a parameter.</H2>
<FORM>
<INPUT TYPE="button" VALUE="Open window #1" onClick="popItUp('one')">
<INPUT TYPE="button" VALUE="Open window #2" onClick="popItUp('two')">
<INPUT TYPE="button" VALUE="Open window #3" onClick="popItUp('three')">
</FORM>
```

The code in Listing 7-2 defines a function called popItUp() that takes a single parameter. When a user clicks the Open Window #1 button, the 'one' string is sent to the popItUp() function. The popItUp() function uses this incoming parameter to identify the name of the window (one) as well as the HTML file to open in the window (one.htm).

You can experiment with the code in Listing 7-2 in your own browser by opening the list0702.htm file, which you find on the companion CD.

Positioning new windows

When you open a new browser window, the browser decides where to place that window, as shown previously in Figure 7-2. However, you can tell the browser exactly where to put it — by using JavaScript, of course!

The following code shows you one way to do just that:

```
var leftPosition = screen.width/2

var newWindow = window.open("one.htm", "secondWindow",
            "width=225,height=200,left=" + leftPosition + ",top=0")
```

The window placement positions that you can control are left and top. The JavaScript code that you see here calculates the value for the left position — in this case, the calculation is equal to half the screen width. The calculated value is stored in the variable leftPosition and used as the value of the left attribute expected by the window.open() function. The upshot? The left side of the newly displayed window appears exactly halfway across the screen.

Working with Frames

Scripted frames are a valuable addition to any Web developer's tool belt. By using a combination of HTML frames and JavaScript, you can present a static, clickable table of contents on one side of a page; then, on the other side of the page, you can present the text that corresponds with each table of contents entry.

Check out Figure 7-5 to see an example of a simple framed table of contents on the left side of the page and content on the right.

One of the benefits of frames is that they allow you to display different HTML files independently from one another. So, for example, as Figure 7-3 shows, the left frame stays visible — even if the user scrolls the right frame. Plus, clicking a link in the frame on the left automatically loads the appropriate content in the frame you see on the right.

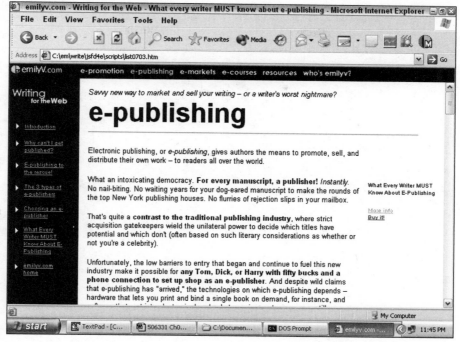

Figure 7-3:
Using
frames to
show a site
index and
the related
content.

This approach, which I explain in the following sections, helps users navigate through the site quickly and is very useful for organizing small sites — or even larger sites that contain mostly text.

Creating HTML frames

Because this book doesn't focus on HTML, I don't go into great detail on creating HTML frames. Instead, I show you the basic syntax you need to know to understand how JavaScript and the document object model fit into the picture. (If you want to know more about creating HTML frames, you might want to pick up a copy of HTML 4 For Dummies, 4th Edition, by Ed Tittel and Natanya Pitts and published by Wiley Publishing, Inc.) Listing 7-3 shows you an excerpt of the code you need to create frames, using the HTM files to hold the frames together. The list0703.htm file pulls together the pub_l.htm file (left frame's table of contents) and the pub_c.htm file (right frame's content).

You can view the complete working example of the code presented in this section by opening these files, which you can find on the companion CD: list0703.htm, pub_l.htm, and pub_c.htm.

Listing 7-3:   HTML Syntax for Creating Index and Content Frames

```
 . . .
<FRAMESET COLS="125, *"
             BORDER="0"
             FRAMESPACING="0"
             FRAMEBORDER="NO">
// Defining the source file, name, and display details
// for the left frame
<FRAME SRC="pub_l.htm"
             NAME="leftnav"
             SCROLLING="AUTO"
             NORESIZE MARGINHEIGHT="0"
             MARGINWIDTH="0"
             LEFTMARGIN="0"
             TOPMARGIN="0"
             TARGET="body">
// Defining the source file, name, and display details
// for the right frame
<FRAME SRC="pub_c.htm"
             NAME="content"
             SCROLLING="AUTO"
             NORESIZE
             MARGINHEIGHT="0"
             MARGINWIDTH="0"
             LEFTMARGIN="0"
             TOPMARGIN="0"
             TARGET="body">
   </FRAMESET>
 . . .
```

Take a good look at the HTML code in Listing 7-3 to find the two frame definitions:

- leftnav (which corresponds to the HTML file pub_l.htm)
- content (which corresponds to the HTML file pub_c.htm)

The file pub_l.htm contains a list of content links (in other words, a table of contents), and the file pub_c.htm contains corresponding text. Figures 7-4 and 7-5 show you what these two files look like when loaded separately into Internet Explorer. (Refer to Figure 7-3 to see what they look like connected.)

Looking at pages separately, before you put them into frames, helps you understand how to combine them for the best effect.

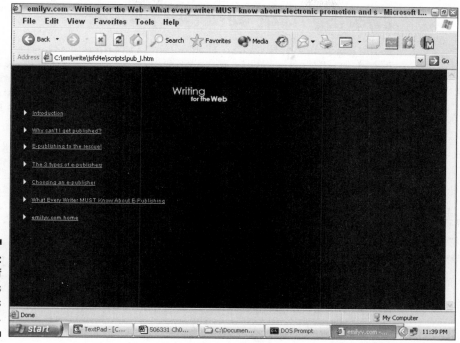

Figure 7-4:
The table of
contents as
it appears
by itself.

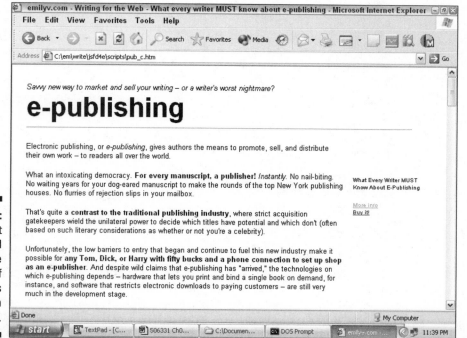

Figure 7-5:
The text that
corresponds
to the
table of
contents
shown in
Figure 7-4.

Sharing data between frames

In the example in this section, the content in the frame on the right reloads based on what a user clicks in the left frame. So, naturally, the code that's responsible for the text reload can be found in the source code for the left frame, pub_1.htm. Take a look at the pertinent syntax shown in Listing 7-4. This code snippet, from pub_1.htm, connects the table of contents links to the appropriate content.

Listing 7-4: Connecting the Index Links to the Content Headings

```
// When a user clicks the Introduction link,
// the anchor located at pro_c.htm#top loads into the
// frame named content

<A HREF="pro_c.htm#top" TARGET="content"
>Introduction</A>


  . . .


// When a user clicks the Why Can't I Get Published? link,
// the anchor located at pro_c.htm#cantget loads into the
// frame named content

<A HREF="pub_c.htm#cantget" TARGET="content"
>Why can't I get published?</A>
  . . .
<A HREF="pub_c.htm#rescue" TARGET="content"
>E-publishing to the rescue!</A>
  . . .
<A HREF="pub_c.htm#types" TARGET="content"
>The 3 types of e-publishers</A>
  . . .
<A HREF="pub_c.htm#choose" TARGET="content"
>Choosing an e-publisher</A>
  . . .
<A HREF="pub_c.htm#epubGuide" TARGET="content"
>What Every Writer MUST Know About E-Publishing</A>
  . . .
// When a user clicks the "emilyv.com home" link, a
// new page (home.htm) replaces the current page

<A HREF="home.htm" TARGET="_top"
>emilyv.com home</A>
```

Each of the links that I define in Listing 7-4 contains a value for the TARGET attribute. Except for the last link, the TARGET attribute is set to content — the name of the frame on the right, which is defined in Listing 7-3, shown earlier in this chapter. Assigning the name of a frame to the TARGET attribute of a link causes that link to load in the named frame, just as you see in Figure 7-3, shown previously.

Right on target

When you create a link (or an anchor, area, base, or form) in HTML, you have the option of specifying a value for the TARGET attribute associated with these HTML elements. Valid values for the TARGET attribute include any previously named frame or window or one of the following built-in values. (See Chapter 11 for an example of specifying the _top value for the TARGET attribute associated with a link.)

Value	What Does It Mean?
_blank	Open the link in a brand-new window
_parent	Open the link in this window or frame's parent window/frame
_self	Open the link in this window or frame
_top	Open the link in the root window or frame

You might want to handle the final link in the listing a bit differently. At the bottom of Listing 7-4, you see that the last defined link assigns a value of _top to the TARGET attribute. When a user clicks the emily.com Home link, the page changes to the contents of home.htm.

_top is a built-in value that translates to "whatever the top-level window in this window/frame hierarchy happens to be." (The sidebar "Right on target" in this chapter describes all the built-in values that you can specify for the TARGET attribute.)

If you specify a value for TARGET that doesn't match either a previously defined frame name or one of the built-in values that you see in the sidebar "Right on target," the associated link loads into a brand-new window. So if you expect a link to open in a frame and it pops up in a new window instead, check your source code. Odds are you made a typo!

The example in this section shows you how to load the contents of one frame based on a user's clicking a link in another. To load two frames based on a user's clicking a link, you can create a JavaScript function similar to the following:

```
function loadTwoFrames(leftURL, contentURL) {

    // Loads the first passed-in URL
    // into the container frame previously defined
    // as "leftNav" in an HTML file such as the one
    // you see in Listing 7-3

    parent.leftNav.location.href=leftURL
```

```
        // Loads the second passed-in URL
        // into the container frame previously defined
        // as "content"

        parent.content.location.href=contentURL
}
```

Then pass the `loadTwoFrames()` function two URL strings. For example:

```
<A HREF="javascript:loadTwoFrames('some.htm', 'another.htm')">
```

or

```
<INPUT TYPE="button" VALUE="Load Two Frames" onClick="loadTwoFrames('some.htm',
                'another.htm')">
```

Don't fence me in!

Just as you can display other folks' Web pages inside your frames, so those folks can display *your* Web pages inside *their* frames.

But in some cases, you might want to prevent your site from being framed. For example, say you spend weeks creating a beautiful, graphics-rich site optimized for a particular monitor size and screen resolution. Then, say I come along and add a link to your site from mine — but I choose to display your fabulous, pixel-perfect site by squeezing it into a tiny 2-x-2-inch frame! (Worse yet, I'm a cat lover, so I surround the 2-x-2-inch frame with an image of my beloved Fifi — so your site appears to be peeking out of my cat's mouth.)

To prevent other sites from displaying your document in a frame, you can add the following short script to your document's head:

```
<HEAD>
 . . .
<SCRIPT LANGUAGE="JavaScript">
<!-- Start hiding from non-JavaScript-support browsers

// If this page has been loaded into a frame...
if (top != self) {
    // Replace the original framing page with the framed page
    top.location.href = location.href;
}
// Stop hiding -->
</SCRIPT>
 . . .
</HEAD>
```

Part III

Making Your Site Easy For Visitors to Navigate and Use

The 5th Wave   By Rich Tennant

@RICHTENNANT

"I couldn't get this 'job skills' program to work on my PC, so I replaced the motherboard, upgraded the BIOS and wrote a program that links it to my personal database. It told me I wasn't technically inclined and should pursue a career in sales."

In this part . . .

In this part, you find practical ways to make your Web pages easy for visitors to navigate and use. Chapter 8 shows you how to create rollovers, hotspots, and navigation bars (fancy terms for graphic images that respond when users click on or roll their mouses over those images). In Chapter 9, you see how to create spiffy pull-down and sliding menus. Chapter 10 demonstrates how you can describe the contents of your site by adding a JavaScript site map, and Chapter 11 rounds out this part by showing you how to create tooltips — helpful hints that appear to your visitors when they mouse over a designated area of your site.

Chapter 8

Creating Interactive Images

• •

• •

A s anyone who's surfed the Web can tell you, a good picture is worth a thousand words. Images add visual punch to your site. They also let you incorporate information that would be downright impossible to present in any other way. (Can you imagine trying to describe a collection of antique lamps without using photo images?)

Because images are represented as programmable objects in JavaScript, you can go above and beyond the static image by creating interactive images — images that respond appropriately when a user clicks or drags a mouse over them. Read on for all the juicy details!

Creating Simple Animations

Typically, when you see a cool animation on a Web page, you're looking at one of the following:

✔ **A Java applet:** Java applets are small software applications written in the Java programming language that your browser downloads from a Web server to your machine when you load a page.

✔ **A plug-in:** A plug-in is special software that you can download that plugs in to your browser and allows an application to execute inside a Web page. Flash is one popular animation plug-in (from the good folks at Macromedia).

✔ **An animated GIF:** GIF stands for graphics interchange format, and it describes a special way of compressing image files. Regular GIF files are used to transfer images on the Web. Animated GIFs are a bunch of regular GIFs packaged together — much like those cartoon flipbooks that you might have had as a child, where each page contains a separate drawing. When you flip the flipbook pages (or load an animated GIF), those separate images flow from one to another to create an animated effect.

Animated GIFs are a popular choice for Web-based animations because

- Most browsers support them.
- No separate download is required (unlike plug-ins).
- They don't hog a lot of client resources (unlike some Java applets).

You can create simple animations with JavaScript, as well. You might want to do so for two very good reasons:

✔ Creating JavaScript animations saves your users time. (JavaScript animations don't require any downloads, either upfront like plug-ins or during animation execution like applets.)

✔ Creating JavaScript animations saves you the trouble of figuring out another programming language, such as Java, or figuring out how to use an animation construction tool, such as Macromedia's Fireworks.

The downside? Because JavaScript wasn't designed specifically to create animations, it isn't optimized for this purpose — meaning that specially built functions and the compression techniques necessary for hard-core animation execution don't exist in JavaScript. In other words, JavaScript animations are best kept simple. Fortunately, many times, simple animations are all you need!

In this section, I demonstrate the basis of all animations: the humble image.

You add an image to a Web page by including the HTML <IMG> tag into your HTML source code, like this:

```
<IMG SRC="somePicture.jpg" . . . >
```

For example, take a look at the HTML snippet shown in Listing 8-1, which appears in full on the CD as the file list0801.htm.

Listing 8-1:   Creating an Image Object with the HTML <IMG> Tag

```
. . .
<IMG SRC="splash.jpg" WIDTH=241 HEIGHT=208
   TITLE="Essential resources for the professional and aspiring writer"
   ALT="Writing for the Web splash image"
>
```

The code you see in Listing 8-1 accomplishes the following tasks:

- ✔ Inserts an image file named `splash.jpg` into a space 241 pixels wide by 208 pixels high using the `SRC`, `HEIGHT`, and `WIDTH` attributes of the `<IMG>` tag, respectively.

- ✔ Defines a tooltip message by using the `TITLE` attribute of the `<IMG>` tag.

  The contents of the `TITLE` attribute appear automatically when a user running Microsoft Internet Explorer 6.x or Netscape Navigator 7.x mouses over this image.

- ✔ Defines an alternative text description for the image by using the `ALT` attribute of the `<IMG>` tag.

  The contents of the `ALT` attribute appear in browsers that can't display images, in browsers that have been configured not to display images, and in situations where an image just plain doesn't exist. Figure 8-1 shows you how the code in Listing 8-1 appears in Internet Explorer 6.0 with image loading turned off.

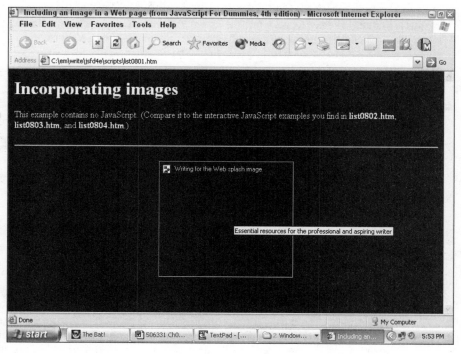

Figure 8-1:
Users who disable image loading in their browsers see the contents of the image's ALT or TITLE attribute instead of a picture.

Picture this

One thing to keep in mind when you create interactive images with JavaScript is that users have the ability to turn off image loading in their browsers. If you rely on an image to convey the bulk of your page's information and interactivity, and your users have configured their browsers so that images don't appear, your page will be ineffective, to say the least!

If you're wondering why a Web surfer would choose not to see images, it's because image files are relatively large and take a long time to download at modest connection speeds. Not every user has a cable modem; plenty of users are making do with 56K dial-up connections that are subject to occasional cutoffs. Because images are often gratuitous (yours won't be, I'm sure!), users without a lot of time to spend might choose to turn off image loading to get their online tasks accomplished in the shortest amount of time.

These are the steps your users take to turn off image loading:

Navigator users

1. **Choose Edit⇨Preferences.**

2. **Click the Privacy & Security option.**

3. **Click the Images option.**

4. **Select the Do Not Load Any Images check box.**

Internet Explorer users

1. **Choose Tools⇨Internet Options.**

2. **Click the Advanced tab.**

3. **Scroll down to Multimedia and deselect the Show Pictures check box.**

Check out Figure 8-1 to see how the line of HTML code in Listing 8-1 appears in Internet Explorer 6.0. Placing your mouse cursor over an image in Internet Explorer 6.0 or Netscape Navigator 7.1 displays the contents of the image's TITLE attribute.

As you can see from Figures 8-1 and 8-2, the TITLE attribute that you define as part of the HTML <IMG> tag provides a bit of interactivity. It displays a helpful message automatically when a user running Internet Explorer 6.0 or Netscape Navigator 7.1 mouses over the defined image.

But what if you want more interactivity? What if you want to display your helpful message more discreetly — say, at the bottom of the window? (Some professional Web designers consider this approach less confusing to Web novices than creating a message that temporarily obscures everything around the mouse pointer.) What if you want different parts of an image to pop up different messages or respond to different mouse clicks?

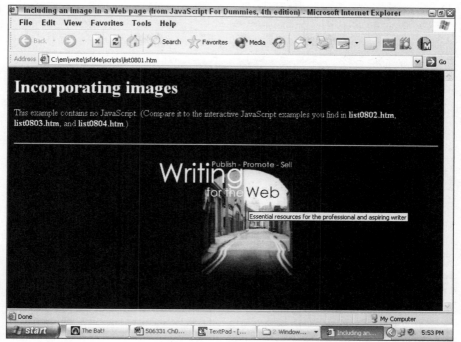

Figure 8-2:
Displaying
an image by
using HTML.

Well, you're in luck: Those scenarios are tailor-made for JavaScript! As you
see in the following sections, making plain old HTML images interactive is a
simple matter of adding a few JavaScript event handlers.

Now you see it, now you don't: Turning images on and off

The simplest animation of all is an image that changes from its original view
and then changes back again. Take a look at Figures 8-3 and 8-4 to see how
my smiley face changes, thanks to the recursive invocation of the built-in
JavaScript function setTimeout().

The relevant code responsible for this simple animation is shown in Listing 8-2.
Check out the simple on/off animation by using image manipulation and the
built-in JavaScript setTimeout() function. If you want to load and experiment with the animation example, use the file list0802.htm from the companion CD.

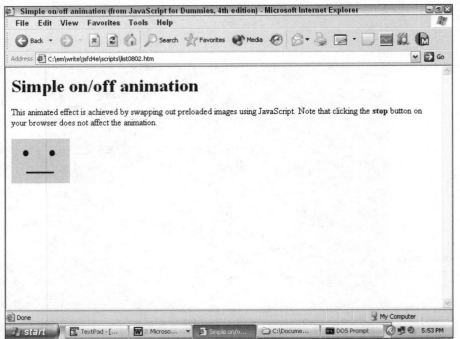

Figure 8-3:
The neutral
face . . .

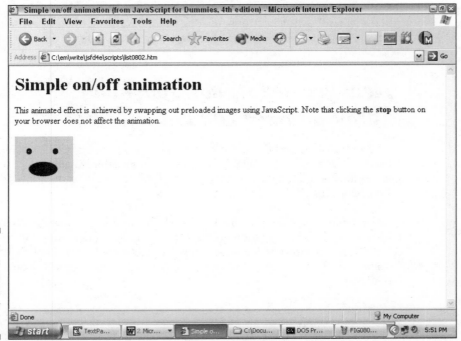

Figure 8-4:
. . . changes
into a
surprised
face every
second.

Listing 8-2: **Creating a Simple Animation with JavaScript's setTimeout() Function**

```
. . .
//Global variable declarations
var whichImg = 1
var nextImage

/////////////////////////////////////////////////
// The swap() function replaces the image
// associated with the first input
// parameter (id) with the image specified
// for the second input parameter (newSrc).
/////////////////////////////////////////////////

function swap(id, newSrc) {
    var theImage = findImage(document, id, 0);
    if (theImage) {
        theImage.src = newSrc;
    }
}

/////////////////////////////////////////////////
// This function swaps the current image
// for the incoming parameter newImage;
// then it calls itself every second,
// passing itself a different newImage
// each time. The result is a simple
// on/off animation.
/////////////////////////////////////////////////
function animate(newImage) {

        swap('animatedFace', newImage);

        if (whichImg == 1) {
            nextImage = "surprised.gif"
            whichImg = 0
        }
        else {
            nextImage = "neutral.gif"
            whichImg = 1
        }
//setTimeout() sets up the continuous swap
// that creates the animation.
        setTimeout("animate(nextImage)", 1000)
}
. . .
// stop hiding -->
</SCRIPT>
</HEAD>
```

(continued)

Listing 8-2 *(continued)*

```
//The animate() function is called as soon as the page loads.
<BODY onLoad="animate('surprised.gif')">
 . . .
//The animation (image) dimensions are defined.
<IMG NAME="animatedFace" SRC="neutral.gif" WIDTH="104" HEIGHT="80">
</BODY>
</HTML>
```

The JavaScript code in Listing 8-2 depends on two image files to create the animation:

- neutral.gif: This image of a yellow square contains two black eyes and a straight line for a mouth for the neutral look.

- surprised.gif: The image is the surprised face. (Okay, okay, it's just a smiley face with a big circle for a mouth instead of a straight line. It's an artist's rendition!)

Here's the order in which JavaScript interpreter steps through the code in Listing 8-2 — a peek inside the interpreter's mind, as it were:

1. The HTML <IMG> tag names and defines the animation placeholder frame (the spot on the page where the images appear alternately during the animation).

   In the <IMG> tag, the name is animatedFace, and the dimensions are 104 x 80 pixels.

2. As soon as the page loads, the onLoad event handler executes the animate() function and sends it the name of a source file (surprised.gif, to be exact).

3. The animate() function calls the swap() function to swap out the source file associated with the animatedFace placeholder frame.

   Now, instead of the original neutral.gif, the animatedFace placeholder holds surprised.gif.

4. By using the globally defined variables whichImg and nextImage, the animate() function logs which image it just swapped out and queues up the next image by calling the setTimeout() function.

   The setTimeout() function calls the animate() function every second, alternately passing animate() the neutral.gif and surprised.gif filenames.

Slideshow Bob: Displaying a series of images

Sometimes you want to set up a slideshow by using JavaScript: a way for your users to click a button and see a different image, or slide, without necessarily popping to another Web page.

Figures 8-5 through 8-7 show you the process of clicking a button to change the image from one view to another.

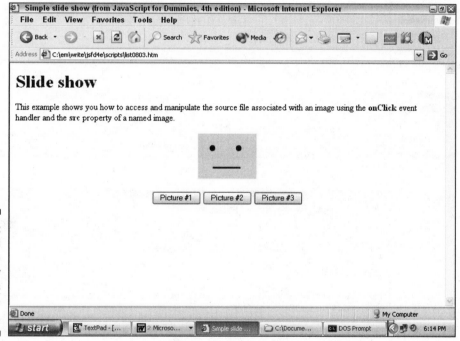

Figure 8-5: A neutral face appears by default as soon as the page loads.

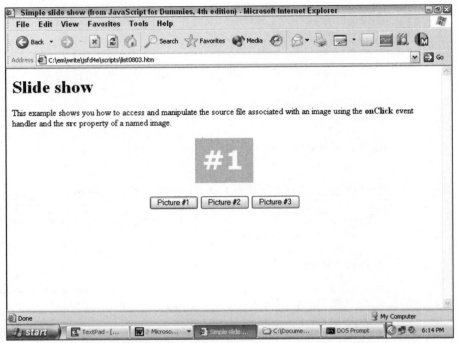

Figure 8-6:
Clicking the
Picture #1
button
automatic-
ally displays
the #1
image.

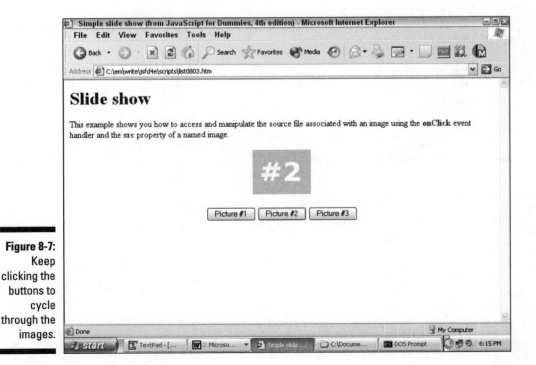

Figure 8-7:
Keep
clicking the
buttons to
cycle
through the
images.

The JavaScript code that's necessary to create the simple slideshow example appears in Listing 8-3.

The code in Listing 8-3 is located on the companion CD in the `list0803.htm` file.

Listing 8-3:   Creating a User-Activated Slideshow

```
. . .

////////////////////////////////////////////////////
// This swap() function constructs a filename
// based on the input parameter and then sets
// the slideshow image's source to that
// filename.
//
// Note: The initial image determines the size
// of the slideshow "frame".  Swapping to
// a larger image causes that larger image to
// be squeezed to fit the initial image "frame".
////////////////////////////////////////////////////
function swap(newImage) {

    var fileName = newImage.toString() + ".gif"
    document.slideshow.src = fileName
}
// stop hiding -->
</SCRIPT>
</HEAD>

<BODY>
<H1>Slide show</H1>
This example shows you how to access and manipulate the source file associated
            with an image using the <B>onClick</B> event handler and the
            <B>src</B> property of a named image.
...

<!-- The initial image (a face) to display is specified here. -->

<IMG NAME="slideshow" SRC="neutral.gif" WIDTH="104" HEIGHT="80">

<P>

<!-- These three onClick event handlers call the swap() function to display the
            user-selected image -->

<INPUT TYPE="button" VALUE="Picture #1" onClick="swap('1')">
<INPUT TYPE="button" VALUE="Picture #2" onClick="swap('2')">
<INPUT TYPE="button" VALUE="Picture #3" onClick="swap('3')">
..
```

See the `<IMG>` tag near the bottom of the Listing 8-3 code listing? That `<IMG>` tag defines the initial image that displays when this page first appears, as shown in Figure 8-5, and names the placeholder for that initial image `slideshow`.

When a user clicks any of the buttons — Picture #1, Picture #2, or Picture #3 — that button's `onClick` event handler springs into action and calls the `swap()` function, passing the `swap()` function the appropriate number: 1, 2, or 3. Inside the `swap()` function are just two lines of JavaScript code:

```
var fileName = newImage.toString() + ".gif"
document.slideshow.src = fileName
```

The first line creates a variable called `fileName` and then assigns to `fileName` a string based on the parameter sent to `swap()` from the `onClick` event handler. (You must use the `toString()` method to convert the value of `newImage` to a string before you can tack on the `.gif`.) After the JavaScript interpreter interprets this first line, `fileName` contains one of the following string values: `1.gif`, `2.gif`, or `3.gif`. (These filenames correspond to actual GIF files located on the companion CD.) The second line of the `swap()` function assigns this new `fileName` to the built-in `src` property of the slideshow placeholder. (You specify a particular image placed in a document by navigating from the `document` object to the `all` object to the named `Image` object.)

Creating Rollovers, Hotspots, and Navigation Bars

Interactive images help you communicate with your users quickly and easily. Three of the most popular approaches to creating interactive images on the Web are

- **Rollovers:** A rollover is an image that changes appearance when a user rolls the cursor over it. Rollovers are typically associated with links, so that when a user clicks a rollover, the user's browser loads a new Web page.

- **Hotspots:** A hotspot is similar to a rollover except that a hotspot refers to an interactive portion of an image. You can carve up a single image to create multiple hotspots.

- **Navigation bars:** Finally, a navigation bar is a group of links — typically displayed as rollovers or as hotspots — that allow your users to surf to all the pages of your Web site.

The following sections show you how to create these cool effects with JavaScript.

Creating a simple rollover

The term rollover describes an image that changes color, font, size, or some other aspect when a user rolls over it with the mouse pointer. Figure 8-8 shows the E-Publishing button as it appears (white) when first loaded into Internet Explorer.

As you can see in Figure 8-9, rolling the mouse over a navigation button that you implement as a rollover provides a visual cue that helps users recognize what they can expect when they click the mouse button. (The change in text color from white to purple lets users know in no uncertain terms that they're hovering over a button!)

Rollovers are most often used to create navigation bars, but you can use rollovers to make any graphic portion of your Web site respond to mouse events.

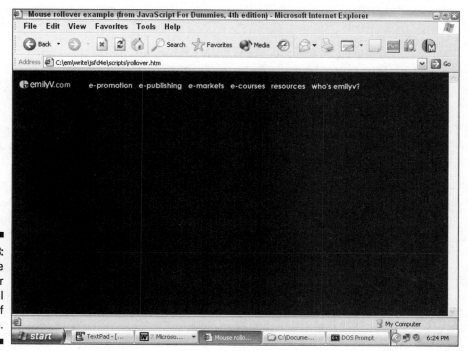

Figure 8-8:
Using white images for the initial version of the button.

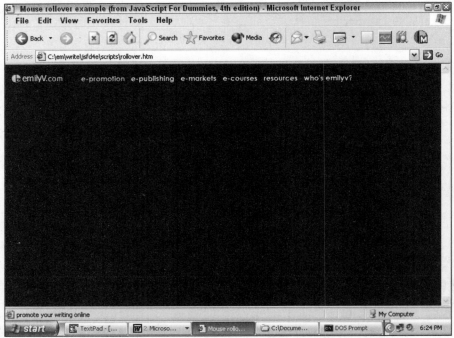

Figure 8-9:
Contrasting
colors
respond
when
the mouse
rolls by.

Creating a mouse rollover is fairly simple. Just follow this plan:

1. **Select two images of precisely the same size: one to display by default, and one to display in response to a** `mouseOver` **event.**

One way to keep the two versions straight is to use on/off terminology. From now on I refer to these images as the off image and the on image, respectively, because one appears when your mouse is resting somewhere off the image and one when your mouse is on it.

You can get images one of two ways:

• You can use predesigned images. Many graphics tools come complete with a library of predesigned images; you can also find images online — some free, some for purchase.

• You can create your own images by using an image-creation tool, such as Paint Shop Pro 6 or later. (You can find a trial copy of Paint Shop Pro 6 on the companion CD-ROM.)

One popular approach is to create a navigation button that you like and save it as the off image — then change the color of the button and immediately save another copy as the on image.

Not graphically inclined? GoGraph offers freely downloadable icons and graphics at www.gograph.com.

2. **Create two JavaScript functions, one attached to the** onMouseOver **event handler and one attached to the** onMouseOut **event handlers.**

The following are two examples that use the custom swap() function to swap the image named mkt_pic from the white version (mkt_w.gif) to the purple version (mkt_p.gif).

```
<A HREF="mkt.htm"
...
        // Example #1: Swapping from white to purple on mouseOver
        onMouseOver="swap('mkt_pic','mkt_p.gif');

        // Example #2: Swapping from purple to white on mouseOut
        onMouseOut="swap('mkt_pic','mkt_w.gif');
        displayMsg(''); return true"
...
IMG NAME="mkt_pic" SRC="mkt_w.gif" WIDTH="72"
HEIGHT="12" BORDER="0"></A>
```

You can find a working version of the code responsible for Figures 8-8 and 8-9 — which includes the swap() function as well as the following JavaScript code — on the companion CD, in the file rollover.htm.

3. **Add an optional (but recommended) JavaScript function that preloads all of the images.**

Preloading images helps ensure that when users mouse over images for the first time, they don't have to wait while additional images download from the Web server one at a time.

I show you how these three steps work together in the following section, where you see how to construct a typical navigation bar with rollover effects step by step.

Creating navigation bars by putting rollovers together

Navigation bars, such as the one shown previously in Figures 8-8 and 8-9, are wonderful tools for helping your users find their way around your Web site. Fortunately — because navigation bars are nothing more than a collection of rollovers combined with links to different Web pages — they're also pretty easy to put together, as you see in the following sections.

The approach to navigation bar creation that I demonstrate in this chapter is the old-fashioned, code-by-hand approach. Point-and-click visual tools, such as Macromedia Dreamweaver, make the process of creating navigation bars even more straightforward and painless.

Preloading images

You aren't required to preload your rollover images, but doing so is a good idea. Using preloaded images makes your rollovers work much more smoothly, which in turn gives your visitors a much better impression of your site.

So, why is preloading images a good idea? By default, browsers fetch images only when they're needed for display the first time. So, by default, browsers don't bother to fetch on images until a user mouses onto a rollover for the very first time. Unfortunately, if the user's connection is slow or the Web server is overloaded, that fetched image can take quite a while to arrive. In the meantime, the browser display doesn't change, and the user doesn't get to see the rollover effect.

Preloading all images helps ensure that users see your rollover effects right away. To preload images, you simply create instances of the Image object by using JavaScript, and then you fill those instances with the names of the image files that you want to preload. You do all this as soon as the page loads; that way, while the user is busy reading the text on your Web page, the images are quietly loading in the background. By the time the user is ready to click an image, all the on images are loaded in memory and ready to go!

I break down this next example in three chunks to help clarify what's happening. Listing 8-4 shows you how to preload images by using a custom function called, appropriately enough, preloadImages(). Watch the comments for the stages of the process, which I outline following the listing.

Listing 8-4:   Preloading Images as Soon as the Web Page Loads

```
function preloadImages() {

// See Step 1 in the following text

    if (document.images) {

    // See Step 2 in the following text

        var imgFiles = preloadImages.arguments;

        // See  Step 3 in the following text

        var preloadArray = new Array();

        // See Step 4 in the following text

        for (var i=0; i < imgFiles.length; i++) {

                // Create a new Image object in the
                // preloadArray array and associate it
                // with a source file, thus loading
```

```
            // that image into memory.

            preloadArray[i] = new Image;
            preloadArray[i].src = imgFiles[i];
      }
    }
}
 . . .

</SCRIPT>
</HEAD>

<BODY BGCOLOR="#000000" TEXT="#FFFFFF" LINK="#FFFFFF" VLINK="#CCCCFFF"
            ALINK="#CCCCFFF">
// This second script calls the preloadImages() function
// defined in the first script.

<SCRIPT LANGUAGE="JavaScript" TYPE="text/javascript">
<!--
// Preload all the images used in this file
// (the logo, plus all white and purple
// navigation buttons).

// See Step 5 in the following text

preloadImages('logo.jpg',
'pro_p.gif', 'pub_p.gif', 'mkt_p.gif', 'crs_p.gif',
'res_p.gif', 'who_p.gif', 'pro_w.gif', 'pub_w.gif',
'mkt_w.gif', 'crs_w.gif', 'res_w.gif', 'who_w.gif');
//-->
</SCRIPT>
```

The code in Listing 8-4 begins with the definition of the `preloadImages()` function.

Here's how the JavaScript interpreter steps through this function:

1. The interpreter checks the `document.images` property to see whether any image placeholders (`<IMG>` tags) appear for this document.

2. If one or more `<IMG>` tags exist in this document, the interpreter creates a variable called `imgFiles` containing all the arguments sent to the `preloadImages()` function.

   The `arguments` property is automatically available for every function that you create.

3. The interpreter creates a new variable, called `preloadArray`, by calling the `new` operator in conjunction with the built-in JavaScript `Array()` constructor.

   The result is an empty array.

4. The interpreter fills the empty `preloadArray` array and preloads all the images necessary for this Web page.

   The interpreter creates new instances of the `Image` object and then immediately associates them with the names of the image files passed into the `preloadImages()` function.

5. The second script that you see in Listing 8-4 — the one placed between the document `<BODY>` and `</BODY>` tags — executes as soon as users load the Web page into their browsers.

   This script calls the `preloadImages()` function, passing to it all of the image files necessary for this page. The upshot? As soon as the page loads, JavaScript immediately begins preloading all the navigation bar images.

You might find it helpful to distinguish your on/off image files by using a simple tagging system in the filenames. The filenames in this example containing _w represent white navigation buttons; _p indicates the purple navigation buttons. So, in this example, `pro_p.gif` is the name of the off image for the E-Promotion navigation button, and `pro_w.gif` is the name of the corresponding on image for the E-Promotion navigation button.

Swapping images on rollover

As soon as the user's browser loads your rollover images into memory by using a scheme like the one that you see in the preceding section, you need some way to swap those images out in response to a `mouseOver` event. You do this by using the `onMouseOver` event handler associated with each navigation button. A detailed explanation follows the listing.

Listing 8-5: Using the mouseOver Event to Swap Images

```
<HEAD>
<SCRIPT LANGUAGE="JavaScript" TYPE="text/javascript">

// Defining the swap() function
function swap(id, newsrc) {
    var theImage = locateImage(id);
    if (theImage) {
        theImage.src = newsrc;
    }
}


///////////////////////////////////////////////////////
// The locateImage() function accepts the name of an
// image and returns the Image object associated
// with that name.
///////////////////////////////////////////////////////

function locateImage(name) {
```

```
        var theImage = false;
        if (document.images) {
            theImage = document.images[name];
        }
        if (theImage) {
            return theImage;
        }
        return (false);
}
</SCRIPT>
</HEAD>

<BODY>

  . . .

<A HREF="pro.htm"
onMouseOut="swap('promo_pic','pro_w.gif')"
//Calling the swap() function from an onMouseOver event handler
onMouseOver="swap('promo_pic','pro_p.gif')" ><IMG NAME="promo_pic"
            SRC="pro_w.gif" WIDTH="81" HEIGHT="12" BORDER="0"></A>
  . . .
```

To help you wade through the code in Listing 8-5, I explain how the `swap()` function works first; then, I explain what happens when you call the `swap()` function from the `onMouseOut` and `onMouseOver` event handlers.

Defining the swap ( ) function

The `swap()` function that you see defined in Listing 8-5 accepts two arguments:

- ✔ `id`, which represents the name of the image that you want to swap
- ✔ `newsrc`, which represents the filename of the new image that you want to display

Here's what's going on inside the body of the `swap()` function:

First, a variable called `theImage` is created and assigned the preloaded `Image` object that you want to swap out. (To create `theImage`, the `locateImage()` function is used. I explain the inner workings of `locateImage()` in the next section.)

Second, the filename of `theImage` is changed, which causes the browser to display the new image. Image swap complete, as shown here:

```
function swap(id, newsrc) {
    var theImage = locateImage(id);
    if (theImage) {  // if an image was found
        theImage.src = newsrc; // swap it out
    }
}
```

Creating the locateImage ( ) function

If you're interested in how the locateImage() function works, you've come to the right place. As you see in the preceding section, the swap() function uses locateImage() to, well, to locate the image it needs to swap out.

Here's the code for the locateImage() function:

```
function locateImage(name) {
//Start with a blank variable called theImage
    var theImage = false;

// If there are images defined for this document . . .
    if (document.images) {
// Assign the image we're looking for to theImage.
        theImage = document.images[name];
    }
// If theImage exists, return it to the calling function.
    if (theImage) {
        return theImage;
    }
// Otherwise, return false (0) to the calling function.
    return (false);
}
```

Calling the swap ( ) function

To perform a rollover, you must swap out images two different times: when a user mouses onto an image, and when a user mouses off again. You do this by calling the swap() function from both the onMouseOver and onMouseOut event handlers, as shown in the following Listing 8-5 excerpt:

```
// Because the image is implemented as a link, clicking
// the image automatically loads the pro.htm file.

<A HREF="pro.htm"
onMouseOut="swap('promo_pic','pro_w.gif')"
onMouseOver="swap('promo_pic','pro_p.gif')" >
<IMG NAME="promo_pic" SRC="pro_w.gif" WIDTH="81" HEIGHT="12" BORDER="0">
</A>
```

Notice in this code that the initial value for the E-Promotion image source is pro_w.gif (the white button); the name of the image is promo_pic. (You know these things because the SRC attribute of the <IMG> tag is set to pro_w.gif and the NAME attribute of the <IMG> tag is set to promo_pic.)

Now take a look at the onMouseOver event handler. This statement swaps the promo_pic image from the white version to pro_p.gif (the purple version).

When the `onMouseOut` event handler fires, the `promo_pic` image changes back again to `pro_w.gif` (back to the white version). Thanks to the HTML `<A>` tag, when the user clicks the image, the user's browser loads a new Web page devoted to all things promotional: `pro.htm`.

Carving up a single image into multiple hotspots

HTML areas (and their associated event handlers) let you carve up images into multiple image hotspots, areas of an image that correspond with a message or action (see Listing 8-6). Mousing over the section of the image marked Publish, as shown in Figure 8-10, causes a publishing-related message to appear in the status bar. Figure 8-11 shows a similar trick for a different section of the image. And, you can designate a larger area for a more general message on the status bar (see Figure 8-12). **Note:** If you're running Internet Explorer and don't see the status bar, choose View⇨Status Bar.

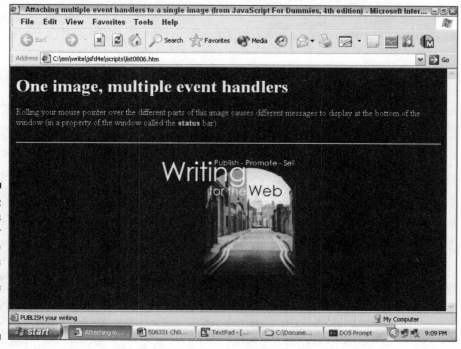

Figure 8-10: The status bar message corresponds to the location of the mouse on a page.

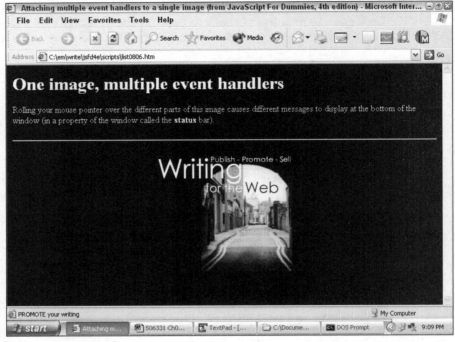

Figure 8-11: Mousing over the section of the image marked Promote causes a promotion-related message to appear on the status bar.

Figure 8-12: A standard message appears on the status bar when the user mouses anywhere on the image.

Listing 8-6 (list0806.htm) shows you how to create a customized message to display on the status bar when a user mouses over a specific area of an image.

Listing 8-6:   Designating Image Hotspots

```
<HTML>
<HEAD>

<TITLE>Attaching multiple event handlers to a single image (from JavaScript For
          Dummies, 4th Edition)</TITLE>

</HEAD>
<BODY BGCOLOR="black" TEXT="white">
<H1>One image, multiple event handlers</H1>
Rolling your mouse pointer over the different parts of this image causes
          different messages to display at the bottom of the window (in a
          property of the window called the <B>status</B> bar).
<P>
<HR>
<P>
<CENTER>
<!--
The HTML areas "carve" up a single image. Defining separate event handlers for
          each area lets you display a different message in the window's
          status bar depending on where a user's mouse moves or clicks.
-->

<IMG height=208 src="splash.jpg" width=241
    useMap=#newsplash border=0>
<MAP name=newsplash>

        <AREA
        onMouseOver="window.status='Writing for the Web'; return true"
        onMouseOut="window.status=''; return true"
        shape=POLY target=_top
        coords=1,2,1,46,78,48,80,197,240,201,239,18,93,12,94,2
        >

        <AREA
        onMouseOver="window.status='SELL your writing'; return true"
        onMouseOut="window.status=''; return true" shape=RECT target=_top
        coords=216,0,241,16
        >

        <AREA
        onMouseover="window.status='PROMOTE your writing'; return true"
        onMouseout="window.status=''; return true" shape=RECT target=_top
        coords=149,0,209,15
        >
        <AREA
        onMouseOver="window.status='PUBLISH your writing'; return true"
```

(continued)

Listing 8-6 *(continued)*

```
        onMouseOut="window.status=''; return true" shape=RECT target=_top
        coords=94,0,140,14
        >
</MAP>

</CENTER>
</BODY>
</HTML>
```

HTML areas are the constructs that let you carve an image into separate pieces. The image itself stays where it is, and the areas that you define just let you define arbitrary ways of interacting with that image.

You can define as many areas for an image as you want, sized and shaped however you like (courtesy of the `coords` attribute). You define an area by using the HTML `<AREA>` and `<MAP>` tags, as shown in Listing 8-6. Each area gets to define its own event handlers.

Four separate areas are defined in Listing 8-6:

- ✔ The portion of the image that says `Publish`. The `onMouseOver` event handler associated with this area displays the message `PUBLISH your writing`.

- ✔ The portion of the image that says `Promote`. The `onMouseOver` event handler associated with this area displays the message `PROMOTE your writing`.

- ✔ The portion of the image that says `Sell`. The `onMouseOver` event handler associated with this area displays the message `SELL your writing`.

- ✔ The rest of the image not described by the preceding areas. The `onMouseOver` event handler associated with this leftover area displays the generic message `Writing for the Web`.

To add a link to a hotspot, all you need to do is define a value for the `HREF` attribute of the `<AREA>` tag, as the following code shows:

```
<AREA
onMouseover="window.status='PROMOTE your writing'; return true"
onMouseout="window.status=''; return true" shape=RECT target=_top
coords=149,0,209,15 href="http://www.somePromotionPage.com"
>
```

To create distinct areas within an image, you need to know the x,y coordinates that describe that area. Most graphic-manipulation tools on the market today, including Macromedia Fireworks and Adobe ImageReady, allow you to import a picture, outline which areas you want to create, and then — boom! — they generate the necessary coordinates for you.

Chapter 9

Creating Menus

· ·

In This Chapter

▶ Using DHTML to create pull-down menus

▶ Creating dynamic sliding menus

▶ Taking advantage of third-party DHTML menu tools

· ·

Dynamic HTML, or DHTML, refers to the collection of client-side languages and standards that you use to create Web pages that change appearance dynamically after they're loaded into a user's Web browser.

The languages and standards that contribute to DHTML include

✔ HTML

✔ JavaScript

✔ Cascading style sheets

✔ The document object model (DOM)

My focus in this chapter is on JavaScript and the document object model and how they combine to contribute to DHTML — in short, how you can use JavaScript to access and manipulate the DOM and create cool dynamic effects, including pull-down and sliding menus. I also steer you toward a handful of third-party menu components (in case you'd rather purchase and customize menus than code them yourself).

 Although the examples in this chapter include HTML and cascading style sheet code, I don't spend a lot of time describing these two languages in depth. If you're interested in finding out more about DHTML, including HTML and cascading style sheets, you might want to check out a good book devoted to these subjects. One worth checking out is Dynamic HTML: The Definitive Reference, 2nd Edition, by Danny Goodman (O'Reilly & Associates).

Chapter 4 describes the document object model (DOM) and shows you how to access it. Appendix C presents both Internet Explorer's and Netscape Navigator's DOMs.

Getting Acquainted with Menus

A menu in Web-speak is much the same as a menu in a restaurant: a collection of options. Menus help you organize your content attractively — and help your users find what they're looking for quickly and easily. Figure 9-1 shows you an example of a simple menu.

Because menus typically involve dynamic content positioning and hiding, you don't create menus by using JavaScript alone; instead, you use DHTML — a combination of HTML, cascading style sheets, JavaScript, and the DOM. In the following sections, I demonstrate two types of menus: pull-down menus and sliding menus.

Pull-down menus

If your computer runs Windows, you might be familiar with pull-down menus: Click a menu item, and additional items appear.

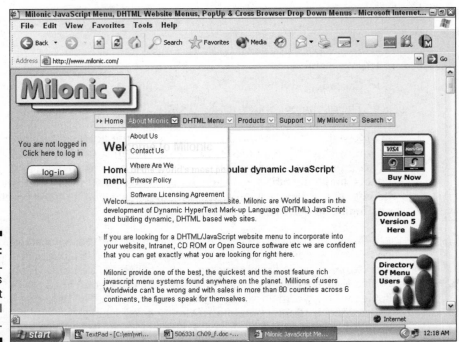

Figure 9-1:
This DHTML menu makes a great navigational tool.

Pull-down menus, such as the one that you see in Figure 9-2, are useful because they allow you to organize your Web content efficiently — and because they're user-directed. In other words, the menu display doesn't change until a user clicks her mouse. Because many users are familiar with pull-down menus — and because many users prefer Web page interfaces that don't change until they direct it to change by clicking something — pull-down menus are a popular approach to menu creation.

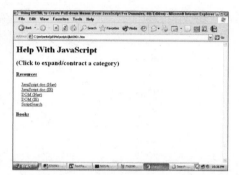

Figure 9-2:
A simple pull-down menu allows users to choose additional menu items.

The code in Listing 9-1 creates the pull-down menu that you see in Figure 9-2. As you peruse the code, notice that much of the code is HTML and style sheet code. The only JavaScript code that you see consists of:

- ✔ The custom function `displayMenu()`

- ✔ Two calls to `displayMenu()` associated with the `onClick` event handlers for the two expandable menu options, Resources and Books

You can find the working code in Listing 9-1 on the companion CD under the filename `list0901.htm`.

Listing 9-1:   Creating a Simple Pull-Down Menu

```
<HTML>
<HEAD>
<TITLE>Using DHTML to Create Pull-down Menus (From JavaScript For Dummies, 4th
            Edition)</TITLE>
<SCRIPT LANGUAGE="JavaScript" TYPE="text/javascript">
<!-- Hide from older browsers

function displayMenu(currentMenu) {

    var thisMenu = document.getElementById(currentMenu).style
```

(continued)

Listing 9-1 *(continued)*

```
    // Custom JavaScript function that expands/contracts menus as
    // appropriate
    // If the menu is expanded, contract it
    if (thisMenu.display == "block") {
        thisMenu.display = "none"
    }
    else {
        // If the menu is contracted, expand it
        thisMenu.display = "block"
    }
    return false
}

// End hiding-->
</SCRIPT>

<STYLE TYPE="text/css">
<!--

// Style definition of the "menu" class
.menu {display:none; margin-left:20px}

-->
</STYLE>

</HEAD>

<BODY BGCOLOR="#FFFFFF">

<H1>Help With JavaScript</H1>
<H2>(Click to expand/contract a category)</H2>

<H3>
// Call to display resource menu.
<a href="dummy1.html" onClick="return displayMenu('resMenu')">Resources</a>
</H3>
<span class="menu" id="resMenu">
<a href="jhttp://channels.netscape.com/ns/browsers/default.jsp">JavaScript doc
            (Nav)</a><br />
<a href="http://www.microsoft.com/windows/ie/default.htm">JavaScript doc
            (IE)</a><br />
<a href="http://www.mozilla.org/docs/dom/domref/dom_shortTOC.html">DOM
            (Nav)</a><br />
<a href="http://msdn.microsoft.com/workshop/author/dhtml/reference/objects.asp">
            DOM (IE)</a><br />
<a href="http://www.scriptsearch.com/JavaScript">ScriptSearch</a><br />
</span>

<H3>
```

```
// Call to display book menu.
<a href="dummy2.html" onclick="return displayMenu('bookMenu')">Books</a>
</H3>

<span class="menu" id="bookMenu">
<a href="http://www.dummies.com">Dummies</a><br />
<a href="http://www.powells.com">Powells</a><br />
<a href="http://www.amazon.com">Amazon</a><br />
<a href="http://www.ebay.com">eBay</a><br />
<a href="http://www.bn.com">Barnes & Noble</a><br />
</span>
</BODY>
</HTML>
```

Unless you're an HTML and CSS guru, the code in Listing 9-1 might seem daunting. Not to worry! Taken a step at a time, the code unravels. The following four items (which are boldface in the code in Listing 9-1) are the most important:

- ✓ **The JavaScript** `displayMenu()` **function.** The `displayMenu()` function accepts a single parameter representing the current menu.

  1. The JavaScript code inside the `displayMenu()` function gets the document object associated with the current menu and stores it in the variable called `thisMenu`.

  2. The code uses the `thisMenu` object's `display` property to determine whether the current menu is expanded or contracted.

  3. If the current menu is expanded, the code contracts it; if the current menu is contracted, the code expands it.

- ✓ **The cascading style sheet definition of the** menu **class.** The HTML `<STYLE>` tags define a class of style sheet called `menu`. Every HTML component associated with the `menu` class (see the last bullet in this list) shares the display characteristics defined between the `<STYLE>` tags.

- ✓ **The JavaScript calls to the** `displayMenu()` **functions that are associated with each of the** `onClick` **event handlers: one for the Resources hyperlink and one for the Books hyperlink.** When users click either the Resources or Books hyperlink shown in Figure 9-2, the JavaScript code associated with the `onClick` event handler for each of these hyperlinks sends the current menu to the `displayMenu()` function, causing the current menu to contract (if it's already expanded) or expand (if it's contracted).

- ✓ **The HTML definition of the resMenu and bookMenu layers.** Each of these layers, which are defined using the HTML `<span>` tag, associates the layer itself with the CSS `menu` class. The result?

- The browser displays both the resMenu and bookMenu layers by using the same menu class definition.

- Both the resMenu and bookMenu layers are stored as document objects whose display property is accessible (and manipulable) via JavaScript.

The first item in this list has more information on the display property.

HTML and CSS are broad, complex topics. If you'd like more in-depth info on these topics than I present here, WebDeveloper.com offers a wealth of free HTML and CSS resources. Check them out at http://webdeveloper.com/html and http://webdeveloper.com/html/html_css_links.html, respectively.

Sliding menus

Sliding menus differ from pull-down menus in one important way: In a sliding menu, menu options appear dynamically in response to a mouseOver event. In other words, when it comes to sliding menus, users don't have to click a menu item to see additional menu items; all they have to do is move their mouses over an item, and bingo! More items appear, as if by magic.

The menu shown previously in Figure 9-1 is a sliding menu, and so is the menu that you see in Figure 9-3.

Figure 9-3:
Mousing over a sliding menu causes the menu to display additional menu items.

Take a peek at the code in Listing 9-2, which creates the sliding menu shown in Figure 9-3. (It's a bit ugly, but I describe the important parts in detail in the remainder of this section.) As you glance through the code, notice a single JavaScript function — displayMenu() — as well as calls to displayMenu() associated with the onMouseOver and onMouseOut event handlers.

I've included the working code in Listing 9-2 on the companion CD under the filename list0902.htm.

Listing 9-2:   Creating a Sliding Menu

```
<HTML>
<HEAD>
<TITLE>Using DHTML to Create Sliding Menus (From JavaScript For Dummies, 4th
          Edition)</TITLE>
<SCRIPT LANGUAGE="JavaScript" TYPE="text/javascript">
<!-- Hide from older browsers

// Custom JavaScript function displayMenu()
function displayMenu(currentPosition,nextPosition) {

    // Get the menu object located at the currentPosition
    // on the screen.
    var whichMenu = document.getElementById(currentPosition).style;

    if (displayMenu.arguments.length == 1) {
        // Only one argument was sent in, so we need to
        // figure out the value for "nextPosition"

        if (parseInt(whichMenu.top) == -5) {
            // Only two values are possible: one
            // for mouseOver
            // (-5) and one for mouseOut (-90). So we want
            // to toggle from the existing position to the
            // other position: for example, if the position
            // is -5, set nextPosition to -90...
            nextPosition = -90;
        }
        else {
            // Otherwise, set nextPosition to -5
            nextPosition = -5;
        }
    }

    // Redisplay the menu using the value of "nextPosition"
    whichMenu.top = nextPosition + "px";
}

// End hiding-->
</SCRIPT>

// Style sheet definition
<STYLE TYPE="text/css">
<!--
```

(continued)

Listing 9-2 *(continued)*

```
.menu {position:absolute; font:12px arial, helvetica, sans-serif; background-
            color:#CCCCCC; layer-background-color:#CCCCCC; top:-90px}
#resMenu {left:10px; width:130px}
#bookMenu {left:145px; width:160px}
A {text-decoration:none; color:#000000}
A:hover {background-color:pink; color:blue}

 -->

</STYLE>
</HEAD>

<BODY BGCOLOR="white">

// Associating the call to displayMenu() with the onMouseOver and onMouseOut
// event handlers.
<div id="resMenu" class="menu" onMouseOver="displayMenu('resMenu',-5)"
            onMouseOut="displayMenu('resMenu',-90)"><br />
<a href="jhttp://channels.netscape.com/ns/browsers/default.jsp">JavaScript doc
            (Nav)</a><br />
<a href="http://www.microsoft.com/windows/ie/default.htm">JavaScript doc
            (IE)</a><br />
<a href="http://www.mozilla.org/docs/dom/domref/dom_shortTOC.html">DOM
            (Nav)</a><br />
<a
            href="http://msdn.microsoft.com/workshop/author/dhtml/reference/ob
            jects.asp">DOM (IE)</a><br />
<a href="http://www.scriptsearch.com/JavaScript">ScriptSearch</a><br />
<b><a href="javascript:displayMenu('resMenu')">JavaScript Resources</a></b>
</div>

// Associating the call to displayMenu() with the onMouseOver and onMouseOut
// event handlers.
<div id="bookMenu" class="menu" onMouseOver="displayMenu('bookMenu',-5)"
            onMouseOut="displayMenu('bookMenu',-90)"><br />
<a href="http://www.dummies.com">Dummies</a><br />
<a href="http://www.powells.com">Powells</a><br />
<a href="http://www.amazon.com">Amazon</a><br />
<a href="http://www.ebay.com">eBay</a><br />
<a href="http://www.bn.com">Barnes & Noble</a><br />
<b><a href="javascript:displayMenu('bookMenu')">JavaScript Books</a></b>
</div>

</BODY>
</HTML>
```

Sliding menus rely heavily on three items:

- ✔ **Cascading style sheets:** When you create a sliding menu, you use a style sheet to define such display characteristics as how you want the browser to display the menu before a user mouses over it and after a user mouses over it and what color you want the hyperlinks to be.

- ✔ **Display screen (monitor) properties:** You use screen properties to specify where you want the browser to display the menu initially, as well as after a user mouses over the menu.

- ✔ **JavaScript:** You use JavaScript to tie the menu display (the first bullet in this list) and positioning (the second bullet) to the onMouseOver and onMouseOut event handlers associated with the menu options. When users mouse over a menu option, as shown in Figure 9-3, the menu automatically appears — and then disappears after the mouse pointer moves away.

As you examine the code shown in Listing 9-2, pay special attention to the following three callouts, which implement the preceding three points:

- ✔ **The custom JavaScript function** displayMenu(). The displayMenu() function accepts up to two parameters: currentPosition and nextPosition. The JavaScript code uses these parameters to determine where on the screen to display the menu. If only one parameter was sent to the displayMenu() function, the code calculates the value of the second parameter by determining whether the menu is currently expanded or contracted — and then the code displays it the opposite way.

- ✔ **The style sheet definition describing how the browser should display menus.** All the code between the <STYLE> and </STYLE> tags constitutes the cascading style sheet definition:

  - • Display characteristics common to both menus appear next to the .menu keyword.

  - • Display characteristics specific to the Resources menu appear next to the #resMenu keyword.

  - • Display characterstics specific to the Books menu appear next to the #bookMenu keyword.

  - • Display characteristics for the hyperlink menu items — as well as the hyperlinks when a mouse is positioned over them — appear next to the A and A:hover keywords, respectively.

✔ **The JavaScript calls to** `displayMenu()` **associated with the** `onMouseOut` **and** `onMouseOver` **event handlers.** The HTML `<div>` and `</div>` tags specify how the browser is to display the Resources and Books menus initially — but it's the JavaScript calls to the `displayMenu()` function, associated with both the Resource hyperlink's `onMouseOut` and `onMouseOver` event handlers and the Books hyperlink's `onMouseOut` and `onMouseOver` event handlers, that cause the menus to slide open and closed.

Taking Advantage of Third-Party DHTML Menu Components

As you might notice if you peruse Listings 9-1 and 9-2, creating DHTML menus from scratch takes quite a bit of programming savvy, not just with respect to JavaScript but to HTML and cascading style sheets, as well. If you don't want to invest the time and trouble in coding DHTML menus by hand (and not everyone does), you're in luck: Several companies offer tools that you can use to get cool menu effects with a minimum of effort. The following list represents just a handful of the products available. (Many are low cost or offer free trial versions.)

✔ **OpenCube's Visual QuickMenu Pro** is a point-and-click tool you can use to create customized menus quickly and easily. You must be running Windows to create your menus using Visual QuickMenu Pro, but the menus you create run on multiple browsers. You can find a free trial version of this product at `www.opencube.com`.

✔ **Milonic Solutions' industrial-strength DHTML Menu** works with Navigator, Internet Explorer, and other Web browsers, and is available in professional and corporate versions. Find out more at `www.milonic.com`.

✔ **Apycom Software offers DHTML Menu,** as well as a ton of online examples demonstrating how to use their product to create customized menus. You can download a free trial version of DHTML Menu from `http://dhtml-menu.com`.

✔ **SmartMenus DHTML menu** is a shareware product you can download and use for a minimal fee. Check out SmartMenus on the Web at `www.smartmenus.org` for details.

Chapter 10

Creating Expandable Site Maps

●●

●●

In Chapter 9, I demonstrate creating a simple pull-down menu by using Dynamic HTML, or DHTML. (DHTML, as you see in Chapter 9, combines HTML, JavaScript, the document object model, and cascading style sheets into a powerful approach to creating interactive Web pages.)

Although the examples in this chapter include HTML and cascading style sheet code, I don't spend a lot of time describing these two languages. If you're interested in finding out more about DHTML, including HTML and cascading style sheets, you might want to check out a good book devoted to these subjects. One worth checking out is Dynamic HTML: The Definitive Reference, 2nd Edition, by Danny Goodman (O'Reilly).

In this chapter, I show you one way to transform the simple pull-down menu that you see in Chapter 9 into a useful site navigation tool called an expandable site map. Expandable site maps — similar to those used in popular software applications such as Microsoft Windows (see Figure 10-1) — can help the folks who visit you on the Web find information on your site quickly and easily.

Site Map Basics

A site map, such as the one you see in Figure 10-1, is a menu that organizes the contents of your Web site in a nice, neat, user-friendly order.

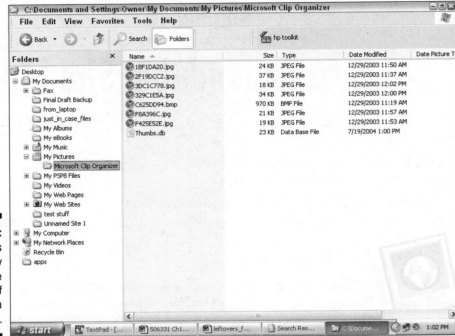

Figure 10-1:
Site maps
display
multiple
levels of
content at a
glance.

Because the purpose of a site map is to help visitors find content quickly, site maps are best designed as no-frills lists of organized links. If you think of site content as a book, the site map is the table of contents.

Typically, you add a site map link, such as the one shown in the top-right corner of Figure 10-1, to each and every Web page in your site. When users click the site map link, a page containing a drop-down list (similar to the one in Figure 10-1) appears.

Only large, complex Web sites need site maps. If your Web site contains fewer than 25 pages, you probably don't need to add a site map — although you certainly can if you'd like!

A site map — no matter how cleverly designed — can't make up for poorly organized content. Think of a site map as an additional navigational tool, not a substitute for an orderly, well-planned-out site.

Many approaches to creating site maps exist. In the following sections, I demonstrate one popular approach: combining pull-down menus with frames to create a site map that stays visible on one side of the page while displaying content on the other side of the page.

The pull-down menu revisited

In Chapter 9, you see an example of a simple pull-down menu for a fictitious knitting site created by using a combination of HTML, JavaScript, and cascading style sheets. In this chapter, I show you how to adapt that pull-down menu — by using frames, which I discuss in Chapter 7 — to create the site map shown in Figure 10-2.

Creating the site map shown in Figure 10-2 involves three steps, which I explain further in this section and in the following two sections:

1. Creating a pull-down menu

2. Adding a frameset

3. Adding targeted hyperlinks

You use a combination of HTML, JavaScript, and cascading style sheets to create a site map. The code that you see in Listing 10-1 is responsible for the site map shown in Figure 10-2.

Figure 10-2:
Clicking a bolded selection expands or contracts the site map.

The code shown in Listing 10-1 is on the companion CD under the filename `sitemap.htm`.

Listing 10-1:   A Simple Pull-Down Menu

```
<HTML>
<HEAD>
<TITLE>Using DHTML to Create a Site Map (From JavaScript For Dummies, 4th
            Edition)</TITLE>
<SCRIPT LANGUAGE="JavaScript" TYPE="text/javascript">
<!-- Hide from older browsers

function displayMenu(currentMenu) {

    var thisMenu = document.getElementById(currentMenu).style

    // If the menu is expanded, contract it.
    if (thisMenu.display == "block") {
        thisMenu.display = "none"
    }
    else {
        // If the menu is contracted, expand it.
        thisMenu.display = "block"
    }
    return false
}

// End hiding-->
</SCRIPT>

<STYLE TYPE="text/css">
<!--

.menu {display:none; margin-left:20px;}

-->
</STYLE>

</HEAD>

<BODY BGCOLOR="#FFFFFF">

<H3>
<a href="dummy1.html" onClick="return displayMenu('basicMenu')">Knitting
            Basics</a>
</H3>
<span class="menu" id="basicMenu">
<b><a href="dummy3.htm" onClick="return displayMenu('subMenu')">Planning a
            project</a></b><br />
```

```
<span class="menu" id="subMenu">
<a>Choosing yarn</a><br />
<a>Swatching</a><br />
</span>

<b><a>The knit stitch</a></b><br />
<b><a>The purl stitch</a></b><br />
</span>

<H3>
<a href="dummy2.html" onClick="return displayMenu('advMenu')">Advanced Topics</a>
</H3>

<span class="menu" id="advMenu">
<a>Circular needles</a><br />
<a>Cables</a><br />
<a>Felting</a><br />
<a>Finishing</a><br />
</span>
</BODY>
</HTML>
```

To understand how the code in Listing 10-1 works, take a better look at the following code elements (each of which appears bold in the code):

1. **The JavaScript** `displayMenu()` **function.** The `displayMenu()` function accepts a single parameter representing the current menu. First, the JavaScript code inside the `displayMenu()` function gets the document object associated with the current menu and stores it in the variable called `thisMenu`. Then the code uses the `thisMenu` object's `display` property to determine whether the current menu is expanded or contracted. If the current menu is expanded, the code contracts it; if the current menu is contracted, the code expands it.

2. **The cascading style sheet definition of the** `menu` **class.** The HTML `<STYLE>` tags define a class of style sheet called `menu`. Every HTML component associated with the `menu` class (see Step 4) shares the display characteristics defined between the `<STYLE>` tags.

3. **The JavaScript calls to** `displayMenu()` **associated with each of the** `onClick` **event handlers: one for the Knitting Basics hyperlink and one for the Advanced Topics hyperlink.** When users click either the Knitting Basics or Advanced Topics hyperlink shown in Figure 10-2, the JavaScript code associated with the `onClick` event handler for each of these hyperlinks sends the current menu to the `displayMenu()` function, causing the current menu to contract (if it's already expanded) or expand (if it's contracted).

4. **The HTML definition of the** `basicMenu` **and** `resMenu` **layers.** Each of these layers, which are defined using the HTML `<span>` tag, associates the layer itself with the CSS `menu` class defined in Step 2. The result: The browser displays both the `basicMenu`, `subMenu`, and `advMenu` layers using the same `menu` class definition — and the `basicMenu`, `subMenu`, and `advMenu` layers are stored as `document` objects whose `display` property is accessible (and manipulable) through JavaScript. (Check out Step 1 for more information on the `display` property.)

Adding frames to the pull-down menu

As you might notice, the site map shown previously in Figure 10-2 consists of two frames. One frame (the one on the left) contains the expandable pull-down menu. The other (the frame on the right) contains the site content. When a user clicks a pull-down menu selection in the left frame, the appropriate content displays in the frame on the right.

In the preceding section, I show you how to create a pull-down menu. In this section, I show you how to create a frameset — and add the pull-down menu to the left frame. (**Note:** For additional scoop on how frames work, check out Chapter 7.)

First, take a look at the code in Listing 10-2.

Experimenting with frames helps you understand how they work. Check out the frame code in Listing 10-2 by loading the file `list1002.htm`, located on the companion CD, into your Web browser.

Listing 10-2:   Creating a Frameset Containing Two Frames

```
<HTML>
<HEAD><TITLE>Site navigation example (from JavaScript For Dummies, 4th
          Edition)</TITLE></HEAD>
        <FRAMESET COLS="170, *" BORDER="0" FRAMESPACING="15"
          FRAMEBORDER="YES" FRAMEBORDER="0">
          <FRAME SRC="sitemap.htm" NAME="sitemap" SCROLLING="AUTO"
        NORESIZE MARGINHEIGHT="15" MARGINWIDTH="5" LEFTMARGIN="0"
        TOPMARGIN="0" TARGET="body">
          <FRAME SRC="content.htm" NAME="content" SCROLLING="AUTO" NORESIZE
        MARGINHEIGHT="0" MARGINWIDTH="0" LEFTMARGIN="0" TOPMARGIN="0"
        TARGET="body">
        </FRAMESET>
</HTML>
```

As you read through the code in Listing 10-2, pay special attention to the HTML tags `<FRAMESET>`, `</FRAMESET>`, and `<FRAME>`. (I've bolded these tags so you can find them easily.)

The `<FRAMESET>` and `</FRAMESET>` tags create a holder for two frames, named `sitemap` and `content`, respectively, which are created by the two `<FRAME>` tags. The source for the left frame is `sitemap.htm`, and the source for the right frame is `content.htm`. If you take a look at the `sitemap.htm` file (located on the companion CD), you find it contains the code in Listing 10-1. If you take a look at the `content.htm` file (also located on the companion CD) you find it contains the heading shown previously in Figure 10-2, `Welcome to my knitting site!`

The upshot? When you load the file `list1002.htm` into a Web browser, the `<FRAMESET>`, `</FRAMESET>`, and `<FRAME>` tags display the pull-down menu (stored as `sitemap.htm`) in the left frame and the initial content (stored as `content.htm`) in the right frame. Check out the following section for details.

Putting it all together: Adding targeted hyperlinks

A site map isn't much good without hyperlinks; after all, the whole point of a site map is to direct users to different Web pages in your site.

You add a hyperlink by using the HTML `<A>` tag, like so:

```
<A HREF="someFile.htm">
```

When you use frames, however, you need to define the `TARGET` attribute as well as the `HREF` attribute. When you define the `TARGET` attribute, you specify the value of the frame in which you want the hyperlinked content to appear, like this:

```
<A HREF="someFile.htm" TARGET="someFrameName">
```

If you've had a chance to glance through Listing 10-2, you notice that the name of the frame on the right is `content`. So to add a targeted hyperlink to the code in Listing 10-1, you define `TARGET="content.htm"`, as shown here:

```
<a href="yarn.htm" TARGET="content">Choosing yarn</a><br />
<a href="swatching.htm" TARGET="content">Swatching</a><br />
...

<a href="knit.htm" TARGET="content">The knit stitch</a><br />
<a href="purl.htm" TARGET="content">The purl stitch</a><br />
...
<a href="circular.htm" TARGET="content">Circular needles</a><br />
```

```
<a href="cables.htm" TARGET="content">Cables</a><br />
<a href="felting.htm" TARGET="content">Felting</a><br />
<a href="finishing.htm" TARGET="content">Finishing</a><br />
```

As you see from this code, clicking the Choosing Yarn link causes the HTML file yarn.htm to appear in the content frame (the right frame, which Listing 10-2 describes.) Clicking the Swatching link causes the HTML file swatching.htm to appear in the content frame; and so on.

Listing 10-3 shows you the updated site map code containing all eight targeted hyperlinks. Together with the code in Listing 10-2, the code in Listing 10-3 and the referenced content files (yarn.htm, swatching.htm, knit.htm, purl.htm, circular.htm, cables.htm, feling.htm, and finishing.htm) represent a complete, frame-enhanced site map.

You can test the site map code for yourself by loading the file list1002.htm that you find on the companion CD.

Listing 10-3:   Putting It All Together: The Site Map Code Updated to Reflect Targeted Hyperlinks

```
<HTML>
<HEAD>
<TITLE>Using DHTML to Create a Site Map (From JavaScript For Dummies, 4th
            Edition)</TITLE>
<SCRIPT LANGUAGE="JavaScript" TYPE="text/javascript">
<!-- Hide from older browsers

function displayMenu(currentMenu) {

    var thisMenu = document.getElementById(currentMenu).style

    // If the menu is expanded, contract it.
    if (thisMenu.display == "block") {
        thisMenu.display = "none"
    }
    else {
        // If the menu is contracted, expand it.
        thisMenu.display = "block"
    }
    return false
}

// End hiding-->
</SCRIPT>

<STYLE TYPE="text/css">
<!--

.menu {display:none; margin-left:20px;}
```

```
-->
</STYLE>

</HEAD>

<BODY BGCOLOR="#FFFFFF">

<H3>
<a href="dummy1.html" onclick="return displayMenu('basicMenu')">Knitting
          Basics</a>
</H3>
<span class="menu" id="basicMenu">
<b><a href="dummy3.htm" onclick="return displayMenu('subMenu')"
          TARGET="content">Planning a project</a></b><br />

<span class="menu" id="subMenu">
<a href="yarn.htm" TARGET="content">Choosing yarn</a><br />
<a href="swatching.htm" TARGET="content">Swatching</a><br />
</span>

<b><a href="knit.htm" TARGET="content">The knit stitch</a></b><br />
<b><a href="purl.htm" TARGET="content">The purl stitch</a></b><br />
</span>

<H3>
<a href="dummy2.html" onclick="return displayMenu('advMenu')">Advanced
          Topics</a>
</H3>

<span class="menu" id="advMenu">
<a href="circular.htm" TARGET="content">Circular needles</a><br />
<a href="cables.htm" TARGET="content">Cables</a><br />
<a href="felting.htm" TARGET="content">Felting</a><br />
<a href="finishing.htm" TARGET="content">Finishing</a><br />
</span>
</BODY>
</HTML>
```

Taking Advantage of Third-Party Site-Mapping Tools

No doubt about it: Creating DHTML site maps from scratch takes quite a bit of programming know-how — not just with respect to JavaScript but to HTML and cascading style sheets, as well. If you don't want to invest the time and trouble in figuring out everything you need to know to code DHTML site maps by hand, you might find a third-party site-mapping tool is just what the doctor ordered. Third-party site-mapping tools — some of which you can find for low or even no cost on the Web — allow you to create customized site maps with a minimum of effort. (The downside, of course, is that these scripts might not look or behave quite the same as one you create yourself.)

The following list — which represents just a fraction of the tools available — is a good place to begin looking for the perfect third-party site-map script:

✔ Download Likno Software's menu-creation product AllWebMenus (for free) and get instant access to an easy-to-use site-map generator. For details, check out Likno Software on the Web at www.likno.com.

✔ Good for large Web sites, Xtreeme's SiteXpert 7 allows you to automate site-map creation and updates. (If you frequently add or delete pages from your site, you might find automatic updating to be indispensable.) Find out more at www.xtreeme.com/sitexpert.

✔ CDR's Site Map Pro 2.1 uses a wizard (an easy-to-use, walk-you-through-it interface) to make creating cross-browser site maps as simple as possible. You can get the latest version from www.sitemappro.com.

Chapter 11

Creating Pop-Up Help (Tooltips)

• •

• •

*I*f you use Internet Explorer or Netscape Navigator to surf the Web, you might be familiar with the helpful messages that pop up when you move your mouse over important areas of some Web pages. These helpful messages, called tooltips, are designed to give users extra information — anything from the definition of the word that the mouse pointer is over to a fancy scholarly citation. Because tooltips can make navigating a Web site easier and more enjoyable, they're worth adding to your own Web pages.

You can add basic tooltips to a Web page by using plain old HTML tags. The problem is that Internet Explorer supports one tag attribute (ALT) and Netscape Navigator supports another (TITLE). (Beginning with version 6.x, Internet Explorer 6.x now supports TITLE, too, but some users may have earlier versions of Internet Explorer installed.) And if you want to customize your tooltips — add an image, for example, or display large-size text over an eye-catching yellow background — you're out of luck. The HTML ALT and TITLE tag attributes don't allow for such customization.

Does that mean you have to give up your hopes of customized tooltips? No! As I demonstrate in this chapter, you can add customized tooltips that appear the same in both Internet Explorer and Navigator (as well as other browsers) by using dynamic HTML.

Dynamic HTML, or DHTML, refers to the combination of HTML, JavaScript, and cascading style sheets — a collection of client-side languages and standards you use to create Web pages that change appearance dynamically, after they're loaded into a user's Web browser.

Although the examples in this chapter include HTML and cascading style sheet code, I don't spend a lot of time describing these two languages. (This is a JavaScript book, after all!) If you're interested in finding out more about DHTML, including HTML and cascading style sheets, you might want to check out a good book devoted to these subjects. One worth checking out is Dynamic HTML: The Definitive Reference, 2nd Edition, by Danny Goodman (O'Reilly).

Creating Plain HTML Tooltips

In the example in Figures 11-1 and 11-2, you see a DHTML tooltip and a plain HTML tooltip.

As you can see in Figure 11-1, the DHTML tooltip — the one that says "Left cousin" — appears in large print. The HTML tooltip ("Sarah"), in contrast, is small. Moving the mouse pointer to another part of the image causes the tooltips to disappear. Other tooltips appear as appropriate; for example, moving the mouse pointer over the girl on the right displays the "Right cousin" DHTML tooltip.

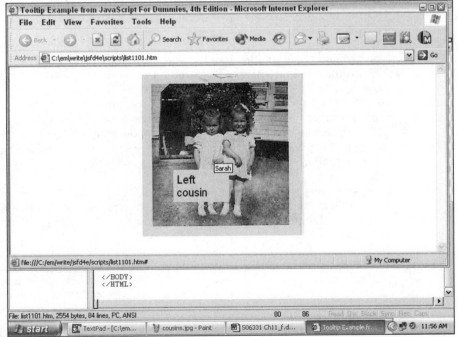

Figure 11-1:
You can customize DHTML tooltips, which is a distinct advantage over plain HTML tooltips.

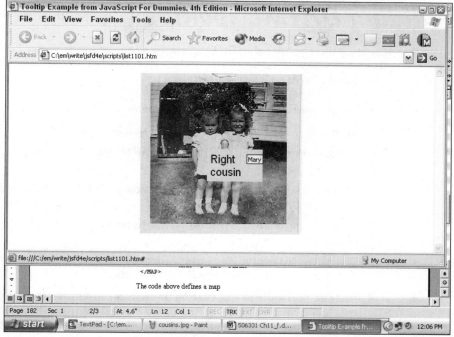

Figure 11-2:
Moving the
mouse
pointer over
another part
of the photo
displays
different
tooltips.

To create the plain HTML tooltip shown in Figure 11-1, you specify a value for the ALT attribute associated with the <AREA> tag as shown below :

```
<MAP name="PicMap" id="PicMap">
...
        <AREA SHAPE="rect" COORDS="112,91,136,315" HREF="#" ALT="Sarah">
        <AREA SHAPE="rect" COORDS="180,81,200,320" HREF="#" ALT="Mary" />
</MAP>
...
        <IMG SRC="cousins.jpg" USEMAP="#PicMap" HEIGHT="289" WIDTH="289" />
```

This code displays a 289 x 289 pixel image overlaid by a map (named PicMap) that defines two rectangular areas. When a user mouses over one area (whose coordinates happen to be 112,91,136,315), the HTML tooltip Sarah appears. When a user mouses over another area of the picture (defined by the coordinates 180,81,200,320) the tooltip Mary appears.

To create a tooltip that appears in Netscape Navigator, you use the TITLE attribute in place of the ALT attribute: for example, TITLE="Mary".

As you see in the following section, the code required to create a DHTML tooltip is a bit more involved.

Building DHTML Tooltips

Creating tooltips by using DHTML involves four separate steps. I describe these four steps here, and in the following sections I provide you with the example code responsible for Figures 11-1 and 11-2.

1. **Create an HTML map containing one or more designated areas.**

   This step is identical to the step you use to create plain HTML tooltips.

2. **Define a style for the tooltip using the HTML <STYLE> and </STYLE> tags.**

   Defining a style for the tooltip automatically creates a JavaScript-accessible object for that tooltip.

3. **Create custom JavaScript functions to access and change the tooltip object.**

   The purposes of the JavaScript functions are to display the tooltip if it's not already visible and hide it if it is visible.

4. **Include two calls to the custom JavaScript functions (see Step 2): one call associated with the** onMouseOver **event handler (to display the tooltip), and one call associated with the** onMouseOut **event handler (to hide the tooltip).**

   These calls cause the tooltip to appear when the mouse pointer enters the designated area and disappear when the mouse pointer leaves the designated area.

Creating an HTML map and designating active areas

The first thing you need to do when you create DHTML tooltips is define which areas of your Web page you want to be active — that is, which areas of your Web page you want to display tooltips in response to a user's mouse pointer. After you decide which areas of your page you want to be active, you use HTML to create a map and one or more active areas, as shown in Listing 11-1.

Listing 11-1:   Defining an HTML Map and Designating Active Areas

```
...
// From <MAP> to </MAP> defines an HTML and active areas.
<MAP NAME="PicMap" ID="PicMap">
    <AREA SHAPE="rect" COORDS="112,91,136,315" HREF="#" ALT="Sarah" />
    <AREA SHAPE="rect" COORDS="180,81,200,320" HREF="#" ALT="Mary" />
```

```
    <AREA SHAPE="rect" COORDS="59,26,208,64" HREF="#" ALT="bougainvillea" />
    <AREA SHAPE="rect" COORDS="226,25,303,82" HREF="#" ALT="needs paint" />
</MAP>
...

// Overlaying a map on top of an image
<IMG SRC="cousins.jpg" USEMAP="#PicMap" HEIGHT="289" WIDTH="289" BORDER="0"
            ALT="Two cousins" />
```

You can use a graphics program such as Paint, which comes installed with Windows, to get the upper-left and lower-right x,y coordinates for each active area.

The code in Listing 11-1 defines a map named PicMap and four separate rectangular areas. Then, near the bottom of Listing 11-1, you see the HTML <IMG> tag, which places an image on the page and overlays that image with the PicMap map.

After you define your active areas, you're ready to define a style for the tooltip, which I demonstrate in the following section.

Defining a style for the tooltip

You define a style for a Web page object by using the HTML <STYLE> and </STYLE> tags. Defining a style for your tooltips accomplishes two important tasks:

- ✔ It allows you to specify how you want your tooltips to appear: bolded, large font, and so on.
- ✔ It allows you to create a named, JavaScript-accessible tooltip object that you can make visible and invisible.

In Listing 11-2, you see an example of the <STYLE> and </STYLE> tags in action.

Because cascading style sheets are so powerful and flexible, they're also relatively complex. You might want to check out a book, such as Designing CSS Web Pages, by Christopher Schmitt (New Riders). Alternatively, you could pick up a good HTML book — many devote a chapter or two to the <STYLE> and </STYLE> tags and cascading style sheet syntax.

Listing 11-2:   Using the <STYLE> and </STYLE> Tags to Define
                a Tooltip Style

```
<STYLE type="text/css">
<!--

.tooltipStyle {background-color: pink; border: pink 1px solid;  layer-
               background-color: pink; width: 100px; font: 20px arial, helvetica,
               sans-serif; padding: 5px; position: absolute; visibility: hidden}
-->
</STYLE>
```

The code you see in Listing 11-2 defines a tooltip style called, appropriately enough, `tooltipStyle`. The code specifies that tooltip text should appear as a relatively large 20 pixels on a nice bright-pink background.

Creating custom JavaScript functions to display and hide tooltips

You use JavaScript to access the correct tooltip and then to display that tooltip (as a user's mouse pointer moves into the active area) or hide it (if a user's mouse pointer moves away from the active area).

In Listing 11-3, you see two JavaScript functions defined: `displayTip()` and `hideTip()`. Take a peek at the code, and then see the human-readable description that follows.

Listing 11-3:   The displayTip() and hideTip() Functions

```
...

function displayTip(theEvent,currentElement) {

    if (latestBrowser) {
        tooltip = document.getElementById(currentElement).style
             }
    else {
        tooltip = eval("document." + currentElement)
    }

    if (document.all) {
        tooltip.pixelTop = parseInt(theEvent.y)+2
        tooltip.pixelLeft = Math.max(2,parseInt(theEvent.x)-
                     75)
    }
```

```
    else {
        if (latestBrowser) {
          tooltip.top = parseInt(theEvent.pageY)+2 + "px"
          tooltip.left =  Math.max(2,parseInt(theEvent.pageX)-75) + "px"
        }
        else {
            tooltip.top = parseInt(theEvent.pageY)+2
            tooltip.left =  Math.max(2,parseInt(theEvent.pageX)-75)
        }
    }
    tooltip.visibility = "visible"
}

function hideTip(currentElement) {
    if (latestBrowser) {
        tooltip = document.getElementById(currentElement).style
    }
    else {
        tooltip = eval("document." + currentElement)
    }
    tooltip.visibility = "hidden"
}
```

The displayTip() function accepts two parameters: theEvent (the value of which at runtime is either the mouseOver or mouseOut object) and currentElement (the value of which at runtime is the name of the tooltip to manipulate).

The first if-else statement in displayTip() obtains the tooltip style object. The second if-else statement sets the x,y coordinates for the tooltip. Finally, the third if-else statement turns the visibility of the tooltip on.

The hideTip() function is much shorter than the displayTip() function. The hideTip() function simply obtains the tooltip to manipulate and then hides it.

The displayTip() and hideTip() functions don't execute unless they're attached to event handlers. Fortunately, the following section demonstrates how to do just that.

Calling custom functions in response to the onMouseOver and onMouseOut events

For tooltips to be effective, they must appear when a user mouses over something on a page and disappear when the mouse pointer moves away. Fortunately, accomplishing this feat is easy with JavaScript, as the code in Listing 11-4 shows.

Listing 11-4: **Attaching the displayTip() and hideTip() Calls to Mouse Events**

```
<MAP name="PicMap" id="PicMap">
        <AREA SHAPE="rect" COORDS="112,91,136,315" HREF="#"
            onMouseOut="hideTip('tooltip1')"
            onMouseOver="displayTip(event,'tooltip1')" ALT="Sarah" />
        <AREA SHAPE="rect" COORDS="180,81,200,320" HREF="#"
            onMouseOut="hideTip('tooltip2')"
            onMouseOver="displayTip(event,'tooltip2')" ALT="Mary" />
        <AREA SHAPE="rect" COORDS="59,26,208,64" HREF="#"
            onMouseOut="hideTip('tooltip3')"
            onMouseOver="displayTip(event,'tooltip3')" ALT="bougainvillea" />
        <AREA SHAPE="rect" COORDS="226,25,303,82" HREF="#"
            onMouseOut="hideTip('tooltip4')"
            onMouseOver="displayTip(event,'tooltip4')" ALT="needs paint" />
</MAP>
<SPAN CLASS="tooltipStyle" ID="tooltip1">Left cousin</SPAN>
<SPAN CLASS="tooltipStyle" ID="tooltip2">Right cousin</SPAN>
<SPAN CLASS="tooltipStyle" ID="tooltip3">Tree</SPAN>
<SPAN CLASS="tooltipStyle" ID="tooltip4">Shutters</SPAN>
```

Much of the code in Listing 11-4 also appears in Listing 11-1 earlier in this chapter. The new parts of the code added here are the onMouseOut and onMouseOver definitions. (See the bold portions of the code.)

As you can see from Listing 11-4, the JavaScript function displayTip() is attached to the onMouseOver event handlers for the each of the active areas, and the JavaScript function hideTip() is attached to the onMouseOut event handlers for those same active areas. (To check out the JavaScript code for the displayTip() and hideTip() functions, flip to Listing 11-3.)

If you're interested in finding out more about events and event handlers, including onMouseOut and onMouseOver, flip to Chapter 13, which is devoted to these topics.

What all this means is that at runtime, when a user mouses over one of the active areas (active areas are defined using the <AREA> tag) the JavaScript interpreter calls the displayTip() function, sending the following two parameters:

1. The appropriate event, which is mouseOver

2. The name of the tooltip to display: tooltip1, tooltip2, tooltip3, or tooltip4. (The tooltip names and content are defined by using the <SPAN> and </SPAN> tags, as shown in Listing 11-4.)

Then, when a user mouses away from the active area, the JavaScript interpreter calls the hide() function, sending the name of the tooltip to hide.

Putting it all together: Using DHTML code to create simple tooltips

Sometimes you find it useful to experiment with a working script containing all the necessary elements for DHTML tooltips: HTML code that defines the active areas for which you want to create tooltips, style sheet code that defines how you want your tooltips to appear, and JavaScript code that tells the Web browser to display (or hide) the appropriate tooltips depending on mouse pointer position.

In Listing 11-5, a complete, working script is exactly what you find. Listing 11-5 pulls together the code you see in Listings 11-1 through 11-4 to demonstrate how each piece fits together.

You can find the code in Listing 11-5 on the companion CD under the filename `list1105.htm`.

Listing 11-5:   The Whole Enchilada: A Working Tooltip Script

```
<HTML>
<HEAD>
<TITLE>Tooltip Example from JavaScript For Dummies, 4th Edition</TITLE>
<SCRIPT type="text/javascript" language="Javascript">
<!-- Hide script from older browsers

    if (document.getElementById) {
            latestBrowser = true
    }
    else {
            latestBrowser = false
    }

    function displayTip(theEvent,currentElement) {
        if (latestBrowser) {
          tooltip = document.getElementById(currentElement).style
        }
                else {
              tooltip = eval("document." + currentElement)
        }

        if (document.all) {
            tooltip.pixelTop = parseInt(theEvent.y)+2
                tooltip.pixelLeft =  Math.max(2,parseInt(theEvent.x)-75)
        }
        else {
            if (latestBrowser) {
                    tooltip.top = parseInt(theEvent.pageY)+2 + "px"
```

(continued)

Listing 11-5 *(continued)*

```
                            tooltip.left = Math.max(2,parseInt(theEvent.pageX)-75) +
            "px"
                }
                  else {
                    tooltip.top = parseInt(theEvent.pageY)+2
                        tooltip.left = Math.max(2,parseInt(theEvent.pageX)-75)
                    }
            }
        tooltip.visibility = "visible"
    }

    function hideTip(currentElement) {
            if (latestBrowser) {
                tooltip = document.getElementById(currentElement).style
            }
            else {
                tooltip = eval("document." + currentElement)
            }
            tooltip.visibility = "hidden"
    }

    // End hiding script -->

    </SCRIPT>

    <STYLE type="text/css">
    <!--

            .tooltipStyle {background-color: pink; border: pink 1px solid;
            layer-background-color: pink; width: 100px; font: 20px arial,
            helvetica, sans-serif; padding: 5px; position: absolute;
            visibility: hidden}
      -->
      </STYLE>
</HEAD>

<BODY>

<MAP name="PicMap" id="PicMap">
            <AREA SHAPE="rect" COORDS="112,91,136,315" HREF="#"
            onMouseOut="hideTip('tooltip1')"
            onMouseOver="displayTip(event,'tooltip1')" alt="Sarah" />

            <AREA SHAPE="rect" COORDS="180,81,200,320" HREF="#"
            onMouseOut="hideTip('tooltip2')"
            onMouseOver="displayTip(event,'tooltip2')" alt="Mary" />

            <AREA SHAPE="rect" COORDS="59,26,208,64" HREF="#"
            onMouseOut="hideTip('tooltip3')"
            onMouseOver="displayTip(event,'tooltip3')" alt="bougainvillea" />
```

```
                <AREA SHAPE="rect" COORDS="226,25,303,82" HREF="#"
                onMouseOut="hideTip('tooltip4')"
                onMouseOver="displayTip(event,'tooltip4')" alt="needs paint" />
</MAP>

<SPAN CLASS="tooltipStyle" ID="tooltip1">Left cousin</SPAN>
<SPAN CLASS="tooltipStyle" ID="tooltip2">Right cousin</SPAN>
<SPAN CLASS="tooltipStyle" ID="tooltip3">Tree</SPAN>
<SPAN CLASS="tooltipStyle" ID="tooltip4">Shutters</SPAN>

<DIV align="center">
                <IMG SRC="cousins.jpg" USEMAP="#PicMap" HEIGHT="289" WIDTH="289"
                BORDER="0" alt="Two cousins" />
</DIV>

</BODY>
</HTML>
```

Taking Advantage of Third-Party Tooltips Scripts

Creating DHTML tooltips from scratch, as you see from Listing 11-5, takes not just JavaScript expertise but expertise in HTML and CSS programming, too. If your heart is set on adding custom tooltips to your site but you don't want to invest the time and trouble in finding out everything you need to know to code them by hand, you're in luck: Third-party scripts are available, and they take most of the hard work out of creating custom tooltips.

Lots of shareware tooltips scripts are available for download over the Web. If you're interested, you might want to start your search for the perfect tooltips tool by checking out the following two sites:

✔ With Walter Zorn's DHTML Tooltips you can create cross-platform, cross-browser tooltips containing images as well as text. More information about this cool shareware tool is available at `www.walterzorn.com/tooltip/tooltip_e.htm`.

✔ Dan Allen's DOM Tooltip is a shareware tool you can use to create tooltips that work not just in Internet Explorer and Navigator but also in other browsers, such as Opera. You can find download instructions and tons of examples at `www.mojavelinux.com/cooker/demos/domTT/index.html`.

Part IV

Interacting with Users

The 5th Wave   By Rich Tennant

"You're part of an 'Insect—Clothing Club' on the Web? Neat!
Where do you get buttons that small?"

In this part . . .

Part IV is jam-packed with information for making professional-looking Web pages that are so cool you just might shock yourself! Chapter 12 shows you how to gather and verify input from the folks who visit your Web site — including time-tested tips to help you design user-friendly Web pages and communicate effectively with your users. In Chapter 13, you see how to turn a simple Web page into a Web-based application by hooking your script to a user-initiated event, such as key press or a mouse click. And finally, Chapter 14 introduces you to JavaScript error-handling techniques that you can use to replace generic error messages (which can frustrate your visitors) with specific, appropriate, user-friendly error messages.

Chapter 12

Handling Forms

In This Chapter
▶ Getting information from your users
▶ Verifying user input
▶ Giving your users helpful feedback

*I*f you're familiar with HTML fill-in forms, you know how useful they can be. Adding an HTML form to your Web page lets your visitors communicate with you quickly and easily. Users can enter comments, contact information, or anything else into an HTML form. Then that information is transmitted automatically to you (okay, technically, to your Web server) the instant your users submit the form.

Although HTML forms are great all by themselves, JavaScript makes them even better! By using JavaScript, you can create intelligent forms — forms that instantly correct user input errors, calculate numeric values, and provide feedback. In developer-talk, what JavaScript gives you is a way to perform client-side data validation (sometimes referred to as data scrubbing), which is an essential component of any well-designed piece of software, from simple Web page to full-blown online application.

Capturing User Input by Using HTML Form Fields

JavaScript adds two very useful features to plain old HTML forms:

✔ JavaScript lets you examine and validate user input instantly, right on the client.

✔ JavaScript lets you give users instant feedback.

I explain both of these features in the following two sections.

Creating an input-validation script

Back in the old days, Web developers had to write server-side Common Gateway Interface (CGI) programs to process user input. That approach, which is still in use, is effective — but inefficient.

For example, imagine that you want to allow your visitors to sign up for your monthly e-newsletter, so you create an HTML form containing a single input field called E-mail Address. Then imagine that a visitor accidentally types XYZ into that field (instead of a valid e-mail address such as janedoe@aol.com). The contents of the E-mail Address field have to travel all the way from that user's Web browser to your Web server before your CGI program can examine the information and determine that XYZ is invalid.

By using JavaScript, on the other hand, you can instantly determine whether an input value is valid, right inside the user's browser — saving the user valuable time. (And saving yourself the trouble of having to figure out how to create a CGI program in C, C++, or Perl!)

Different strokes for different folks: Data validation using regular expressions

Writing scripts is like anything else in life: Usually, more than one way exists to approach any given problem. Some JavaScript programmers like to spell things out much the way I demonstrate in the code that you see in this chapter — in other words, to use as many lines of script as necessary to create a human-readable, working script. Other JavaScript programmers sacrifice human readability for brevity, reasoning that fewer lines of code means fewer lines to debug.

For those of you in the latter camp, *regular expressions* can come in mighty handy. A regular expression is a special kind of pattern that you can use to specify text strings. For example, here's a regular expression that describes a somebody@someplace.some_suffix e-mail address:

```
/^\w+@\w+(\.\w{3})$/
```

Scary stuff! But when you break it down into little pieces, you understand how it works, as you can see in Table 12-1.

Input validation generally falls somewhere in one of the following three categories:

- ✓ **Existence:** Tests whether a value exists.
- ✓ **Numeric:** Ensures that the information is numbers only.
- ✓ **Pattern:** Tests for a specific convention, such as the punctuation in a phone number, an e-mail address, a Social Security number, or a date.

In Listing 12-1, you see the JavaScript code required to validate the oh-so-common pattern category: an e-mail address. (The order form script section in this chapter demonstrates examples of existence and numeric validation, as well as pattern validation.)

Figure 12-1 shows you this code in action. You can experiment with these techniques by loading the `list1201.htm` file from the companion CD into your Web browser.

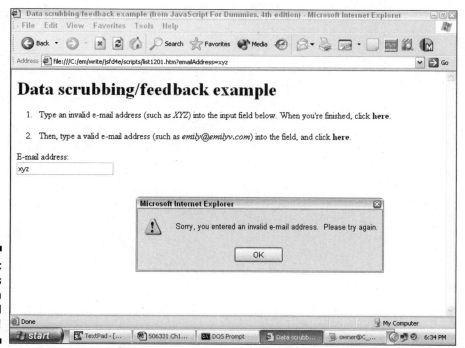

Figure 12-1:
Hey, that's not an e-mail address!

Listing 12-1:   A Script That Validates the E-Mail Address Pattern

```javascript
<SCRIPT LANGUAGE="JavaScript" TYPE="text/javascript">

////////////////////////////////////////////////////
// This function tests for the punctuation characters
// (. and @) found in a valid e-mail address.
////////////////////////////////////////////////////

function isAValidEmail(inputValue) {

    var foundAt = false
    var foundDot = false
    var atPosition = -1
    var dotPosition = -1

    // Step through each character of the e-mail
    // address and set a flag when (and if) an
    // @ sign and a dot are detected.

    for (var i=0; i<=inputValue.length; i++) {
      if (inputValue.charAt(i) == "@" ) {
          foundAt = true
          atPosition = i
      }
      else if (inputValue.charAt(i) == ".") {
          foundDot = true
          dotPosition = i
      }
    }

    // If both an @ symbol and a dot were found, and
    // in the correct order (@ must come first)...

    if ((foundAt && foundDot) && (atPosition < dotPosition)) {

        // It's a valid e-mail address.

        alert("Thanks for entering a valid e-mail address!")
        return true
    }
    else {

        // The e-mail address is invalid.

      alert("Sorry, you entered an invalid e-mail address.  Please try again.")
        return false
    }
}
```

In Listing 12-1, you see that the isAValidEmail() function accepts a single parameter, called inputValue. (I show you an example of calling this function in Listing 12-2.)

Inside isAValidEmail(), the for loop steps through each character of the input e-mail address, one character at a time, looking for an at symbol (@) and a dot (.). If the interpreter finds both of these characters in the input e-mail address — and if the @ symbol appears before the . — that e-mail address passes the test as valid.

If you want to perform additional checks — for example, a check to ensure that at least one character precedes both the @ and the . or one to ensure that the last three characters are com, org, edu, or net — you can add the additional JavaScript statements to isAValidEmail() to do so. As a developer, the criteria that define a valid pattern are solely up to you. Whether the additional JavaScript statements necessary to catch all conceivable errors are worth the trouble and complexity is your decision, as well. In this example, I figure that the most likely mistake users make is forgetting to type an @ or a period, so the code in Listing 12-1 fits the bill nicely.

Table 12-1   Examining a Few Regular Expression Symbols

Regular Expression Symbol	Meaning
/	Beginning of the pattern
^	Beginning of a string
\w+	One or more letters, numbers, or underscores
@	The @ symbol
\w+	One or more letters, numbers, or underscores
(\.\w{3})	A dot followed by three letters, numbers, or underscores
$	Ending of a string
/	Ending of the pattern

Listing 12-2 puts it all together to show how you can use a regular expression to validate an e-mail address in JavaScript. (Note how many fewer lines this e-mail validation script uses than the one I offer in Listing 12-1 earlier in this chapter.)

Listing 12-2:   Using a Regular Expression to Validate an E-Mail Address

```
function validateEmail(input) {
    // JavaScript recognizes regular expressions and automatically
    // designates the variable "emailPattern" as a RegExp object.
    var emailPattern = /^\w+@\w+(\.\w{3})$/

    // test() is a built-in method of the RegExp object.
    if (emailPattern.test(input)) {
        alert("This is a valid e-mail address.")
    }
    else {
        alert("Error: this is NOT a valid e-mail address")
    }
}
...
<BODY>
<FORM>
Please enter an e-mail address and click somewhere else on the page:
<INPUT TYPE="text" SIZE="25" onBlur="validateEmail(this.value);">
```

Regular expressions are fairly complex animals, and I can't go into all the
nitty-gritty details of them here. Fortunately, Microsoft maintains a great
primer on regular expressions (and the built-in JScript object RegExp) at

```
http://msdn.microsoft.com/library/default.asp?url=/library/en-
            us/jscript7/html/jsreconIntroductionToRegularExpressions.asp
```

Oh, no! Everything's blurry!

The name for the onBlur event handler relates
to the concept of focus. An object is said to
receive focus when you click it. So, by default, the
object becomes *blurry* when you click something else, and that object *loses* focus.

Here's a quick rundown of when the JavaScript
interpreter executes a few common blur-related
event handlers:

✔ onFocus executes when an element
receives focus (a user tabs to it or clicks it).

✔ onBlur executes when a user clicks an
element (the element gets focus) and then

clicks somewhere else without changing
anything (the element loses focus, or *blurs*).

✔ onChange executes when an element
loses focus *and* its contents are modified.

✔ onSelect executes when a user selects
some or all text (inside a text or textarea
element). The behavior of onSelect is
similar to onFocus except that onSelect
occurs when the element receives focus
and the user selects text.

You can find the regular expression code from Listing 12-2 on the companion CD. Just look for the file regexp.htm.

Calling a validation script

To someone surfing the Web, few things are more annoying than typing a bunch of information into a form, clicking the form's Submit button, and then — after a lengthy wait — seeing a generic error message that says something like You filled something out incorrectly.

JavaScript lets you check each individual input field, if you like, and pop up instant feedback to let your users know (before they tab clear down to the end of a long form) that they need to make a correction.

In the JavaScript code shown in Listing 12-3, the isAValidEmail() function (which I define in Listing 12-1) is called from the HTML text element's onBlur event handler. The result? Entering an e-mail address into the text element and clicking elsewhere on the Web page causes the isAValidEmail() function to execute (refer to Figure 12-1).

Listing 12-3:   Calling the isAValidEmail() Function from an onBlur Event Handler

```
<BODY>
<H1>Data scrubbing/feedback example</H1>
<OL>
<LI>Type an invalid e-mail address (such as <I>XYZ</I>) into the input field
           below. When you're finished, click <B>here</B>.
<P>
<LI>Then, type a valid e-mail address (such as <I>emily@emilyv.com</I>) into the
           field, and click <B>here</B>.
</OL>
<P>
<FORM NAME="myForm">

E-mail address:
<BR>
//Calling isAValidEmail() with the value typed into the emailAddress text field.
<INPUT TYPE="text" SIZE="25" NAME="emailAddress"
           onBlur="isAValidEmail(this.value)">
</FORM>

</BODY>
```

Putting It All Together: The Order Form Validation Script

In the example in this section, you see how to create an intelligent form that validates user data two different ways:

✔ **At the field level:** You can validate independent fields as soon as the user tabs away from them. An independent field is one that you require (such as a credit card number for a credit card purchase), regardless of what a user types for any other field. (You see an example of field-level validation in "Creating an input-validation script" earlier in this chapter.)

✔ **At the form level:** You want to validate dependent fields when the user finishes filling out a form and clicks the form's Submit button. A dependent field is one that you might or might not validate, depending on what a user types for one or more other fields. For example, you might not require an e-mail address unless your users specify that they want to receive your e-mail newsletter.

Numerical assistance

JavaScript offers a handful of built-in functions that help you identify whether a value is numeric:

✔ `parseInt()`: Tries to turn a value into an integer; returns either the integer value or `false` (if the value can't be turned into a number). These two lines illustrate:

```
var result = parseInt("123")
```

The `result` variable is set to the numeric value 123.

```
var result = parseInt("Emily")
```

The `result` variable is set to NaN (Not a Number).

✔ `parseFloat()`: Tries to turn a value into a floating-point (decimal) number; returns either the floating-point value or `false` (if the value can't be turned into a number). These example show you how:

```
var result = parseFloat("45.6")
```

The `result` variable is set to the numeric value 45.6.

```
var result = parseInt("grumpy")
```

The `result` variable is set to NaN.

✔ `isNaN()`: This function, which stands for *is Not a Number*, returns `true` if the value passed to it is not a number and `false` if the value passed to it *is* a number. (Yeah, I know — double negatives are confusing, aren't they?) Here are two examples:

```
var result = isNaN(3)
```

The `result` variable is set to `false` because 3 is a number.

```
var result = isNaN("George Clooney")
```

The `result` variable is set to `true` because a string value is not a number.

The example that you see in this chapter is for a fictitious Web design company called Webmeister. To allow visitors to request a personalized quote for Web design services, the company decided to create an HTML form and attach JavaScript scripts to meet these design goals:

- ✔ **Validate the existence of entries in required fields:** To submit a successful quote request, Webmeister's visitors must enter a service category, a first and last name, and at least one contact method (telephone or e-mail). In the code in the following section, the `exists()` function implements these validation checks. Existence validation takes place in this example at both the field and form levels.

- ✔ **Validate two pattern fields:** The scripts must check the phone number and e-mail address to ensure they're valid. The `isAValidPhoneNumber()` and `isAValidEmail()` functions implement these validation checks, respectively, on a form level.

- ✔ **Validate numeric fields:** The generic `isANumber()` function assists in validating phone numbers on a form level.

Figure 12-2 shows you what the completed quote request example looks like.

To see the code responsible for Figure 12-2, `list1207.htm`, in its entirety, open the file from the companion CD-ROM.

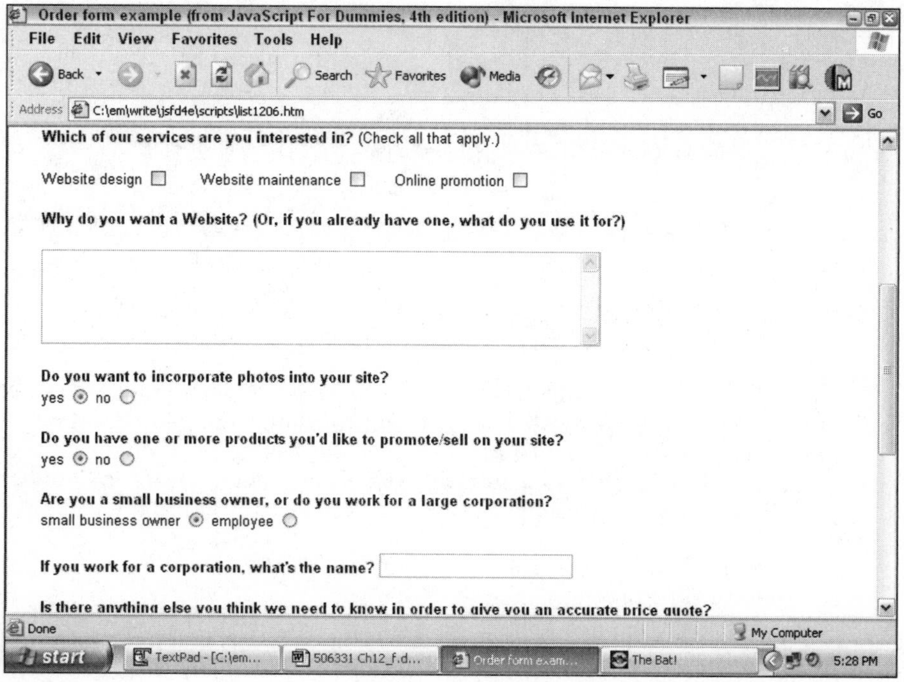

Figure 12-2:
An order form for the fictitious Webmeister company.

Testing for existence

You can require that users provide a value for an HTML form field by attaching an existence-validation script to one of that field's event handlers.

In this example, the Webmeister developers want to ensure that folks requesting a quote enter both their first and last names. Listing 12-4 shows you the JavaScript code necessary to implement this common design requirement.

Listing 12-4:   Testing for the Existence of an Input Value

```
function exists(inputValue) {

    var aCharExists = false

    // Step through the inputValue, using the charAt()
    // method to detect non-space characters.

    for (var i=0; i<=inputValue.length; i++) {
      if (inputValue.charAt(i) != " " && inputValue.charAt(i) != "") {
          aCharExists = true
          break
      }
    }

    return aCharExists
}
...
//The value of the firstName field is sent to the exists() function as soon as
            the user tabs away.
<INPUT TYPE="TEXT" NAME="firstName" SIZE="25" onBlur="if (!exists(this.value)) {
            alert('Please enter a first name'); }">

//The value of the lastName field is sent to the exists() function as soon as
            the user tabs away.

<INPUT TYPE="TEXT" NAME="lastName" SIZE="35" onBlur="if (!exists(this.value)) {
            alert('Please enter a last name') }">
```

The code in Listing 12-4 works on these principles: The exists() function accepts an input value (named, appropriately enough, inputValue). As soon as the exists() function receives this value, it checks the value to see whether it contains a non-white-space character. Either the non-white-space character or the default value of false is returned to the calling code.

If you look lower in the listing, you see the two input fields that call the exists() function, including this one:

```
<INPUT TYPE="TEXT" NAME="firstName" SIZE="25" onBlur="if (!exists(this.value)) {
              alert('Please enter a first name'); }">
```

The preceding JavaScript statement defines a value for the firstName field's onBlur event handler. When a user blurs the firstName field, the value of the firstName field is passed to the exists() function. If exists() returns a value of false (the ! operator is shorthand for "if this thing is false"), a pop-up message appears to remind the user to enter a first name. Now, when the user clicks in the Your First Name field and then tabs away without entering a value, the code causes a reminder message to appear (see Figure 12-3).

Testing for a numeric value

You can require that users provide a valid number for an HTML form field by attaching a numeric validation script to one of that field's event handlers. For an example of the JavaScript code required to perform this validation, take a peek at Listing 12-5.

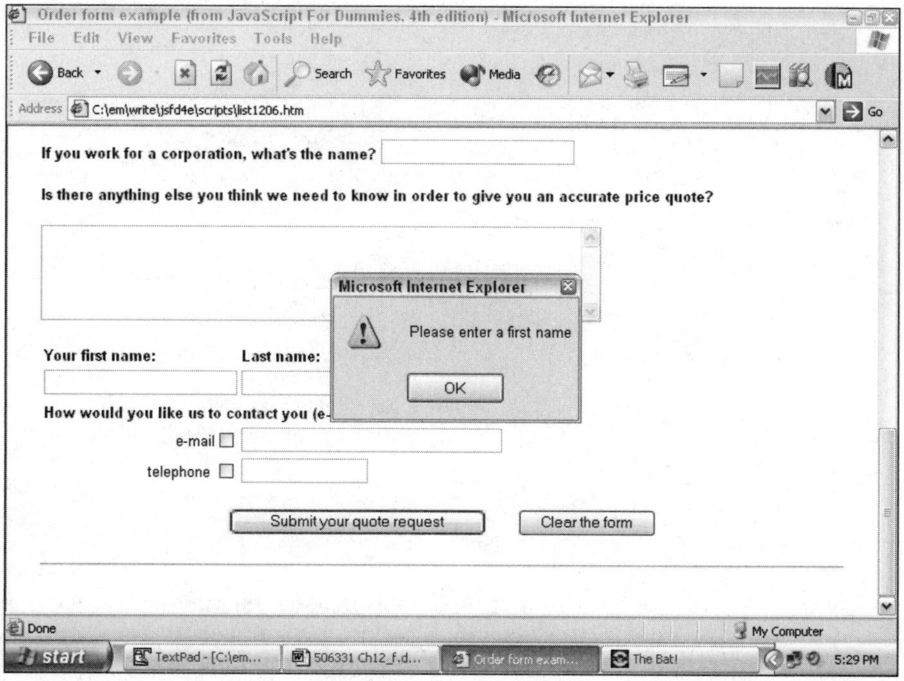

Figure 12-3:
Everybody
must have
(and enter)
a name.

Listing 12-5: Testing to Ensure That a Value Is Numeric

```
//Defining the isANumber() function
function isANumber(inputValue){

    // Assume everything is okay right off the bat.
    var result = true

    // If parseFloat() returns false, a non-numeric
    // character was detected in the first position.

    if (!parseFloat(inputValue)) {
        result = false
    }

    // Otherwise, check the
    // rest of the digits.

    else {
        for (var i=0; i<inputValue.length; i++) {
            if (inputValue.charAt(i) != " ") {
                if (!parseFloat(inputValue.charAt(i))) {
                    result = false
                    break
                }
            }
        }
    }
    // Return true (inputValue is a valid number) or
    // false (it's invalid).

    return result
}

...

function isAValidPhoneNumber(inputValue) {
    ...
    for (var i=0; i<=inputValue.length; i++) {
//Calling the isANumber() function from inside another custom function
        if (isANumber(inputValue.charAt(i))) {
            digitsFound++
        }
    }
```

The isANumber() function definition uses the built-in JavaScript function parseFloat() to weed out all values beginning with something other than a number. (The parseFloat() function returns a value of NaN if the first character that it encounters can't be converted to a number.)

In the event that the first character is a number but subsequent characters aren't (for example, to catch a mistake like 5F5-1212), isANumber() steps through all the remaining characters in inputValue to see whether it can detect a non-numeric character.

The last few statements in Listing 12-5 show you an example of how you can call the isANumber() function. In this example, the isAValidPhoneNumber() function (which you get to examine in detail in the next section) calls the isANumber() function as part of its own validation routine.

Testing for patterns

Listing 12-1, shown previously in this chapter, demonstrates how you might go about validating a very common pattern: the e-mail address. Here, you see an example of another common use for pattern validation: making sure a user types a valid telephone number. Listing 12-6 shows you what I mean.

Listing 12-6: Validating a Phone Number

```
//Defining the isAValidPhoneNumber() function
function isAValidPhoneNumber(inputValue) {
    var digitsFound = 0

    // Step through the inputValue to see how
    // many digits it contains.
    for (var i=0; i<=inputValue.length; i++) {
      if (isANumber(inputValue.charAt(i))) {
          digitsFound++
      }
    }

    // If inputValue contains at least 10
    // digits, assume it is a valid phone number.
    if (digitsFound >= 10) {
        return true
    }
    else {
        return false
    }
}
...
//Calling the isAValidPhoneNumber() function
if (!isAValidPhoneNumber(inputValue) {
    alert("We can't contact you via phone unless you give us your phone number
            (make sure to include your area code).  Thanks!")
}
```

The code you see in Listing 12-6 checks to see that a value contains at least ten digits; if so, that value passes the test as a valid telephone number.

Sometimes you want to create more rigid patterns than this. For example, you may want to ensure that users include parentheses and dashes in their telephone numbers. For an example of how to accomplish this (and some caveats), see the sidebar "An alternative approach to pattern-matching."

Form-level validation

Sometimes you want to validate fields immediately, as soon as a user enters a value or tabs away from the field. (Listing 12-4 shows you an example of independent field validation.)

But sometimes you want to wait until the user finishes entering information before you begin your validation. For example, the Webmeister form allows users to specify whether they want to be contacted by e-mail or by telephone. At least one option must be selected, but triggering validation the instant a user tabs away from the e-mail field would be useless (and annoying). After all, that user might very well be intending to select the phone number option; you have no way of knowing until the user finishes filling out the entire form.

An alternative approach to pattern-matching

If you need to define a more rigid pattern than the telephone number example that I describe in Listing 12-6, take a look at the JavaScript code in this sidebar, which requires that users enter a phone number in the following format:

```
(512)555-1212
```

As you see in the following example, the `sub-string()` method associated with the built-in JavaScript `string` object lets you break a value into chunks and ensure that each chunk is valid. For example, this code instructs the interpreter to extract and inspect the parentheses, area code, exchange, and line portions of the phone number separately.

The benefit of this approach? It ensures that users type exactly what you want them to type, which reduces the chance of miscommunication. The drawback is that you're expecting a user to type a bunch of characters exactly the way you want — a process that is difficult at best! (Keep in mind that the Web is global, and patterns that might be familiar to you might not be familiar at all to folks in other parts of the world.)

A good design rule to follow is this: If you absolutely must gather information in a specific format, by all means adapt this example of JavaScript code for your own purposes. But if you can get by with fewer checks (like the phone number validation routine that I describe in Listing 12-6), go for it.

```
function isAPhoneNumber(entry){
    if (entry) {
            // Set openParen = to the first character of entry.
        var openParen = entry.substring(0,1)

            // Set areaCode = to the next 3 characters.
        var areaCode = entry.substring(1,4)

            // Set closeParen = to the 5th character.
        var closeParen = entry.substring(4,5)

            // Set exchange = to characters 6, 7, and 8.
        var exchange = entry.substring(5,8)

            // Set dash = to the 9th character.
        var dash = entry.substring(8,9)

            // Set line = to the 10th through 13th characters.
        var line = entry.substring(9,13)

        // The following if statement checks all the pieces,
        // like so:
        // if openParen is not equal to "("
        // OR the areaCode is not a number
        // OR the closeParen is not equal to ")"
        // ... and so on.

        if (
            (openParen != "(")      ||
            (!isANumber(areaCode)) ||
            (closeParen != ")")     ||
            (!isANumber(exchange)) ||
            (dash != "-")           ||
            (!isANumber(line))
           ){
        alert("Incorrect phone number.  Please re-enter in the
following format: (123)456-7890")
        }
    }
}
. . .
<FORM NAME="feedbackForm">
<BR>Please enter your home phone number
<BR>in the following format: (123)456-7890
<INPUT TYPE="text" NAME="homePhone" VALUE="" SIZE=13
onBlur="isAPhoneNumber(this.value)">
. . .
```

Giving 'em a piece of your mind

Giving users appropriate, timely feedback can be the difference between a confusing Web site and one that is efficient and pleasant to use. The following are a few things to keep in mind as you decide when and how to interact with your users.

DON'T SHOUT!! Nobody likes being yelled at, and messages THAT ARE IN ALL UPPERCASE LIKE THIS AND END IN EXCLAMATION POINTS ARE YELLS! Say what you need to say; just use normal capitalization and punctuation.

In general, be specific. Sometimes, you don't particularly care what a user types (for example, if you're asking for free-form comments on your product). At other times, what the user types is crucial. For the times when it's crucial, be sure to let the user know up front, right on the page, what format is expected.

When you *do* need to pop up an error message, make sure that it tells users precisely what's wrong with their input. (`Invalid format. Please retry.` doesn't count!)

Give your users a break. Just because you're now a card-carrying expert at validating user input doesn't mean you have to pop up an error message *every* time you detect an error. In some cases, you might be able to *massage* (geek-speak for *modify*) the input data to suit yourself without bugging the user at all. For example, just because you'd like to see a value in uppercase letters doesn't mean the user has to enter it in uppercase letters. Instead of displaying an error and requesting that the user retype the entry, for example, you can just as easily take the input and change it to uppercase yourself using the `toUpperCase()` method of the `string` object.

Pat your users on the back. Don't reserve feedback for only those times when a user enters something incorrectly. Reassuring users that things are proceeding as planned is just as useful. For example, let users know when a form passes all validation checks.

Test 'til you drop. Make sure (and this *should* go without saying, but you never know) that you test your form carefully for every conceivable error (and series of errors) that a user might reasonably be expected to make. Few things are more frustrating to users than getting tangled in an endless loop of errors that refuse to go away, even *after* the user has figured out what's wrong and corrected it!

A better approach for dependent field validation is to wait until users try to submit their forms before executing your validation scripts, as shown in Listing 12-7. Now, if the user attempts to submit a form without entering either a phone number or an e-mail address, the script generates an error and prevents the form from being submitted. To see how this code behaves at runtime, take a look at Figure 12-4.

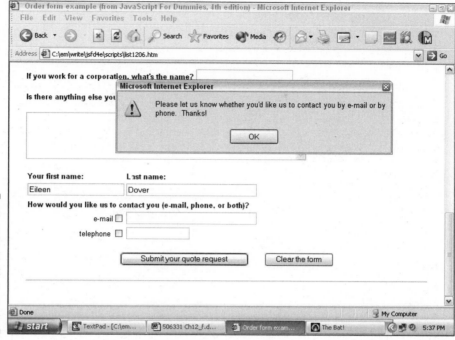

Figure 12-4:
Using
form-level
validation to
ensure that
at least one
option is
filled.

Listing 12-7: Implementing Dependent Validation Checks with the validateForm() Function

```
<HTML>
<HEAD>
<TITLE>Order form example (from JavaScript For Dummies, 4th Edition)</TITLE>

<SCRIPT LANGUAGE="JavaScript" TYPE="text/javascript">
<!-- hide this script from non-javascript-enabled browsers

///////////////////////////////////////////////////////////
// Checks to see whether a value contains non-numeric data.
///////////////////////////////////////////////////////////
function isANumber(inputValue){

    // Assume everything is okay.
    var result = true
```

(continued)

Listing 12-7 *(continued)*

```
        // If parseFloat() returns false, a non-numeric
        // character was detected in the first position,
        if (!parseFloat(inputValue)) {
            result = false
        }

        // Otherwise, we still have to check the rest of
        // the digits, so step through the inputValue one
        // character at a time and set result = false
        // if any non-numeric digits are encountered.
        else {
        for (var i=0; i<inputValue.length; i++) {
                if (inputValue.charAt(i) != " ") {
                    if (!parseFloat(inputValue.charAt(i))) {
                        result = false
                        break
                    }
                }
            }
        }
    }

        // Return true (inputValue is a valid number) or
        // false (it's invalid).

        return result
}

////////////////////////////////////////////////////////
// Checks to see whether an input value contains "@"
// and "."
////////////////////////////////////////////////////////
function isAValidEmail(inputValue) {

    var foundAt = false
    var foundDot = false

    // Step through the inputValue looking for
    // "@" and "."

    for (var i=0; i<=inputValue.length; i++) {
      if (inputValue.charAt(i) == "@" ) {
          foundAt = true
      }
      else if (inputValue.charAt(i) == ".") {
          foundDot = true
      }
```

```
      }

   // If both "@" and "." were found, assume
   // the e-mail address is valid; otherwise,
   // return false so the calling code knows
   // the e-mail address is invalid.

   if (foundAt && foundDot) {
      return true
   }
else {
      return false
   }
}


///////////////////////////////////////////////////////
// Checks to see if an input value contains ten or more
// numbers. This approach lets users type in U.S.-
// style phone formats, such as (123)456-7890, as
// well as European-style (such as 123.456.7890).
///////////////////////////////////////////////////////
function isAValidPhoneNumber(inputValue) {
   var digitsFound = 0

   // Step through the inputValue to see how
   // many digits it contains.

   for (var i=0; i<=inputValue.length; i++) {
     if (isANumber(inputValue.charAt(i))) {
        digitsFound++
     }
   }

   // If inputValue contains at least 10
   // digits, assume it is a valid phone number.
   if (digitsFound >= 10) {
      return true
   }
   else {
      return false
   }
}


///////////////////////////////////////////////////////
// Check for the existence of characters.
// (Spaces aren't counted.)
///////////////////////////////////////////////////////
```

(continued)

Listing 12-7 *(continued)*

```
function exists(inputValue) {

    var aCharExists = false

    // Step through the inputValue, using the charAt()
    // method to detect non-space characters.

    for (var i=0; i<=inputValue.length; i++) {
      if (inputValue.charAt(i) != " " && inputValue.charAt(i) != "") {
          aCharExists = true
          break
      }
    }

    return aCharExists
}

//////////////////////////////////////////////////////
// Perform cross-field checks that can't be performed
// until all of the data has been entered.
//////////////////////////////////////////////////////

// validateForm() performs all dependent field validation

function validateForm() {

    var rc = true

    // Dependent check #1: ensuring a service category is selected

    //////////////////////////////////////////////////////
    // Visitors need to check one of the following
    // choices in order to receive an accurate quote:
    // whether they're interested
    // in design, maintenance, or promotion services.
    //////////////////////////////////////////////////////

    if (!document.quoteForm.designChoice.checked &&
        !document.quoteForm.maintChoice.checked &&
        !document.quoteForm.promoChoice.checked) {
            alert("Please check whether you're interested in our design,
                maintenance, or promotion services so we can give you a more
                accurate quote.  Thanks!")
        rc = false
    }

    // Dependent check #2: ensuring that a company name exists if a
    // user checked "employee"
```

```
/////////////////////////////////////////////////////
// If visitors are employees, they need to specify
// the name of their company.
/////////////////////////////////////////////////////

if (document.quoteForm.bizChoice[1].checked) {
    if (!document.quoteForm.corpName.value) {
        alert("You've specified that you're an employee, so could you please
            type in the name of the company you work for?  Thanks!")
        rc = false


    }
}

// Dependent check #3: double-checking that both first and
// last names exist

/////////////////////////////////////////////////////
// Visitors need to include their first and last
// names.
/////////////////////////////////////////////////////

if (!document.quoteForm.firstName.value ||
    !document.quoteForm.lastName.value) {
    alert("Please type in your entire name (both first and last).  Thanks!")
    rc = false
}

// Dependent check #4: ensuring that users enter either an e-mail
// address or a phone number

/////////////////////////////////////////////////////
// Visitors need to specify either an e-mail
// address or a telephone number.
/////////////////////////////////////////////////////
if (!document.quoteForm.emailChoice.checked &&
    !document.quoteForm.phoneChoice.checked) {
    alert("Please let us know whether you'd like us to contact you by e-mail
            or by phone.  Thanks!")
    rc = false
}

// Dependent check #5: ensuring that an e-mail address exists
// (if a user chose the e-mail contact option)

/////////////////////////////////////////////////////
// If visitors tell us they want us to contact them
// by e-mail, alert them if they haven't put in
// their e-mail address (same with telephone).
/////////////////////////////////////////////////////
```

(continued)

Listing 12-7 *(continued)*

```
    if (document.quoteForm.emailChoice.checked &&
        !isAValidEmail(document.quoteForm.emailAddr.value)) {
            alert("We can't contact you via e-mail unless you give us a valid
                e-mail address. Thanks!")
        rc = false
    }
    else {
        if (document.quoteForm.phoneChoice.checked &&
        !isAValidPhoneNumber(document.quoteForm.phoneNumber.value)) {
            alert("We can't contact you via phone unless you give us your phone
                number (make sure to include your area code).  Thanks!")
        rc = false
        }
    }

    if (rc) {
        // If the rc variable is non-zero, then the form data
        // passed with flying colors!
        alert("Thanks! We'll contact you with a quote shortly.")
    }
    return rc
}

// -->
</SCRIPT>
</HEAD>

<BODY>
<H1>Order form example</H1>
<HR>

...

<P>
<HR>
<TABLE WIDTH="100%" CELLSPACING="10" CELLPADDING="10" BORDER=0>
<TR>
<TD>
<FONT FACE="Helvetica, Arial, Verdana" SIZE="2">
//Dependent validation checks execute when the user attempts to submit the form
<FORM NAME="quoteForm" onSubmit="return validateForm();">
<P>
<B>Which of our services are you interested in?</B> (Check all that apply.)
<P>
Website design <INPUT TYPE="CHECKBOX" NAME="designChoice" VALUE="design">
                 
Website maintenance <INPUT TYPE="CHECKBOX" NAME="maintChoice"
            VALUE="maint">     
Online promotion
<INPUT TYPE="CHECKBOX" NAME="promoChoice" VALUE="promo">

<P>
```

```
<B>Why do you want a Website? (Or, if you already have one, what do you use it
            for?)</B>
<P>
<TEXTAREA NAME="purpose" COLS="60" ROWS="5" WRAP="VIRTUAL">
</TEXTAREA>
<P>
<B>Do you want to incorporate photos into your site?</B>
    <BR>
yes <INPUT TYPE="RADIO" NAME="pixChoice" VALUE="hasPix" CHECKED>
no <INPUT TYPE="RADIO" NAME="pixChoice" VALUE="hasNoPix">
<P>
<B>Do you have one or more products you'd like to promote/sell on your site?</B>
<BR>
yes <INPUT TYPE="RADIO" NAME="cdChoice" VALUE="hasProducts" CHECKED>
no <INPUT TYPE="RADIO" NAME="cdChoice" VALUE="hasNoProducts">
<P>
<B>Are you a small business owner, or do you work for a large corporation?</B>
<BR>
small business owner <INPUT TYPE="RADIO" NAME="bizChoice" VALUE="isOwner"
            CHECKED>
employee <INPUT TYPE="RADIO" NAME="bizChoice" VALUE="isEmployee">
<P>
<B>If you work for a corporation, what's the name?</B>
<INPUT TYPE="TEXT" NAME="corpName" SIZE="25">
<P>
<B>Is there anything else you think we need to know in order to give you an
            accurate price quote?</B>
<P>
<TEXTAREA NAME="extraInfo" COLS="60" ROWS="5" WRAP="VIRTUAL">
</TEXTAREA>
<P>

<TABLE>
<TR>
<TD>
<FONT FACE="Helvetica, Arial, Verdana" SIZE="2">
<B>Your first name:</B>
</TD>
<TD>
<FONT FACE="Helvetica, Arial, Verdana" SIZE="2">
<B>Last name:</B>
</TD>
</TR>
<TR>
<TD>
<INPUT TYPE="TEXT" NAME="firstName" SIZE="25" onBlur="if (!exists(this.value)) {
            alert('Please enter a first name'); }">
</TD>
<TD>
<INPUT TYPE="TEXT" NAME="lastName" SIZE="35" onBlur="if (!exists(this.value)) {
            alert('Please enter a last name') }">
</TD>
```

(continued)

Listing 12-7 *(continued)*

```
</TR>
<TR>
</TR>
<TR>
<TD COLSPAN="2">
<FONT FACE="Helvetica, Arial, Verdana" SIZE="2">
<B>How would you like us to contact you (e-mail, phone, or both)?</B>
</FONT>
</TD>
</TR>

<TR>
<TD ALIGN="RIGHT">
<FONT FACE="Helvetica, Arial, Verdana" SIZE="2">
e-mail<INPUT TYPE="CHECKBOX" NAME="emailChoice" VALUE="email">

</FONT>
</TD>
<TD>

<INPUT TYPE="TEXT" NAME="emailAddr" SIZE="35">
</TD>
</TR>
<TR>
<TD ALIGN="RIGHT">
<FONT FACE="Helvetica, Arial, Verdana" SIZE="2">
telephone <INPUT TYPE="CHECKBOX" NAME="phoneChoice" VALUE="phone">

</TD>

<TD>
<INPUT TYPE="TEXT" NAME="phoneNumber" SIZE="15">
</TD>
</TR>
</TABLE>
<P>
<CENTER>
<INPUT TYPE="SUBMIT" VALUE="Submit your quote request">
      <INPUT TYPE="RESET" VALUE="Clear the form">
...
</HTML>
```

In the code in Listing 12-7, the validateForm() function, which performs five dependent field validation routines, executes when the user attempts to submit the form. (Attaching the vaidateForm() function to the quoteForm form's onSubmit event handler sees to that!)

Chapter 13

Handling User-Initiated Events

· ·

In This Chapter

▶ Getting acquainted with the difference between events and event handlers

▶ Taking a look at the events associated with different objects

▶ Seeing event handlers in action

· ·

*J*avaScript helps you transform static Web pages into interactive Web-based applications. And what's the feature that makes this client-side interactivity possible? The humble and lovable event handler. You can think of event handlers as little software bungee cords that bind custom JavaScript code to events, such as clicking a button or a link, loading a page, typing data into an input field, and so on.

You see examples of event handlers throughout this book. For this chapter, I focus on the event handlers that most developers find most useful — the event handlers associated with window, mouse, form, and keyboard events. Here you find out how to create and attach essential scripts to such user-driven events as opening a Web page window, moving a mouse pointer, interacting with an HTML form, and pressing keys.

The Skinny on Events and Event Handlers

In Web programming terms, an event is anything that happens to a Web page. Examples of events include

✔ A window or frame opening or closing

✔ A mouse pointer moving onto or off of an image, a link, or an HTML form

✔ A mouse clicking or double-clicking anywhere on a page

✔ A key being pressed

By using JavaScript, you can perform an action in response to any event. For example, you can play a welcoming tune when a user opens a Web page; display explanatory text when a user mouses over a certain area of a Web page; validate form data as soon as a user enters it; and create hot keys that perform a custom function in response to a keystroke.

Handling Events

You handle events in JavaScript by attaching event handlers to individual Web page elements. Event handlers are simply attribute-value pairs that allow you to capture and respond to events as they occur.

For example, the following code defines an HTML button that, when clicked, calls a custom JavaScript function. In this sample code, the name of the event handler is `onClick`, and the name of the JavaScript function is `calc()`.

```
<INPUT TYPE="button" NAME="pushButton" VALUE="Calculate Total" onClick="calc()">
```

Table 13-1 lists the events (in addition to `click`) that you can handle in both Navigator and Internet Explorer by using JavaScript — along with the Web page elements, or objects, that support those events.

Netscape Navigator and Internet Explorer provide different levels of support for event handlers, as they do for so many other features of JavaScript and HTML and HTML extensions and . . . well, you get the picture. In addition, because event handling is inherently platform-dependent, browsers implemented on Macintosh and Unix systems offer differing levels of support for events. For additional event handling information, point your browser to

```
http://msdn.microsoft.com/workshop/author/dhtml/reference/events.asp
```

Table 13-1	Common Cross-Browser Web Page Elements (Objects) That Support Event Handlers	
Event Handler	*Supporting Objects*	*Event (Event Handler Triggered When . . .)*
onAbort	Image	The image loading is interrupted.
onBlur	Button, Checkbox, FileUpload, Password, Radio, Reset Select, Submit, Text, Textarea, window (frame)	The element loses input focus. (Clicking out of or tabbing away from an element takes away that element's input focus.)

Event Handler	Supporting Objects	Event (Event Handler Triggered When . . .)
onChange	Checkbox, FileUpload, Password, Radio, Select, Text, Textarea	The element changes (for example, the user types text into a Text element or clicks a Radio button) *and* loses input focus.
onClick	Button, Checkbox, document, FileUpload, Image, Link, Password, Radio, Reset, Select, Submit, Text, Textarea	The element is clicked a single time (combination of onMouseDown and onMouseUp).
onDblClick	Button, Checkbox, document, FileUpload, Image, Link, sion Password, Radio, Reset, Select, Submit, Text, Textarea	The element is clicked twice in quick succes- (double-clicked).
onError	Image	The image doesn't finish loading for some reason. (Perhaps the image file doesn't exist or is corrupted.)
onFocus	Button, Checkbox, FileUpload, Frame, Password, Radio, Reset, Select, Submit, Text, Textarea, window (frame)	The element gains input focus.
onKeyDown	Button, Checkbox, document, FileUpload, Image, Link, Password, Radio, Reset, Select, Submit, Text, Textarea	The user presses a key.
onKeyPress	Button, Checkbox, document, FileUpload, Image, Link, Password, Radio, Reset, Select, Submit, Text, Textarea onKeyUp event handlers).	The user presses and releases a key (which combines the onKeyDown and
onKeyUp	Button, Checkbox, document, FileUpload, Image, Link, Password, Radio, Reset, Select, Submit, Text, Textarea	The user releases a previously pressed key.
onLoad	Image, window (frame)	The element loads successfully.

(continued)

Table 13-1 *(continued)*

Event Handler	Supporting Objects	Event (Event Handler Triggered When . . .)
onMouseDown	Button, Checkbox, document, FileUpload, Image (and Area), Link, Password, Radio, Reset, Select, Submit, Text, Textarea	The user presses a mouse button (but doesn't release it).
onMouseOut	Image (and Area), Link	The mouse moves off the element.
onMouseOver	Image (and Area), Link	The mouse moves onto the element.
onMouseUp	Button, Checkbox, document, FileUpload, Image (and Area), Link, Password, Radio, Reset, Select, Submit, Text, Textarea	The user releases a previously clicked mouse button.
onMove	window (frame)	The user moves or resizes the window or frame.
onReset	form	The form is reset; either the user clicks a Reset button, or the programmer invokes the form.reset() method.
onResize	window (frame)	The user resizes the window or frame.
onSubmit	form	The form is submitted; either the user clicks a Submit button, or the programmer invokes the form.submit() method.
onUnload	window	The user unloads a document (by closing the browser or by loading another document).

Many programmers find four categories of event handlers to be the most useful: window-related events, mouse-related events, form-related events, and key-related events. In the following four sections, I show you examples of each of these four important event categories.

The Event's the thing

Both Navigator and Internet Explorer support the concept of an Event object designed for advanced event-handling scenarios. In theory, you can use the Event object to capture and examine nitty-gritty details about an event that occurs. For example, if a user clicks a mouse button, you can use the methods and properties associated with the Event object to determine which mouse button the user clicks and even the coordinates of the pointer at the time of the click. If a user presses a key, you can use the methods and properties associated with the

Event object to determine which key (or key combination) your visitor presses. The possibilities are numerous. However, JavaScript support for the Event object isn't consistent between browsers at the time of this writing — and documentation for Navigator support is virtually nonexistent. For more information on the Event object and how it's implemented in Internet Explorer, visit

http://msdn.microsoft.com/workshop/ author/dhtml/reference/objects/obj_ event.asp

Window events

One window event that most Web surfers are familiar with is the pop-up advertisement — a tiny (or not-so-tiny) window that appears automatically when you load certain Web pages into your browser. Pop-up ads are attached to the onLoad event handler (and sometimes the onUnload event handler, too, which can pelt you with additional pop-up ads as you try to surf away from a site).

In addition to the onLoad and onUnload event handlers, windows — and frames, which are a special type of window — support event handlers including onBlur, onFocus, onMove, and onResize, as Table 13-2 describes.

Table 13-2	Window- and Frame-Related Event Handlers
Event Handler	*Event (Event Handler Triggered When . . .)*
onBlur	The element loses input focus. (Clicking out of or tabbing away from an element takes away that element's input focus.)
onFocus	The element gains input focus.
onLoad	The element loads successfully.
onMove	The user moves or resizes the window or frame.
onResize	The user resizes the window or frame.
onUnload	The user unloads a document (by closing the browser or by loading another document).

You trigger JavaScript code for a window event by defining a value for the window's event handler. For example, the following code displays a goodbye message when a user unloads (closes or surfs away from) a Web page.

```
<BODY onUnload="alert('Goodbye, and thank you for stopping by my Web site');">
```

Mouse events

Mouse events make cool interactive effects such as rollovers (see Chapter 8) and tooltips (see Chapter 11) possible. No such object as mouse exists. Rather, mouse events occur when a mouse pointer moves — or is clicked — over some other object. For example, the following code ties two functions (displayToolTip() and hideToolTip()) to the onMouseOver and onMouseOut event handlers associated with an HTML-defined area.

```
<MAP name="PicMap" id="PicMap">
<AREA SHAPE="rect" COORDS="226,25,303,82" HREF="#"
              onMouseOut="hideTooltip('tooltip4')"
              onMouseOver="displayTooltip(event,'tooltip4')"/>
```

Table 13-3 describes additional mouse events — and the objects and event handlers associated with those events.

Table 13-3	**Mouse-Related Event Handlers**	
Event Handler	*Supporting Objects*	*Event (Event Handler Triggered When . . .)*
onMouseDown	Button, Checkbox, document, FileUpload, Image (and Area), Link, Password, Radio, Reset, Select, Submit, Text, Textarea	The user presses a mouse button (but doesn't release it).
onMouseOut	Image (and Area), Link	The mouse moves off the element.
onMouseOver	Image (and Area), Link	The mouse moves onto the element.
onMouseUp	Button, Checkbox, document, FileUpload, Image (and Area, Link, Password, Radio, Reset, Select, Submit, Text, Textarea	The user releases a previously clicked mouse button.

Form events

HTML defines a handful of form elements, or controls (push buttons, radio buttons, check boxes, and so on). Each of these elements is associated with appropriate event handlers.

For example, in the life of a button, several events can occur. That button can be clicked, double-clicked, receive input focus, and lose input focus, for example. JavaScript event handlers can detect and handle each of these separate events — click, double-click, focus, and blur. Take a look at the following code to see what I mean:

```
<INPUT TYPE="button" NAME="pushButton" VALUE="Push me!"
onClick="doSomething();">
```

This statement, which is a mixture of HTML syntax and inline JavaScript code, defines an HTML button element. Along with the TYPE, NAME, and VALUE attributes, the statement defines an onClick event handler for the button. At runtime, when a user clicks the Push Me! button, the JavaScript interpreter automatically calls the function doSomething(). Table 13-4 lists additional event handlers for form elements.

Table 13-4	Event Handlers for Form Elements	
Event Handler	*Supporting Form Elements*	*Event (Event Handler Triggered When . . .)*
onBlur	Button, Checkbox, FileUpload, Password, Radio, Reset, Select, Submit, Text, Textarea	The element loses input focus. (Clicking out of or tabbing away from an element takes away that element's input focus.)
onChange	Checkbox, FileUpload, Password, Radio, Select, Text, Textarea	The element changes (for example, the user types text into a Text element or clicks a Radio button) *and* loses input focus.
onClick	Button, Checkbox, FileUpload, Password, Radio, Reset, Select, Submit, Text, Textarea	The element is clicked a single time (which combines the onMouseDown and onMouseUp event handlers).

(continued)

Table 13-4 *(continued)*

Event Handler	Supporting Form Elements	Event (Event Handler Triggered When . . .)
onDblClick	Button, Checkbox, FileUpload, Password, Radio, Reset, Select, Submit, Text, Textarea	The element is clicked twice in quick succession (double-clicked).
onFocus	Button, Checkbox, FileUpload, Password, Radio, Reset, Select, Submit, Text, Textarea	The element gains input focus.
onKeyDown	Button, Checkbox, FileUpload, Password, Radio, Reset, Select, Submit, Text, Textarea	The user presses a key.
onKeyPress	Button, Checkbox, FileUpload, Password, Radio, Reset, Select, Submit, Text, Textarea	The user presses and releases a key (which combines the onKeyDown and onKeyUp event handlers).
onKeyUp	Button, Checkbox, FileUpload, Password, Radio, Reset, Select, Submit, Text, Textarea	The user releases a previously pressed key.
onMouseDown	Button, Checkbox, FileUpload, Password, Radio, Reset, Select, Submit, Text, Textarea	The user presses a mouse button (but doesn't release it).
onMouseUp	Button, Checkbox, FileUpload, Link, Password, Radio, Reset, Select, Submit, Text, Textarea	The user releases a previously clicked mouse button.
onReset	form	The form is reset; either the user clicks a Reset button, or the programmer invokes the form.reset() method.
onSubmit	form	The form is submitted; either the user clicks a Submit button, or the programmer invokes the form.submit() method.

Using window events for good, not evil

Some folks think pop-up ads are inherently evil, and some think they're a legitimate use of Web technology. Wherever you fall in the debate, be aware that pop-up-killer software exists, which some surfers download and install to avoid seeing pop-up ads. Know, too, that many surfers refuse to revisit sites which bombard them with pop-up ads.

Keyboard events

Keyboard-related events occur when a user presses a key while a Web page is loaded. In addition to capturing the overall keyPress event, you can separately capture (and respond to) the user's pressing the key and then releasing the key.

The following sample code ties a custom JavaScript function named disallowInput() to the onKeyPress event handler associated with the document object:

```
<BODY onKeyPress="disallowInput();">
```

For details on the other objects that support keyboard events, check out Table 13-5.

Table 13-5	Keyboard-Related Event Handlers	
Event Handler	*Supporting Objects*	*Event (Event Handler Triggered When . . .)*
onKeyDown	Button, Checkbox, document, FileUpload, Image, Link, Password, Radio, Reset, Select, Submit, Text, Textarea	The user presses a key.
onKeyPress	Button, Checkbox, document, FileUpload, Image, Link, Password, Radio, Reset, Select, Submit, Text, Textarea	The user presses and releases a key (which combines the onKeyDown and onKeyUp event handlers).
onKeyUp	Button, Checkbox, document, FileUpload, Image, Link, Password, Radio, Reset, Select, Submit, Text, Textarea	The user releases a previously pressed key.

Chapter 14

Handling Runtime Errors

. . . .

In This Chapter

▶ Getting familiar with runtime errors and exceptions

▶ Taking a peek at the try, catch, and throw statements

. . . .

*S*upport for exception handling — a technique for anticipating and recovering gracefully from errors that has long been supported in languages like C++ — was finally implemented for JavaScript in Internet Explorer 5.x and Navigator 6.x.

Exceptional Basics

Technically, an exception is any unexpected condition, good or bad, that occurs during the processing of a script. Practically speaking, however, an exception is virtually always an error. Exceptions can result from

🗸 A JavaScript error

🗸 An unanticipated user-input error

🗸 A problem with a user's browser, operating system, or hardware configuration

Trying to make your code access objects (such as array elements, properties, files, and so on) that don't exist is a common source of exceptions that might occur while your JavaScript code is executing in someone's browser.

If you're creating a commercial JavaScript application, you want to make liberal use of JavaScript's exception-handling abilities. Allowing your users to view cryptic, system-generated errors such as `File Not Found` or `No Such Object` is unacceptable in a commercial environment. Although anticipating and handling those errors by using `try` and `catch` blocks might not prevent the errors from occurring, it does give you the opportunity to

- ✔ **Reassure users.** You can use JavaScript's exception-handling functions to display a message telling users that an error has occurred but is being handled appropriately. (This approach is much better than allowing a cryptic system message or blank screen to confuse and alarm users.)

- ✔ **Provide users with helpful, appropriate suggestions.** You can explain the cause of the error and provide users with tips for avoiding that error in the future.

Handling Exceptions

You handle exceptions by creating two special JavaScript functions, or blocks: a `try` block and a `catch` block. Then, in any statement that might generate an error, you use the keyword `throw` to throw an error to the `catch` block. The code in Listing 14-1 shows you how.

Look for the code in Listing 14-1 in the file `list1401.htm` on the companion CD.

Listing 14-1: **Handling Exceptions with** `try-catch` **and** `throw`

```
. . .
<SCRIPT LANGUAGE="JavaScript" TYPE="text/javascript">

function getMonthName (monthNumber) {

    // JavaScript arrays begin with 0, not 1, so
    // subtract 1.
    monthNumber = monthNumber - 1

    // Create an array and fill it with 12 values
    var months = new Array("Jan","Feb","Mar","Apr","May","Jun","Jul",
                            "Aug","Sep","Oct","Nov","Dec")

    // If the monthNumber passed in is somewhere
    // between 0 and 11, fine; return the corresponding
    // month name.

    if (months[monthNumber] != null) {
        return months[monthNumber]
    }

    // Otherwise, an exception occurred, so throw
    // an exception.
```

```
    else {
        // This statement throws an error
        // directly to the catch block.
        throw "InvalidMonthNumber"
    }
}


/////////////////////////////////////////////////////////
// The try block wraps around the main JavaScript
// processing code. Any JavaScript statement inside
// the try block that generates an exception will
// automatically throw that exception to the
// exception handling code in the catch block.
/////////////////////////////////////////////////////////

// The try block
try {

    // Call the getMonthName() function with an
    // invalid month # (there is no 13th month!)
    // and see what happens.

    alert(getMonthName(13))

    alert("We never get here if an exception is thrown.")

}

// The catch block
catch (error) {

    alert("An " + error + " exception was encountered.  Please contact the
             program vendor.")

    // In a real-life situation, you might want
    // to include error-handling code here that
    // examines the exception and gives users specific
    // information (or even tries to fix the problem,
    // if possible.)
}
```

Take a look at Figure 14-1 to see the error that running the code in Listing 14-1 generates in Internet Explorer.

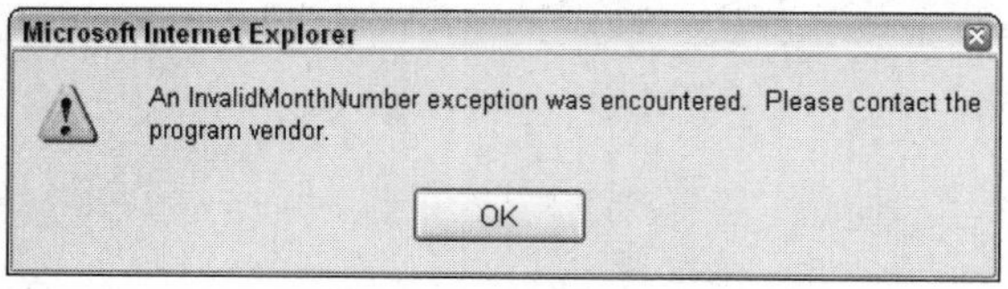

Figure 14-1:
Houston,
we have
an error.

Microsoft Internet Explorer

An InvalidMonthNumber exception was encountered. Please contact the
program vendor.

OK

The first code executed in Listing 14-1 is the code that you see defined in the try block:

```
alert(getMonthName(13))
```

Because only 12 months are defined in the months array, passing a value of 13 to getMonthName() causes an exception ("InvalidMonthNumber") to be thrown, as shown here:

```
function getMonthName(monthNumber) {
    . . .
    throw "InvalidMonthNumber"
```

All thrown exceptions are processed automatically by whatever code exists in the catch block, so the message that you see in Figure 14-1 (and defined in the catch block code shown in Listing 14-1) appears automatically when the exception is thrown.

If you want to write truly airtight JavaScript code, you need to identify all the events that could possibly cause an exception in your particular script (such as actions the user could take, error conditions the operating system could generate, and so on), and implement a try-catch block for each.

Depending on your application, you might want to include more processing code in the catch block than the simple pop-up message shown in Figure 14-1. For example, you might want to include JavaScript statements that examine the caught exception, determine what kind of exception it is, and process it appropriately.

You aren't limited to a string literal when it comes to identifying a thrown exception. Instead of InvalidMonthNumber, you can create and throw an elaborate custom exception object (by using the function and new operators that I describe in Chapter 3).

For more information on how Netscape implements exception handling (including examples), visit

```
http://developer.netscape.com/docs/manuals/js/core/jsguide/stmtsov.htm#1011537
```

To see how Microsoft does the same for Internet Explorer, check out this page:

```
http://msdn.microsoft.com/library/default.asp?url=/library/en-
            us/jscript7/html/jsstmtrycatch.asp
```

Part V
The Part of Tens

The 5th Wave   **By Rich Tennant**

"I don't know how it happened, but there's an applet in the toaster and some guy in Norway keeps burning my toast."

In this part . . .

*P*art V begins with a list of some great JavaScript-related Web sites that are full of useful information about all aspects of JavaScript. If you feel the need to communicate with real people about your JavaScript scripts, Chapter 15 even provides you with a list of some user groups that enable you to do just that.

These online resources are followed by a chapter explaining the most common mistakes that people run into when implementing Web pages (along with tips on how to avoid them). And finally, no programming book worth its salt would be complete without at least a few handy debugging techniques. Chapter 17 provides you with lots of bug-related tips that make debugging at least entirely bearable, if not downright pleasant!

Chapter 15

Top Ten (Or So) Online JavaScript Resources

In This Chapter

▶ Finding and using JavaScript tutorials

▶ Finding cool JavaScript examples online

▶ Taking advantage of the essential JavaScript-related newsgroups

*G*etting help on how to do something has never been easier than it is right now. Why? The Internet, of course! From its roots in government and university installations, the Internet remained a close-knit, mostly academic community until as recently as a decade ago. Inevitably, commercialism reared its ugly head and has had a tremendous effect — and not all bad, either — on all things Net. (For example, the commercialism of the Internet is directly responsible for the proliferation of Web tools and languages such as JavaScript.)

Although marketing and advertising have become common on the Internet, the spirit of sharing and intellectual collaboration hasn't yet been snuffed out. Helping other people (and maybe showing off a little in the process) is a fundamental joy. And because access to the Internet is relatively cheap and easy, everybody and their dog indulges — as you see when you visit the URLs and newsgroups that I list in this chapter.

Ten Web Sites to Check Out

With no further ado, then, on to the good stuff: a list of irresistible JavaScript-related Web resources. You find tips, tricks, tutorials, examples, and up-to-the-minute documentation. The site's URL follows a description of the goodies offered.

Netscape

The Netscape DevEdge site contains a wealth of information on getting started with JavaScript, including a complete language reference, how-to articles, and sample code. It also offers a downloadable JavaScript debugger.

```
http://devedge.netscape.com
```

Microsoft

Microsoft maintains an information-packed site devoted to its JavaScript-compatible language, JScript. Documentation, tutorials, sample code, and access to JScript-related newsgroups are just some of the great resources that you find here.

```
http://msdn.microsoft.com/scripting/jscript/default.htm
```

Builder.com

The JavaScript section at CNET Builder.com features tips and tutorials in addition to copy-and-paste JavaScript code.

```
http://builder.com.com/1200-31-5084860.html
```

Webmonkey

Webmonkey maintains a killer JavaScript code library containing not just a wealth of scripts but a handy browser reference chart, cheat sheets on HTML and CSS, and more — all free for the taking.

```
http://hotwired.lycos.com/webmonkey/reference/javascript_code_library
```

Project Cool's JavaScript QuickStarts

Project Cool's JavaScript QuickStarts offer hands-on JavaScript (and DHTML) tutorials. From basic to advanced, all are organized into neat, bite-sized chunks perfect for beginning JavaScript programmers.

```
www.devx.com/projectcool
```

Stop, thief!

Most of the sites that I describe in this chapter are commercial sites, and without exception, the JavaScript source code they offer is clearly marked "for free download." (You might have to register your e-mail address before you can download, though, so these companies can stick you on their electronic mailing lists.)

But if you're looking for scripts, you're not limited to commercial sites. You can cut and paste embedded JavaScript source code from *any* site, with or without that Webmaster's permission, simply by clicking View⇨Source (from Internet Explorer) or View⇨Page Source (Navigator). (This is one reason why password protection and other highly sensitive features aren't typically implemented in JavaScript!)

One caveat: If you run across source that includes a copyright notice, contact the author or Webmaster and ask for permission before using it. If in doubt, don't copy a file line for line; instead, take a look at how the programmer solved the problem and base your solution on the overall approach.

EarthWeb.com

The EarthWeb.com JavaScript site offers a huge repository of cut-and-paste scripts — scripts for everything from navigation to multimedia.

```
http://webdeveloper.earthweb.com/webjs
```

About.com

The Focus on JavaScript Web page at About.com contains articles, tutorials, and downloadable scripts on every conceivable JavaScript-related topic — including my personal favorite, troubleshooting.

```
http://javascript.about.com/compute/javascript
```

1RT.org

Internet Related Technologies' JavaScript section offers an exhaustive knowledge base of frequently asked (and answered) script-related questions.

```
http://developer.irt.org/script/script.htm
```

WebReference.com

WebReference.com's homegrown JavaScript resource list contains links to online JavaScript magazines, script archives, and much more.

```
www.webreference.com/programming/javascript/index.html
```

ScriptSearch.com

ScriptSearch.com maintains a giant database of JavaScript scripts, from ad banners to visual effects.

```
http://scriptsearch.internet.com/JavaScript/
```

Not-to-Be-Missed Newsgroups

The Web sites listed in the preceding sections are a great source of information. Sometimes, though, you just have to send a message to a real live person and ask a point-blank question. Newsgroups can be a great timesaver, especially when it comes to researching specific how-to's and known bugs.

To access newsgroups, you need to have a news server defined. Generally, you set up both a Web server and a news server as part of the browser installation and configuration process, but you can always add news support later.

To participate in a user group, by viewing other peoples' messages or by posting your own, you need to switch from surfing the Web to perusing the news. To do this, choose Window⇨Mail & Newsgroups from the Navigator menu or Tools⇨Mail and News⇨Read News if you're an Internet Explorer fan.

 For detailed instructions on configuring your browser software to access newsgroups, check with your browser provider (in other words, contact technical support at Microsoft or Netscape) or check out a good book on the topic, such as The Internet For Dummies, 9th Edition, by John R. Levine, Carol Baroudi, and Margaret Levine Young (Wiley Publishing, Inc.).

 Collectively, newsgroups are known as Usenet. For more information about newsgroups — including where to find news, how to write effective posts, and even how to create your own — visit

```
http://groups.google.com
```

Although user groups come and go, the following have established themselves as the best places to be for JavaScript-related development:

- If you follow only one user group, make it the following one. This group is very well attended and is currently the premier JavaScript information group for newbies and advanced scripters alike:

  `comp.lang.javascript`

  (The `it.comp.lang.javascript` and `de.comp.lang.javascript` newsgroups are high-traffic Italian- and German-language versions.)

- Get answers to HTML questions answered here:

  `comp.infosystems.www.authoring.html`

- Microsoft's public scripting newsgroup focuses on JScript tips and questions:

  `microsoft.public.scripting.jscript`

Chapter 16

Ten (Or So) Most Common JavaScript Mistakes (And How to Avoid Them)

In This Chapter

▶ Catching typographical errors

▶ Fixing unmatched pairs

▶ Putting scripting statements between HTML tags

▶ Nesting quotes incorrectly

▶ Treating numbers as strings

▶ Treating strings as numbers

▶ Finding logic errors

*E*very JavaScript author makes mistakes. (Actually, I like to think of it in the reverse — it's the JavaScript interpreter that makes the mistakes by not figuring out what the programmer means by something. Yeah! That's it!) Most of the time, the errors you make fall into one of the categories listed in this chapter. The good news is that the errors are all easy to correct. The better news is that the JavaScript interpreter tells you quickly — and in no uncertain terms — when it encounters an error.

Check out this book's companion CD to see the sample listings scattered throughout this chapter. I've named the files after the listings so you can find them easily. For example, you can find Listing 16-1 in the file `list1601.htm`.

HTML woes

Because JavaScript statements are embedded in HTML files, some of the mistakes you might find are actually HTML mistakes. For example, the following is an HTML error (`TYE="button"` should be `TYPE="button"`):

```
<INPUT TYE="button" NAME="testButton" VALUE="test"
onClick='test()'>
```

In this case, the JavaScript interpreter doesn't display an error message because the error doesn't concern it. What *does* happen is that your `button` element fails to display properly.

If your page doesn't behave as expected and JavaScript doesn't alert you, you're probably dealing with an HTML error. If this happens (and you can't find the solution in this chapter), check out a good HTML reference such as *HTML For Dummies,* 4th Edition, by Ed Tittel and Natanya Pitts (Wiley Publishing, Inc.).

Typing-in-a-Hurry Errors

Spelling and capitalization errors easily take first prize for being the most common mistakes that all JavaScripters make, from the greenest beginner to the most highly seasoned veteran.

The JavaScript interpreter is a stickler for correct spelling: You simply can't access an object, property, method, variable, or function unless you spell its name properly. For example, the second line of the following bit of code generates an error:

```
var identification = "ABC";
alert("The id number is " + identificatoin);
```

The JavaScript interpreter is also case-sensitive, which means you can't substitute uppercase letters for lowercase letters in object, property, method, variable, and function names. The following example generates an error because the correct name of the method is `toLowerCase()` (not `TOLOWERCASE()`):

```
alert("Broadcast network ID = "
    + identification.TOLOWERCASE());
```

To detect and correct these errors:

- ✔ Be aware, as you write your JavaScript code, that consistency in spelling and capitalization is essential to bug-free statements.

- ✔ Take advantage of any spell-checking utilities or point-and-click method name insertion utilities that your text editor provides.

Breaking Up a Happy Pair

JavaScript scripts are typically rife with pairs: pairs of opening and closing tags (courtesy of HTML), pairs of parentheses and curly braces, pairs of single quotes and double quotes. The JavaScript interpreter treats the stuff between the pairs as one entity, so if half of the pair is missing, the interpreter gets confused — mighty confused, in some cases!

The following are specific examples of happy couples that you don't want to break up in JavaScript.

Lonely angle brackets

Looking at the following code, you'd think that the display would include two text elements: one to hold a first name and one to hold a last name. It doesn't, though, because a closing angle bracket is missing.

```
<FORM NAME="myForm">
  . . .
First name: <INPUT TYPE="text" NAME="firstName" LENGTH=15
Last name: <INPUT TYPE="text" NAME="lastName" LENGTH=30>
  . . .
```

If a text element doesn't appear — no error message, no nothing, just blank space where the element should have appeared — the likely suspect is a missing angle bracket on the line directly before the invisible text element.

Lonely tags

The code that you see in Listing 16-1 depicts a tiny little script, perhaps a first attempt at a JavaScript-enabled Web page. At first blush, perhaps you don't see anything amiss. If you were to load this script, though, you'd see that something is definitely amiss!

Listing 16-1:   HTML Source Containing a Missing Tag

```
  . . .
<HEAD>
<SCRIPT LANGUAGE="JavaScript">
function test() {
    var aString = "some text"
```

(continued)

Listing 16-1 *(continued)*

```
    alert("aString is " + aString)
}
//The closing </SCRIPT> tag that should be here is missing.
</HEAD>
<BODY>
<FORM NAME="myForm">
<INPUT TYPE="button" NAME="testButton" VALUE="test"
onClick='test()'>
<P>
First name: <INPUT TYPE="text" NAME="firstName" LENGTH=15>
Last name: <INPUT TYPE="text" NAME="lastName" LENGTH=30>
</FORM>
</BODY>
</HTML>
```

The absence of the closing </SCRIPT> tag in the preceding code snippet causes the page to display nothing — zip, nada, zilch — instead of the button and text elements that you expect.

Whenever elements refuse to appear, check your HTML statements to see whether an opening half of a two-part tag, such as <TITLE>, <SCRIPT>, or <BODY>, is missing its closing half (</TITLE>, </SCRIPT>, and </BODY>, respectively).

Lonely parentheses

When you look closely at the body of the following test() function, you can easily spot the missing parenthesis on line three:

```
function test() {
    var aString = "some text"
    alert("aString is " + aString
}
```

As your JavaScript skills increase, though, you might find yourself putting together whopping long statements. Furthermore, each of the whopping long statements might contain many pairs of parentheses, often nested a few layers deep — and that's when you're most likely to make this kind of mistake.

Unless the editor that you use to create your script provides an automatic parentheses-pair-checking utility, you need to eyeball your code to catch and correct this mistake.

Lonely quotes

Take a good look at the following example:

```
<INPUT TYPE="button" NAME="testButton" VALUE="test"
onClick='test("hello)'>
```

The mistake here is that no closing double quote appears after the word `hello`. The preceding code doesn't generate an error; it just disables the `testButton` object's `onClick` event handler.

Here's how the corrected statement looks:

```
<INPUT TYPE="button" NAME="testButton" VALUE="test"
onClick='test("hello")'>
```

Putting Scripting Statements in the Wrong Places

When you're new to JavaScript, remembering the order of things might be a little difficult. For example, JavaScript statements are valid only when they're placed between the `<SCRIPT>` and `</SCRIPT>` tags or as values assigned to event handlers. If you forget and place them somewhere else, you're bound to get an unexpected result.

The good news is that you find out as soon as you load your page and take a look at it that something is amiss — because your source code appears right there on the page! Check out the source shown in Listing 16-2 to see what I mean.

Listing 16-2:   HTML Source Containing Misplaced Scripting Statements

```
<SCRIPT LANGUAGE="JavaScript" TYPE="text/javascript">
function test(inputValue) {
    alert("Wow, I sure do love JavaScript!" +
     "\nHere's what the public is saying about JavaScript: " +
        inputValue)
}
</SCRIPT>
// The addNumbers() function is incorrectly defined
// below the closing </SCRIPT> tag.
```

(continued)

Listing 16-2 *(continued)*

```
function addNumbers(numberOne, numberTwo) {
    return numberOne + numberTwo
}
</HEAD>
   . . .
```

When you execute the code in Listing 16-2, you don't see a JavaScript error, but you do see the text of the `addNumbers()` function displayed on-screen. (You don't see a JavaScript error because the JavaScript interpreter can't access any statement outside the beginning and ending `<SCRIPT>` tags — unless that statement is a value for an event handler.)

Moving the `</SCRIPT>` tag just after the closing brace of the `addNumbers()` function fixes this script, causing the JavaScript interpreter to interpret the `addNumbers()` function as JavaScript code.

Anytime that you see your well-crafted JavaScript statements displayed in living color on your page, you can be pretty sure that the problem is that your statements are outside the bounds of the `<SCRIPT>` and `</SCRIPT>` tags. Move the statements back to where they belong and they should behave.

Nesting Quotes Incorrectly

Nesting single and double quotes together, like the following lines, is perfectly legitimate:

```
onClick="alert('This is an example of nested quotes.')"
```

```
onClick='alert("This is another example of nested quotes.")'
```

Just make sure that you don't nest double quotes inside double quotes, or single quotes inside single quotes, like this:

```
onClick="alert("Oops! Incorrectly nested quotes generate a syntax error!')'
```

If you must include a mismatched quote, you can — as long as you escape the mismatched quote. Escaping a quote tells the JavaScript interpreter not to expect a matching quote. You escape a quote by preceding that quote with a backslash, like this:

```
onClick="alert('This escaped quote doesn\'t cause a problem.')"
```

Treating Numbers as Strings

Humans tend not to make a big fuss over the difference between text and numbers — at least, not in most contexts. For example, when you write a sentence in English, you don't need to do anything different to include a number. (Even if you write 333 of them!)

Numbers and text strings are two very different things to most programming languages, though, and that includes JavaScript. In JavaScript, trying to treat a number as a string, as shown in Listing 16-3, generates an error every time.

Listing 16-3:   JavaScript Source Containing Statement That Treats a Number Like a String

```
. . .
<SCRIPT LANGUAGE="JavaScript">
function testIt(inputValue) {
// The bold() method you see in the next line is associated
// with the String object (not the Number object).

    document.write(inputValue.bold())
    document.close()
}
</SCRIPT>
    . . .
<FORM NAME="myForm">
// The following onClick event handler
// sends the number 2 to the testIt() function.

<INPUT TYPE="button" NAME="testButton" VALUE="test"
onClick='testIt(2)'>
```

The problem occurs when the number 2 is passed from the definition of the onClick event handler to the testIt() function, which isn't set up to handle numbers. If you look at the testIt() function, you can see that it's taking whatever the input value is (in this case, the number 2) and trying to call the String object's bold() method on it. And that ain't flying. The only thing that you can call a string function on is a string, and 2 isn't a string! (If you'd like more information on what a string is, take a look at Chapter 3.)

Sometimes you are going to want to send a number to a function and have that function deal with it as a string. In these cases, all you need to do is add lines like the following to your function:

```
function testIt(inputValue) {
    // Set up a temporary string variable.
    var aString = ""
```

```
// Place the input value into the temporary
// string variable.
aString += inputValue

// Call the bold() method on the string version of
// the inputValue.
document.write(aString.bold())

}
```

Now you can send whatever value you like to the testIt() function, and testIt()behaves nicely!

Treating Strings as Numbers

The preceding section shows what happens when you treat numbers as strings. As you might guess, the reverse — treating strings as numbers — also causes grief in JavaScript. Let me explain by way of the code snippet shown in Listing 16-4.

Listing 16-4: **JavaScript Source Containing Statement That Treats a String Like a Number**

```
function calculateTax(inputNumber) {
    return inputNumber * .50
}
    . . .
<INPUT TYPE="button" NAME="calculateTaxButton"
    VALUE="Calculate"
onClick='alert("The tax is " + calculateTax("baked"))'>
    . . .
```

When you click the Calculate button, the baked string goes to the calculate Tax() function, where it's immediately multiplied by .50. Now, if you can tell me what the result of baked times .50 is, you're a better mathematician than I'll ever be. (Okay, so maybe it's half-baked!) JavaScript doesn't know, either, so it displays a built-in value NaN, which is JavaScript's way of saying "I don't know what the heck this is, but I do know it's Not a Number!"

Once again, in JavaScript as in life, you can do pretty much anything you like — if you know how to go about doing it. If you want to create a function that expects a number but can deal gracefully with a string, all you need to do is add a few lines to the very top of your function. Listing 16-5 shows you how.

Listing 16-5:   JavaScript Source for a Function That Expects a Number but Deals with a String

```
function calculateTax(inputNumber) {
  // myNumber will be false if inputNumber is a string.
  var myNumber = parseFloat(inputNumber)

  // If the inputNumber was, in fact, a number,
  // perform the necessary calculation.
  if (myNumber) {
    return myNumber * .50
  }
  // Otherwise, display an error.
  else {
      alert("A non-numeric value was passed to a function that expected a
            number")
      return "unknown"
  }
}
  . . .
<INPUT TYPE="button" NAME="calculateTaxButton"
VALUE="Calculate"
onClick='alert("The tax is " + calculateTax("baked"))'>
  . . .
```

In this new, improved, better-tasting version, the first thing the `calculate Tax()` function does is see whether it can convert whatever value it receives into a number. If it can, it converts the value, if necessary, and then goes on to perform its calculations on the converted value. For example, you can pass a number or a string such as `"1234.56"` to `calculateTax()` instead of the string `baked`. If the `calculateTax()` function can't make a conversion (what number does `"baked"` convert to?), it recognizes that it can't convert this value, doesn't bother to perform any calculations, and alerts the user instead.

Missing the Point: Logic Errors

Logic errors are the most difficult errors to track down because they don't generate one specific type of error message. (You never see the JavaScript interpreter spit out a `Clearly, that is not how you calculate the interest on a 20-year loan` message, for example.)

How could the JavaScript interpreter possibly know what you're logically trying to do? Unlike a human, it can't read your code, analyze it, and confer with other interpreters to figure out whether your code comes close to accomplishing some reasonable task. JavaScript just skims your code for syntax errors. If you want to give your users the option to submit a form but then not actually submit the form when they indicate Yes — that's up to you. JavaScript is not your mother!

The only way to track down logic errors is the old-fashioned way: by studying your code, displaying the contents of variables, making changes, and retesting.

The `alert()` method, as you see in the following example, is very handy for displaying the contents of variables throughout your code. Often, when you see the contents of variables, you discover a logic error immediately. (For example, a value you expect to be 1,000 displays as –3 — and so you know that the calculations responsible for that value contain an error.)

```
alert("Made it to the first if-else statement inside the calculateOrder() func-
        tion and the value of someValue is " + someValue);
```

Neglecting Browser Incompatibility

Few things are more frustrating than spending hours creating a fantastic, impressive script, posting it to your Web server, and then having someone who visits your Web site e-mail you with the bad news: It doesn't work in my Web browser!

JavaScript support varies not just between Internet Explorer and Navigator, but among versions of these browsers, as well. If a script behaves as expected in one browser but tanks in another, you've run into the dreaded browser incompatibility problem. Here are four suggestions for overcoming this bane of every Web developer's existence:

✔ **Forego the latest and greatest JavaScript features; stick to core features.**

Don't rush to incorporate the latest JavaScript features in each browser version; instead; try to rely on tried-and-true, lowest-common-denominator features whenever possible.

✔ **Always check the documentation.**

When sticking to core JavaScript features isn't possible (or desirable), go ahead and use proprietary features — just make sure to inspect your target browser's technical documentation to determine how the features you want to use are implemented.

• Netscape's client-side JavaScript language reference:

    http://devedge.netscape.com/central/javascript

• Microsoft's JavaScript-compatible JScript language reference:

    http://msdn.microsoft.com/scripting/jscript/default.htm

✔ **Include browser-detection code.**

Chapter 3 shows you how to create a script that detects a visitor's browser on-the-fly and behaves differently based on different browser capabilities.

✔ **Always test your scripts in multiple browsers before publishing them.**

Documentation can be wrong, and browser-detection code can malfunction. So before you actually post your JavaScript-enabled pages to your Web server (thereby exposing them for all the world to see), always test them yourself in as many browsers as possible.

Although the America Online browser has a fairly large market share, it's often overlooked by JavaScript developers. You can download your own free copy of this browser from `http://free.aol.com`.

Rather than downloading and installing multiple browsers, you can take advantage of an online service, such as NetMechanic, to help you spot cross-browser bugs at this site:

`www.netmechanic.com/cobrands/zdnet/browsercheck`

Chapter 17

Ten (Or So) Tips for Debugging Your Scripts

*I*n Chapter 16, you see some of the most common mistakes (or bugs) that JavaScript programmers tend to make. This chapter expands on that theme by showing you the quickest, most direct ways to pinpoint and correct any bugs that you happen to introduce into your code. Many language compilers and interpreters come complete with tools for debugging. Unfortunately, few debugging tools exist for JavaScript just yet. I introduce you to those tools later in this chapter — along with some great advice for debugging your JavaScript code as quickly and easily as possible.

Debugging is sort of like washing dishes. Neither chore is exactly a ton of fun, but both are necessary, and you always feel better when they're finished. Debugging doesn't have to be a dreaded chore, though. You might find that, with a little help (like the tips presented in this chapter) and a little practice, the job gets easier and easier.

JavaScript Reads Your Code, Not Your Mind!

Strangely enough, the first step in successful bug extermination involves determining whether you've actually encountered one. If your JavaScript script doesn't behave the way that you expect it to, you could be dealing with a bug. However, your script might be working as designed, and the problem is in your understanding of how the script is supposed to work.

In the old days, programmers created flowcharts — pages and pages of little symbols and lines that described how they wanted their programs to behave at runtime. Flowcharts have fallen out of favor — not because they were a bad idea but because they were nearly as time-intensive to create as the programs themselves.

These days, most programmers find it helpful to write pseudocode as part of the design process. Then, during testing, these programmers have something to refer to — a touchstone, as it were, to help them clarify whether a potential bug lies in their JavaScript code or in their programming logic.

Pseudocode is a shorthand combination of JavaScript and the programmer's natural language. Because this tool is designed to be as easy and natural for programmers as possible, no hard-and-fast rules define precisely how to write pseudocode.

Say, for example, that your goal is to calculate the total price (including sales tax, if any) for international orders placed through your Web site. Here's an example of what your pseudocode might look like:

1. **The user presses the Submit button.**

2. **If it's a U.S. order, calculate the tax (look up the tax rate based on** `myForm.state`**) and store the calculated tax in** `totalTax`

   `else` {What to do if non-U.S. orders?!}

3. **Multiply the number of widgets (**`myForm.numWidgets`**) ordered by the price (**`myForm.price`**). . . .**

As useful as writing pseudocode is to helping you clarify the requirements of a Web page, it's absolutely indispensable when it comes to tracking down bugs in your logic after you finish implementing your Web page.

Don't keep your comments to yourself

Getting into the habit of commenting on your JavaScript code as you write it can be a great help when it comes time to debug that code. (You might be surprised at how much you can forget between the time you create a script and the time when your code misbehaves, which can be weeks or even months down the line!)

If you create pseudocode to help you plan and design your scripts, try using that pseudocode as the basis for your JavaScript comments. Doing so helps the future you (or someone else who has to debug your script) understand precisely what the code is trying to accomplish.

Isolating the Bug

If you encounter a genuine bug, you need to try to home in on it and identify precisely which lines of code are affected. Here are some examples to help you work backward from the clues:

- **Does the problem occur the instant the page loads?** If so, the problem is probably either HTML-related or in the JavaScript code you set up to handle the onLoad event.

- **Does the problem occur when users type text in an input field?** Check the onChange and onBlur event handlers associated with that field.

- **When users click a button, do things go haywire?** Check that button's onClick event handling code.

- **Does something go wrong when users close the window?** The culprit is probably lurking in your onUnload event-handling statements.

First, decide on a place to begin your search — say, with the function that's called from one of your onClick event handlers. (I call it buggyFunction().) The next step is to dig a little deeper. For example, try adding a test button to your JavaScript code that exercises that same function as the following one does:

```
<INPUT TYPE="button" NAME="testButton" VALUE="Test"
onClick='buggyFunction(123, "abc")'>
```

In the first line, you're sending the buggy function numeric and string literals. This process helps you determine whether the function itself is buggy or whether the problem lies with the variables that your original code is passing to the function.

If the function behaves incorrectly after you pass it numeric and string literals, you know that the bug is in your function. If it behaves correctly, you need to check the parameters that the original onClick is sending to the function. (See the "Displaying Variable Values" section later in this chapter.)

One way to isolate a bug is to comment out all the code in a function except one or two suspect statements. By using this approach, you can focus on the statements that you want to examine in more detail. To comment out a section of code, you place JavaScript comments before each line, like so:

```
// someVariable = someResult;
```

Make a copy of your original HTML or script file before you make any changes. Few things are more frustrating than modifying a file beyond recognition, only to have it perform even worse than when you started — and then forgetting how the code originally looked! You might also want to look into a version control tool such as CVS (www.cvshome.org). Version control tools allow you to track different versions of files separately so that if you accidentally goof up one version, you can always go back to an earlier, working version.

Consulting the Documentation

The JavaScript Guide and JavaScript Reference are the most up-to-date resources available regarding the JavaScript language as Netscape implements it. Bookmarking or downloading these documents in your browser helps ensure that they're at your fingertips when you need them!

```
http://devedge.netscape.com/central/javascript
```

Internet Explorer implements JavaScript through the Microsoft scripting language JScript. Check out the following URL for a complete description of all things JScript-related:

```
http://msdn.microsoft.com/scripting/jscript/default.htm
```

Displaying Variable Values

A useful debugging technique involves displaying the values of variables at various stages in their lives. For example, suppose that you have a function whose job is to calculate the total cost of an order. Based on your understanding of the way the total should be calculated, you determine that this function always returns an incorrect value; you just don't know why.

Seeing what JavaScript thinks is going on at every stage in the process (from the beginning of the function right down to the statement that calculates the return value) is easy to do with the debugging statements that you see in Listing 17-1.

Listing 17-1:   Tracking Down a Bug with Alert Display Statements

```
. . .

var price=3.50

function calculatePrice(numberWidgets) {
// Examine the variable at the beginning of the function.
    alert("Inside calculatePrice, numberWidgets is " + numberWidgets)

    var totalPrice = 0

    // No tax calculated on orders of 100 or less
    if (numberWidgets >= 10) {
        // Test to see that the if statement
        // is coded correctly.
        alert("Apparently numberWidgets is 11 or higher")
        var tax = calculateTax(numberWidgets * price)
        totalPrice = tax + (numberWidgets * price)
    }

    else {
        alert("numberWidgets is 10 or less so no tax calculated")
        totalPrice = numberWidgets * price
    }

// Displaying all the values that contribute to a calculation
// helps you spot errors.
    alert("totalPrice is $" + totalPrice
                        +  " based on a per-item price of $"
                        + price)
    return totalPrice

}
```

The code in Listing 17-1 contains four alert() calls. Each alert() displays the values of variables at different points in the calculatePrice() logic, as shown in the following series of figures:

✔ Alert number one shows you what the value of the numberWidgets variable is at the beginning of the calculatePrice() function, as shown in Figure 17-1.

✔ Alert number two, shown in Figure 17-2, helps you determine whether your if statement is coded correctly.

✔ Alert number three lets you examine several values at a single point in the code, as shown in Figure 17-3.

Figure 17-1:
Getting
the initial
value in
calculate-
Price().

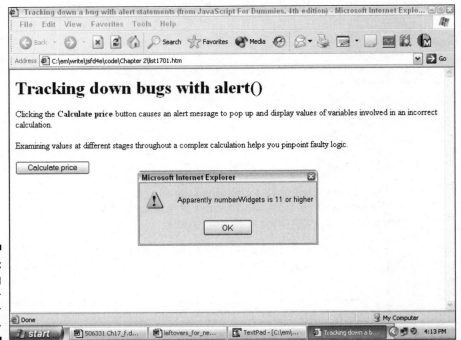

Figure 17-2:
Checking
the if state-
ment's per-
formance.

Figure 17-3:
Examining
several
values in a
block of
code.

The more knotty and complex your logic is, the more this technique can help you pinpoint your bug. But whatever answers you find, keep one thing in mind: After you track down the bugs in your script, make sure that you remember to remove the alert statements. Forgetting to do so can be embarrassing!

I once worked with a programmer who thought he'd removed all his debug statements, but he missed one. The condition causing the debug statement to appear occurred so infrequently that he forgot all about it! Until, that is, dozens of folks — including the programmer's boss, his boss's boss, and the company's most important clients — were evaluating the application in a meeting. You guessed it: Up popped the debug statement! This most unfortunate and embarrassing situation can be avoided if you search for all the occurrences of the `alert()` method in your script by using the search/replace function available in your text editor.

Breaking Large Blocks of Statements into Smaller Functions

Limiting the size of the functions that you create to about a screenful of text is good design practice. (You don't have to take my word for it, though. A time or two debugging a complex, monster-huge function should convince you.)

Limiting function size gives you these breathing-easier advantages:

✔ **Increases your ability to reuse code.** The smaller and more discrete a function is, the more likely you are to be able to reuse that function in another context. For example, say you write a large function called `isAPhoneNumber()` to determine whether an input value is a valid phone number. Removing the statements that deal with numeric validation and organizing those statements into a separate function, called `isANumber()`, gives you a generic function that you can call not just from `isAPhoneNumber()` but from any other function that requires numeric validation (such as `isAValidCreditCardNumber()`, `isAValidAge()`, and so on).

✔ **Decreases your frustration level.** Small functions are much easier to debug than large functions simply because small functions are easier for humans to step through mentally and comprehend than their outsized counterparts.

Functions too big to fit on the average monitor display tend to be poorly designed from a standpoint of reuse. That is, usually (and I say usually because this is just a general rule) when a function gets that big, it's that big because you're trying to make it perform more than one conceptual task. Ideally, a function is an implementation of just one conceptual task.

Honing the Process of Elimination

When you're chasing bugs, sometimes figuring out what isn't causing the problem is just as important as figuring out what is. For example, if you have a bug in your HTML code, no amount of searching and testing your JavaScript code is going to help you correct the problem.

Although I can't tell you exactly how to pinpoint your errors (if I could, I'd be rich!), I can tell you that good programmers have a general pattern they follow when they're debugging:

1. **Create several test cases.**

   A test case is a single, real-life scenario that describes how a user might reasonably interact with your pages. For an educational site, for example, your test cases might include

   • A student searching for a specific piece of information

   • A teacher posting lesson plans

   • A parent interested in school grading policies

2. **For each test case (make sure you have several), load your pages and interact with them.**

   Note the way your site behaves and compare what happened to what you expected would happen for that test case.

If you see a difference between what you expect and what actually happens, the first thing to do is to try to figure out whether the problem is related to your browser, JavaScript script, or HTML statements.

Debugging browser problems

A problem with your browser is unlikely to occur unless you've just downloaded and installed a new version or have been doing something in another application that might have altered the way that your browser works.

Symptoms:

Your browser doesn't come up, or it does come up, but you can't get it to load any local files (as opposed to it's being able to load every file except the file that you're testing).

Home-in strategy:

If you've just reinstalled your browser, try reinstalling it again. If you still have problems, browse the technical help or contact the technical support line.

Tracking HTML bugs

If you're new to JavaScript or HTML, you're likely to make a few HTML errors before you get the hang of it. Not to worry, though . . . HTML is one well-documented animal!

Symptoms:

Your Web page displays only part of what you think it should display (for example, buttons or other elements that you can see defined in your HTML source are missing). Or conversely, your Web page displays more than you expected. (For example, some of your JavaScript statements are splashed on the screen.)

Home-in strategy:

Note exactly what displays (or what doesn't). If only the first two elements that you defined appear, check the source code that defines the second element — and every statement after that line of source code. If the second element is contained within a tag set (for example, between the <BODY> and </BODY> tags), check to see that the closing tag is placed and spelled correctly.

If JavaScript statements appear that shouldn't, note the very first word in the statement that's showing. Then find that word in the HTML source file and check the preceding line. Make sure you've remembered to include both opening and closing <SCRIPT> and </SCRIPT> tags.

Checking the JavaScript code

As a JavaScript programmer, you're likely to make most of your mistakes in — well, in your JavaScript code.

Symptoms:

Any bug that shows its face before a form is submitted is almost certainly a JavaScript bug. Pre-form-submittal bugs can occur in response to a user event (clicking a button, for example, or typing text) or in the course of calculating some numbers.

Home-in strategy:

Here's where your skills at displaying variable values and breaking up functions really pay off. After you trace a bug to an event or calculation, try to isolate that event or calculation. Create a test button that exercises the functions involved.

Exercising a function means calling it with a variety of parameters to see what happens in each case. If a function is long, break it up and exercise each resulting function separately.

Taking Advantage of Others' Experience

When you hit a hard-shelled bug, you really come to appreciate the Usenet user groups (called newsgroups) that Chapter 15 lists. Not only can you browse the groups to see whether someone else has already encountered the problem you're struggling with, but you can also post a message that contains a section of code and a description of the error. Many newsgroup contributors pride themselves on their abilities to debug others' code, and technical support people (including some Netscape and Microsoft gurus) often monitor the newsgroups as part of their jobs.

Keep in mind that no matter how frustrated you are or how urgent your problem is, you should check through the newsgroups archives for a problem similar to your own before posting. Chances are good that some similar problem has been posted at least once (and maybe a dozen times), and your group mates will appreciate your adapting previous posts before making a new post.

Exercising the Time-Honored Trial-and-Error Approach

When all else fails, just do something — anything. Make a change to your code, note the change, and then load the page and see what happens. The JavaScript interpreter makes testing things quick and easy for you. If the code change doesn't work, put the code back the way it was and try again. Whatever you do, don't be afraid to try something. The worst thing you can do is crash your browser — and believe me, browser crashes aren't fatal. (If they were, I sure wouldn't be alive to write this book!)

If you tend, like me, to be on the conservative side, make a habit of copying your source code file to a safe place as soon as it begins to behave and at regular intervals thereafter. That way, if the unthinkable happens, and you accidentally mangle the file while you're editing it, you can always drop back to your most recent good copy.

The best advice that I can give you is to enjoy yourself. The more mistakes you make, the more you can figure things out on your own — and the easier creating your next JavaScript-enabled Web page will be.

Just Try and Catch Me Exception Handling!

Support for exception handling — a technique for anticipating and recovering gracefully from errors that has long been supported in languages like C++ — was finally implemented for JavaScript in the 5.x and 6.x versions of Internet Explorer and Navigator, respectively.

Technically, an exception is any unexpected condition, good or bad, that occurs during the processing of a script. In reality, however, an exception is virtually always an error. Exceptions can result directly from a JavaScript error, an unanticipated user input error, or from a problem with a user's browser, operating system, or even hardware configuration. Trying to make your code access objects (such as array elements, properties, files, and so on) that don't exist is a common source of exceptions that might occur while your JavaScript code is executing in someone's browser.

If you're creating a commercial JavaScript application, you want to make liberal use of JavaScript's exception-handling abilities. Allowing your users to view cryptic, system-generated errors such as `File Not Found` or `No Such Object` is unacceptable in a commercial environment. Although anticipating and handling those errors by using `try` and `catch` blocks might not prevent the errors from occurring, it does give you the opportunity to

✔ **Reassure users.** You can use JavaScript's exception-handling functions to display a message telling users that an error has occurred but is being handled appropriately. (This approach is much better than allowing a cryptic system message or blank screen to confuse and alarm users.)

✔ **Provide users with helpful, appropriate suggestions.** You can explain the cause of the error and provide users with tips for avoiding that error in the future.

You handle exceptions by creating two special JavaScript functions, or blocks: a `try` block and a `catch` block. (Because these two separate blocks are always used together, they're often referred to as the try-catch block.) Then, in any statement that might possibly generate an error, you use the keyword `throw` to throw an error. The code in Listing 17-2 shows you how.

Listing 17-2:   Handling Exceptions with try-catch and throw

```
. . .
<SCRIPT LANGUAGE="JavaScript" TYPE="text/javascript">

function getMonthName (monthNumber) {

    // JavaScript arrays begin with 0, not 1, so
    // subtract 1.
    monthNumber = monthNumber - 1;

    // Create an array and fill it with 12 values.
    var months = new Array("Jan","Feb","Mar","Apr","May","Jun","Jul",
                           "Aug","Sep","Oct","Nov","Dec")

    // If a month array element corresponds to the
    // number passed in, fine; return the array
    // element.

    if (months[monthNumber] != null) {
```

```
            return months[monthNumber]
    }

    // Otherwise, an exception occurred, so throw
    // an exception.

    else {
        // This statement throws an error
        // directly to the catch block.
        throw "InvalidMonthNumber"
    }
}

/////////////////////////////////////////////////////
// The try block wraps around the main JavaScript
// processing code. Any JavaScript statement inside
// the try block that generates an exception will
// automatically throw that exception to the
// exception handling code in the catch block.
/////////////////////////////////////////////////////

// The try block
try {

    // Call the getMonthName() function with an
    // invalid month # (there is no 13th month!)
    // and see what happens.

    alert(getMonthName(13))

    alert("We never get here if an exception is thrown.")

}

// The catch block
catch (error) {

    alert("An " + error + " exception was encountered.  Please contact the
            program vendor.")

    // In a real-life situation, you might want
    // to include error-handling code here that
    // examines the exception and gives users specific
    // information (or even tries to fix the problem,
    // if possible).
}
```

Take a look at Figure 17-4 to see the error that running the code in Listing 17-2 generates in Internet Explorer.

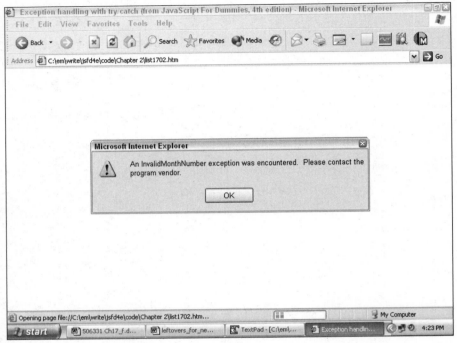

The first code executed in Listing 17-2 is the code that you see defined in the `try` block:

```
alert(getMonthName(13))
```

Because only 12 months are defined in the `months` array, passing a value of 13 to `getMonthName()` causes an exception ("InvalidMonthNumber") to be thrown, as shown here:

```
function getMonthName(monthNumber) {
    . . .
    throw "InvalidMonthNumber"
```

All thrown exceptions are processed automatically by whatever code exists in the `catch` block, so the message that you see in Figure 17-4 appears automatically when the exception is thrown.

If you want to write truly airtight JavaScript code, you need to identify all the events that could possibly cause an exception in your particular script (such as actions the user could take, error conditions the operating system could generate, and so on), and implement a `try-catch` block for each.

Depending on your application, you might want to include more processing code in the `catch` block than the simple pop-up message shown in Figure 17-4. For example, you might want to include JavaScript statements that examine the caught exception, determine what kind of exception it is, and process it appropriately.

You aren't limited to a string literal when it comes to identifying a thrown exception. Instead of `InvalidMonthNumber`, you can create and throw an elaborate custom exception object (by using the function and new operators that I describe in Chapter 3).

For more information on how Netscape implements exception handling (including examples), visit

```
http://developer.netscape.com/docs/manuals/js/core/jsguide/stmtsov.htm#1011537
```

To see how Microsoft does the same for Internet Explorer, check out this page:

```
http://msdn.microsoft.com/library/default.asp?url=/library/
           en-us/jscript7/html/jsstmtrycatch.asp
```

Taking Advantage of Debugging Tools

Both Netscape and Microsoft offer free JavaScript debugging tools. They include

- Netscape Navigator's built-in JavaScript console (available for use with Netscape Navigator 7.x)
- Microsoft Internet Explorer's built-in error display

In addition to the built-in debugging tools that I describe in this section, Netscape and Microsoft offer standalone script debuggers that you can download for free. Venkman is the name of the free JavaScript debugger created for use with Netscape Navigator 7.x. Although support for this JavaScript debugger is spotty at best, you can get the latest documentation (and download your very own copy) from `www.hacksrus.com/~ginda/venkman`. Microsoft offers a script debugger that you can use to debug JScript scripts (as well as scripts written in other scripting languages, such as Microsoft's own VBScript). To download a copy of Microsoft's script debugger, point your browser to

```
www.microsoft.com/downloads/details.aspx?FamilyID=2f465be0-94fd-4569-b3c4-
           dffdf19ccd99&displaylang=en
```

Netscape's JavaScript console

Netscape Navigator 7.x comes complete with a JavaScript debugging tool called the JavaScript console, which you see in Figure 17-5.

You can display the JavaScript console shown in Figure 17-5 by performing either of the following two actions:

✔ **Select Tools➪Web Development➪JavaScript Console from the Netscape Navigator main menu.**

✔ **Type** javascript: **in Netscape Navigator's navigation toolbar and hit Enter.**

After you display the JavaScript console, you can debug JavaScript code two ways:

✔ **Load an HTML file containing a script into Netscape Navigator as usual.** When you do, any errors the script generates appear in the console, as shown in Figure 17-6.

Figure 17-5:
Navigator comes with a script-debugging tool called the Java-Script Console.

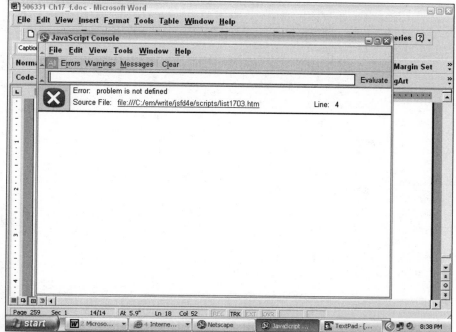

Figure 17-6:
JavaScript errors appear in Netscape's JavaScript console.

ON THE CD

As you can see in Figure 17-6, a JavaScript error was detected on line 4 of the file error.htm.

If you take a look at error.htm (a copy of which you find on the companion CD), you see this HTML/JavaScript code:

```
<HTML>
<HEAD>
<SCRIPT LANGUAGE="JavaScript" TYPE="text/javascript">
alert("This is a " + problem);
...
```

The JavaScript console message shown in Figure 17-6 reads Error: problem is not defined. And sure enough, if you count down to line 4, you see the variable problem isn't defined before it's used. (You see how to define a variable in Chapter 3.)

✔ **Enter JavaScript code directly into the console's evaluation field.** You can type JavaScript code directly into the evaluation field that you find on the JavaScript console and click the Evaluate button for instant feedback. Take a look at Figure 17-7 to see what I mean.

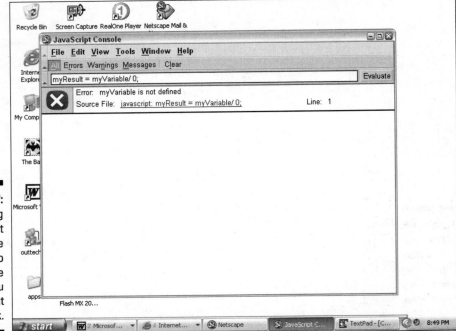

Figure 17-7:
Entering
JavaScript
code
directly into
the console
gives you
instant
feedback.

Microsoft Internet Explorer's built-in error display

When you load a JavaScript error-containing Web page into Internet Explorer, you see an icon in the status bar at the lower-left side of the screen. Double-clicking the icon displays a pop-up window describing the JavaScript error — along with hints for fixing that error. Check out Figure 17-8 to see what I mean.

Figure 17-8 shows that Internet Explorer encountered an error on line 4 of the HTML file: namely, that `problem` is undefined.

Sure enough, if you take a look at the following HTML code (you find a copy of the `error.htm` file on the companion CD) you see that line 4 references an undefined variable called `problem`. (I demonstrate how to define a variable in Chapter 3.)

```
<HTML>
<HEAD>
<SCRIPT LANGUAGE="JavaScript" TYPE="text/javascript">
alert("This is a " + problem);
...
```

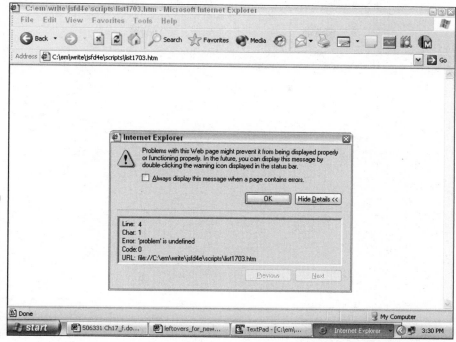

Figure 17-8:
Double-
clicking the
status bar
icon
displays
JavaScript
errors.

Part VI
Appendixes

The 5th Wave   By Rich Tennant

IF BOB DYLAN HAD PURSUED A CAREER IN COMPUTERS

"He's a whiz at developing applications, but thank goodness for email because I can't understand a word he says when he talks."

In this part . . .

1 include numerous resources to help you develop more complex and exciting scripts. Here, you find a list of words that you can't use in your code, as well as plenty of shortcuts and objects that you're sure to incorporate.

JavaScript reserves certain words that you don't want to use as variable names, function names, or other user-defined elements in your code. Appendix A lists these special words. JavaScript also gives you a couple options for making sure that the colors you want in your pages appear the way you intend (or close to it), which you can find out about in Appendix B.

Although Appendix C doesn't include every possible explanation for every possible object, you can find nearly all the objects that you're sure to need with their respective methods and properties, as well as some tips on which ones are browser-conscious. And, finally, you can use the special characters in Appendix D to make sure your Web pages comply with the demands of the global marketplace and the languages of your users.

Appendix A

JavaScript Reserved Words

•••

*T*he words listed in this appendix mean something special to the JavaScript interpreter implemented in the current versions of Navigator and Internet Explorer (or are reserved for future versions). If you try to use any of these words to do anything other than what they are designed to do, the JavaScript interpreter generates an error when you try to run the script. For example, don't try to use any of these words to name a variable, a function, a method, or an object.

In addition to the reserved words listed in this appendix, names of existing objects, properties, and methods are off-limits when it comes to naming your own variables and functions. For example, the JavaScript interpreter ignores a custom function named `toString()` — the name of an existing method. Appendix C lists many of the existing JavaScript objects, properties, and methods.

abstract	boolean	break
byte	case	catch
char	class	comment
const	continue	debugger
default	delete	do
double	else	enum
export	extends	false
final	finally	float
for	function	goto
if	implements	import
in	instanceof	int
interface	label	long
native	new	null
package	private	protected

public	return	short
static	super	switch
synchronized	this	throw
throws	transient	true
try	typeof	var
void	volatile	while
with		

Appendix B

JavaScript Color Values

- -

*T*his appendix offers an alphabetical listing of all predefined colors available to you in JavaScript. When you refer to a color in JavaScript code, you can use either the human-readable color names (for example, alice blue) or their hexadecimal equivalents (F0F8FF). For example, the following two JavaScript statements are equivalent:

```
document.write(someTextString.fontcolor("aqua"))
document.write(someTextString.fontcolor("00FFFF"))
```

To be sure that your color combinations result in readable Web pages, make sure that you test your Web pages before releasing them for all the world to see.

Color	*Hexadecimal*
aliceblue	F0F8FF
antiquewhite	FAEBD7
aqua	00FFFF
aquamarine	7FFFD4
azure	F0FFFF
beige	F5F5DC
bisque	FFE4C4
black	000000
blanchedalmond	FFEBCD
blue	0000FF
blueviolet	8A2BE2
brown	A52A2A
burlywood	DEB887
cadetblue	5F9EA0

(continued)

Color	Hexadecimal
chartreuse	7FFF00
chocolate	D2691E
coral	FF7F50
cornflowerblue	6495ED
cornsilk	FFF8DC
crimson	DC143C
cyan	00FFFF
darkblue	00008B
darkcyan	008B8B
darkgoldenrod	B8860B
darkgray	A9A9A9
darkgreen	006400
darkkhaki	BDB76B
darkmagenta	8B008B
darkolivegreen	556B2F
darkorange	FF8C00
darkorchid	9932CC
darkred	8B0000
darksalmon	E9967A
darkseagreen	8FBC8F
darkslateblue	483D8B
darkslategray	2F4F4F
darkturquoise	00CED1
darkviolet	9400D3
deeppink	FF1493
deepskyblue	00BFFF
dimgray	696969

Color	Hexadecimal
dodgerblue	1E90FF
firebrick	B22222
floralwhite	FFFAF0
forestgreen	228B22
fuchsia	FF00FF
gainsboro	DCDCDC
ghostwhite	F8F8FF
gold	FFD700
goldenrod	DAA520
gray	808080
green	008000
greenyellow	ADFF2F
honeydew	F0FFF0
hotpink	FF69B4
indianred	CD5C5C
indigo	4B0082
ivory	FFFFF0
khaki	F0E68C
lavender	E6E6FA
lavenderblush	FFF0F5
lawngreen	7CFC00
lemonchiffon	FFFACD
lightblue	ADD8E6
lightcoral	F08080
lightcyan	E0FFFF
lightgoldenrodyellow	FAFAD2
lightgreen	90EE90

(continued)

Color	Hexadecimal
lightgrey	D3D3D3
lightpink	FFB6C1
lightsalmon	FFA07A
lightseagreen	20B2AA
lightskyblue	87CEFA
lightslategray	778899
lightsteelblue	B0C4DE
lightyellow	FFFFE0
lime	00FF00
limegreen	32CD32
linen	FAF0E6
magenta	FF00FF
maroon	800000
mediumaquamarine	66CDAA
mediumblue	0000CD
mediumorchid	BA55D3
mediumpurple	9370DB
mediumseagreen	3CB371
mediumslateblue	7B68EE
mediumspringgreen	00FA9A
mediumturquoise	48D1CC
mediumvioletred	C71585
midnightblue	191970
mintcream	F5FFFA
mistyrose	FFE4E1
moccasin	FFE4B5
navajowhite	FFDEAD

Color	Hexadecimal
navy	000080
oldlace	FDF5E6
olive	808000
olivedrab	6B8E23
orange	FFA500
orangered	FF4500
orchid	DA70D6
palegoldenrod	EEE8AA
palegreen	98FB98
paleturquoise	AFEEEE
palevioletred	DB7093
papayawhip	FFEFD5
peachpuff	FFDAB9
peru	CD853F
pink	FFC0CB
plum	DDA0DD
powderblue	B0E0E6
purple	800080
red	FF0000
rosybrown	BC8F8F
royalblue	4169E1
saddlebrown	8B4513
salmon	FA8072
sandybrown	F4A460
seagreen	2E8B57
seashell	FFF5EE
sienna	A0522D

(continued)

Color	Hexadecimal
silver	C0C0C0
skyblue	87CEEB
slateblue	6A5ACD
slategray	708090
snow	FFFAFA
springgreen	00FF7F
steelblue	4682B4
tan	D2B48C
teal	008080
thistle	D8BFD8
tomato	FF6347
turquoise	40E0D0
violet	EE82EE
wheat	F5DEB3
white	FFFFFF
whitesmoke	F5F5F5
yellow	FFFF00
yellowgreen	9ACD32

Appendix C

Document Object Model Reference

● ●

You can think of this appendix as an alphabetical cheat sheet that lists the bulk of the objects, properties, methods, and event handlers that make up the document object model that you interact with in JavaScript. (The built-in functions available to you in JavaScript are also listed in the second half of this appendix.)

The folks who implemented the document object model — Netscape and Microsoft — surely had their reasons for beginning some, but not all, object names with uppercase letters! JavaScript is a case-sensitive language, which means that if an object begins with a lowercase (or uppercase) letter, you must access it that way.

The Document Object Model

I've organized the document object model (DOM) alphabetically, by object. If you need to look up a particular property or method — say, `prompt()` — and don't know what object it belongs to, take a quick peek at the index that you find at the back of this book.

This appendix is as up-to-date as is humanly possible, but because new browser versions appear regularly (each of which might implement a slightly different DOM), you might find some minor differences between the DOM that your browser supports and the one listed here. In fact, both Netscape and Internet Explorer have pledged their intention to continue modifying their DOM until that happy day when they both match the ECMA standard and developers can count on the same object existing and behaving identically in both browsers — but that day hasn't yet arrived. So for the last word in object implementation, including detailed descriptions of any of the elements you find in this appendix, visit Netscape and Microsoft online.

Internet Explorer's DOM:

```
http://msdn.microsoft.com/workshop/author/dhtml/reference/
            objects.asp
```

Netscape Navigator's DOM:

```
http://devedge.netscape.com/library/manuals/2000/javascript/
            1.5/reference
```

Because all the objects in the DOM derive from the `Object` object (try saying that three times fast!), all JavaScript objects inherit the `Object` object's properties and methods. (I tell you this, instead of listing those few properties and methods associated with the `Object` object over and over again for every other object, in the interest of saving space.)

Anchor

Description: The target of a hyperlink.

What creates it: `<A NAME="`*`anchorName`*`">` or `String.anchor("`*`anchorName`*`")`

How to access it: `document.anchors[`*`i`*`]` (individual anchor) or `document.anchors.length` (number of anchors in a document)

Properties: `name`, `text`, `x`, `y`

Methods: None

Event handlers: None

Applet

Description: A reference to a Java applet in a Web page.

What creates it: `<APPLET NAME="`*`appletName`*`">`

How to access it: `document.applets[`*`i`*`]` or `document.`*`appletName`*

Properties: Depends on applet.

Methods: Depends on applet (`start()` and `stop()` supported by convention).

Event handlers: None

Area

Description: Defines an area of an image as an image map.

(See Link.)

arguments

Description: A collection of the arguments passed into a function.

What creates it: `function` `functionName() { functionStatements }`

How to access it: `arguments` (from inside a function body)

Properties: `callee, caller, length`

Methods: None

Event handlers: None

Array

Description: A collection of objects.

What creates it: `arrayName = new Array(arrayLength)` **or** `arrayName = new Array(element0, element1, . . ., elementN)`

How to access it: `arrayName[i]`

Properties: `constructor, index, input, length, prototype`

Methods: `concat(), join(), length(), pop(), push(), reverse(), shift(), slice(), sort(), splice(), toSource(), toString(), unshift(), valueOf()`

Event handlers: None

Boolean

Description: A boolean (true/false) value.

What creates it: *booleanName* = new Boolean(*value*) (constructor) **or** *booleanName* = Boolean(*value*) (conversion function)

How to access it: *booleanName*

Properties: constructor, prototype

Methods: toSource(), toString(), valueOf()

Event handlers: None

Button

Description: A push button included in an HTML form.

What creates it: <FORM NAME="*formName*"> . . . <INPUT TYPE="button" NAME="*buttonName*" . . . ></FORM>

How to access it: document.*formName*.*buttonName* or *formName*.elements[i]

Properties: form, name, type, value

Methods: blur(), click(), focus(), handleEvent()

Event handlers: onBlur, onClick, onFocus, onMouseDown, onMouseUp

Checkbox

Description: A check box included in an HTML form. (A check box is a toggle switch that lets the user turn a value on or off.)

What creates it: <FORM NAME="formName"> . . . <INPUT TYPE="checkbox" NAME="checkboxName" . . . ></FORM>

How to access it: document.*formName*.*checkboxName* or *formName*. elements[i]

Properties: checked, defaultChecked, form, name, type, value

Methods: blur(), click(), focus(), handleEvent()

Event handlers: onBlur, onClick, onFocus

clientInformation

Description: Describes browser configuration details. It is supported only by Internet Explorer. (Internet Explorer also supports the navigator object.)

What creates it: Automatically created by Internet Explorer.

How to access it: window.clientInformation (or just clientInformation)

Properties: appCodeName, appMinorVersion, appName, appVersion, browserLanguage, cookieEnabled, cpuClass, onLine, platform, system Language, userAgent, userLanguage, userProfile

Methods: javaEnabled(), taintEnabled()

Event handlers: None

crypto

Description: This object defines two cryptography-related methods that developers can use to implement digital signatures. It is supported only by Netscape Navigator.

What creates it: Automatically created by Netscape Navigator.

How to access it: window.crypto (or just crypto)

Properties: None

Methods: random(), signText()

Event handlers: None

Date

Description: An object that lets you create, manipulate, and format date and time values.

What creates it:

aDate = new Date()

aDate = new Date(milliseconds)

aDate = new Date(dateString)

aDate = new Date(yr_num, mo_num, day_num
[, hr_num, min_num, sec_num, ms_num])

How to access it: aDate

Properties: constructor, prototype

Methods: getDate(), getDay(), getFullYear(), getHours(),
getMilliseconds(), getMinutes(), getMonth(), getSeconds(),
getTime(), getTimezoneOffset(), getUTCDate(), getUTCDay(),
getUTCFullYear(), getUTCHours(), getUTCMilliseconds(),
getUTCMinutes(), getUTCMonth(), getUTCSeconds(), getYear(),
parse(), setDate(), setDay(), setFullYear(), setHours(),
setMilliseconds(), setMinutes(), setMonth(), setSeconds(),
setTime(), setUTCDate(), setUTCFullYear(), setUTCHours(),
setUTCMilliseconds(), setUTCMinutes(), setUTCMonth(),
setUTCSeconds(), setYear(), toGMTString(), toLocaleString(),
toSource(), toString(), toUTCString(), UTC(), valueOf()

Event handlers: None

document

Description: The currently loaded HTML document; provides methods for displaying HTML output to the user.

What creates it: <BODY> . . . </BODY>

How to access it: window.document (or just document)

Properties: alinkColor, anchors[], applets[], bgColor, cookie, domain,
embeds, fgColor, formName, forms[], images[], lastModified,
linkColor, links[], plugins[], referrer, title, URL, vlinkColor

Netscape Navigator only: `classes`, `height`, `ids`, `tags`, `width`

Internet Explorer only: `activeElement`, `all[]`, `charset`, `children[]`, `defaultCharset`, `expando`, `parentWindow`, `readyState`

Methods: `close()`, `handleEvent()`, `open()`, `write()`, `writeln()`

Netscape Navigator only: `captureEvents()`, `contextual()`, `getSelection()`, `releaseEvents()`, `routeEvent()`

Internet Explorer only: `elementFromPoint()`

Event handlers: `onClick`, `onDblClick`, `onKeyDown`, `onKeyPress`, `onKeyUp`, `onMouseDown`, `onMouseUp`

elements[]

Description: A collection of the form elements included in an HTML document.

What creates it: `<FORM NAME="formName>` . . . `</FORM>`

How to access it: `document.formName.elements[]`

Properties: `checked`, `defaultChecked`, `defaultValue`, `form`, `length`, `name`, `options[]`, `selectedIndex`, `type`, `value`

Methods: `blur()`, `click()`, `focus()`, `select()`

Event handlers: `onBlur`, `onChange`, `onClick`, `onFocus`

event

Description: One of several predefined occurrences in JavaScript, such as a mouse click, a text entry, or a document load. This object is passed as an argument to an event handler automatically when an event occurs.

What creates it: Automatically created by browser.

How to access it: `window.event` (or just `event`)

Properties (Netscape Navigator only): `data`, `height`, `modifiers`, `pageX`, `pageY`, `screenX`, `screenY`, `target`, `type`, `which`, `width`

Properties (Internet Explorer only): `altKey`, `button`, `cancelBubble`, `clientX`, `clientY`, `ctrlKey`, `fromElement`, `keyCode`, `offsetX`, `offsetY`, `reason`, `returnValue`, `screenX`, `screenY`, `shiftKey`, `srcElement`, `srcFilter`, `toElement`, `type`, `x`, `y`

Methods: None

Event handlers: None

FileUpload

Description: A file upload element on an HTML form. (A file upload element lets users select or specify a file as input to a Web application.)

What creates it: `<FORM NAME="`*formName*`">` . . . `<INPUT TYPE="file" NAME="`*fileUploadName*`"` . . . `></FORM>`

How to access it: `document.`*formName*`.`*fileUploadName* or *formName*`.elements[i]`

Properties: `form`, `name`, `type`, `value`

Methods: `blur()`, `focus()`, `handleEvent()`, `select()`

Event handlers: `onBlur`, `onChange`, `onFocus`

Form

Description: An HTML form. HTML forms let users input text and interact with such elements as check boxes, radio buttons, and selection lists. Forms can be configured to post data to a Web server automatically when the user submits the form.

What creates it: `<FORM NAME="`*formName*`">` . . . `</FORM>`

How to access it: `document.`*formName*

Properties: `action`, `elements[]`, `encoding`, `length`, `method`, `name`, `target`

Methods: `handleEvent()`, `reset()`, `submit()`

Event handlers: `onReset`, `onSubmit`

Frame

Description: An HTML display frame.

What creates it: `<FRAME>` . . . `</FRAME>`

(See window.)

Function

Description: A chunk of JavaScript code to be preprocessed by the JavaScript interpreter.

What creates it: `new Function ([arg1[, arg2[, . . . argN]],]` `functionBody)` **or** `function functionName([param[, param[, . . .` `param]]]) { statements }`

How to access it: `functionName`

Properties: `arguments[]`, `arity`, `caller`, `length`, `prototype`

Methods: `apply()`, `call()`, `toSource()`, `toString()`, `valueOf()`

Event handlers: None

Hidden

Description: A nondisplayed HTML form field useful for holding and transmitting calculated values to a Web server.

What creates it: `<FORM NAME="formName">` . . . `<INPUT` `TYPE="hidden" NAME="hiddenName" . . . ></FORM>`

How to access it: `document.formName.hiddenName` **or** `formName.` `elements[i]`

Properties: `form`, `name`, `type`, `value`

Methods: None

History

Description: A collection of URLs that a user has visited.

What creates it: Automatically created by browser.

How to access it: `window.history`, `frame.history`, **or just** `history`

Properties: `current`, `length`, `next`, `previous`

Methods: `back()`, `forward()`, `go()`

Event handlers: None

Image

Description: An image included in an HTML document.

What creates it: `<IMG NAME="imageName">`

How to access it:

`document.imageName`

`document.images[i]`

`document.images.length`

Properties: `border`, `complete`, `height`, `hspace`, `lowsrc`, `name`, `src`, `vspace`, `width`

Methods: `handleEvent()`

Event handlers: `onAbort`, `onError`, `onKeyDown`, `onKeyPress`, `onKeyUp`, `onLoad`

java

Description: A top-level object used to access any Java class in the package `java.*`.

What creates it: Automatically created by Java-supporting browser.

(See JavaPackage.)

JavaArray

Description: The JavaScript representation of a Java array.

What creates it: Any Java method that returns an array.

How to access it: By calling a method defined by an individual Java applet.

Properties: length

Methods: toString()

Event handlers: None

JavaClass

Description: JavaScript representation of a Java class.

What creates it: Automatically created by Java-supporting browser.

(See JavaPackage.)

JavaObject

Description: JavaScript representation of a Java object.

What creates it: Any Java method that returns an object type.

How to access it: By calling a method defined by an individual Java applet.

Properties: Determined by individual Java applet/method.

Methods: Determined by individual Java applet/method.

Event handlers: None

JavaPackage

Description: JavaScript representation of a Java package.

What creates it: Automatically created by Java-supporting browser.

How to access it: Packages.*JavaPackage*

Properties: Determined by individual Java package.

Methods: Determined by individual Java package.

Event handlers: None

Link

Description: A hypertext link included in an HTML document.

What creates it: `<A>`, `<AREA>`, or `String.link()`

How to access it: `document.links[i]` (individual link)or `document.links.length` (number of links in a document)

Properties: `hash, host, hostName, href, pathname, port, protocol, search, target, text, x, y`

Methods: `handleEvent()`

Event handlers: `onDblClick, onMouseOut, onMouseOver` (`<AREA>`), `onClick, onDblClick, onKeyDown, onKeyPress, onKeyUp, onMouseDown, onMouseOut, onMouseUp, onMouseOver` (`<A>` or `String.link()`)

location

Description: The currently loaded URL.

What creates it: Automatically created by browser.

How to access it: `window.location` (or just `location`)

Properties: `hash, host, hostname, href, pathname, port, protocol, search`

Methods: `reload(), replace()`

Event handlers: None

Math

Description: A built-in object containing properties and methods for mathematical constants and functions.

What creates it: Automatically created by browser.

How to access it: Math

Properties: E, LN10, LN2, LOG10E, LOG2E, PI, SQRT1_2, SQRT2

Methods: abs( ), acos( ), asin( ), atan( ), atan2( ), ceil( ), cos( ), exp( ), floor( ), log( ), max( ), min( ), pow( ), random( ), round( ), sin( ), sqrt( ), tan( )

Event handlers: None

MimeType

Description: A MIME type (Multipart Internet Mail Extension, such as .pdf) supported by the browser.

What creates it: Automatically created by Netscape Navigator.

How to access it:

navigator.mimeTypes[*i*]

navigator.mimeTypes["*type*"]

navigator.plugins[*i*].mimeTypes[*j*]

navigator.mimeTypes.length

Properties: description, enabledPlugin, suffixes, type

Methods: None

Event handlers: None

navigator

Description: Browser configuration details.

What creates it: Automatically created by browser.

How to access it: window.navigator (**or just** navigator)

Properties: appCodeName, appName, appVersion, language, mimeTypes, platform, plugins, userAgent

Methods: `javaEnabled()`, `plugins.refresh()`, `preference()`, `save Preferences()`, `taintEnabled()`

Event handlers: None

netscape

Description: A top-level object used to access any Java class in the package `netscape.*`.

What creates it: Automatically created by Netscape Navigator.

(See JavaPackage.)

Number

Description: A JavaScript object wrapper for primitive numeric values.

What creates it: *aNumber* = `new Number(`*value*`)`

How to access it: aNumber

Properties: `constructor`, `MAX_VALUE`, `MIN_VALUE`, `NaN`, `NEGATIVE_ INFINITY`, `POSITIVE_INFINITY`, `prototype`

Methods: `toSource()`, `toString()`, `valueOf()`

Event handlers: None

Object

Description: The primitive JavaScript object type from which all other objects derive.

What creates it:

anObject = `new Object()` **or** *anotherObject* = `new Object(`*anObject*`)`

How to access it: *anObject*, *anotherObject*

Properties: constructor, prototype

Methods: eval(), toSource(), toString(), unwatch(), valueOf(), watch()

Event handlers: None

Option

Description: An option in an HTML select list.

What creates it: <FORM NAME="*formName*"><SELECT NAME="*selectName*"> <OPTION></SELECT></FORM> **or** new Option([*text*[, *value*[, *defaultSelected*[, *selected*]]]])

How to access it: document.*formName*.*selectName*.options[*i*]

Properties: defaultSelected, index, length, selected, text, value

Methods: None

Event handlers: None

Packages

Description: A top-level object that's used to access Java classes from within JavaScript code.

What creates it: Automatically created by Java-supporting browsers.

How to access it: Depends on Java package.

Properties: className, java, netscape, sun

Methods: Depends on Java package.

Event handlers: None

Password

Description: A password field included in an HTML form. When a user enters text into a password field, asterisks (*) hide that text from view.

What creates it: `<FORM NAME="`*formName*`">` . . . `<INPUT TYPE="password" NAME="`*passwordName*`"` . . . `></FORM>`

How to access it: `document.`*formName*`.`*passwordName* **or** *formName*`.elements[i]`

Properties: `defaultValue, form, name, type, value`

Methods: `blur(), focus(), handleEvent(), select()`

Event handlers: `onBlur, onFocus`

Plugin

Description: A plug-in application module installed in Netscape Navigator.

What creates it: Netscape Navigator (on browser plug-in install).

How to access it: `navigator.plugins[`*i*`]`

Properties: `description, filename, length, name`

Methods: None

Event handlers: None

Radio

Description: A radio button in a set of radio buttons included in an HTML form. The user can use a set of radio buttons to choose one item from a list.

What creates it: `<FORM NAME="`*formName*`">` . . . `<INPUT TYPE="radio" NAME="`*radioName*`"` . . . `></FORM>`

How to access it: `document.`*formName*`.`*radioName* **or** *formName*`.elements[i]`

Properties: checked, defaultChecked, form, name, type, value

Methods: blur(), click(), focus(), handleEvent()

Event handlers: onBlur, onClick, onFocus

RegExp

Description: Contains the pattern of a regular expression. This object provides properties and methods for using that regular expression to find and replace matches in strings.

What creates it: /pattern/flags

new RegExp("pattern"[, "flags"])

How to access it: Regular expressions are tricky animals. You use regular expressions for pattern-matching applications. The following gives an example:

```
<SCRIPT LANGUAGE="JavaScript1.2">
aRegularExpression = /(\w+)\s(\w+)/;
oldString = "John Smith";
newString=oldString.replace(aRegularExpression, "$2, $1");
document.write(newString)
</SCRIPT>
```

(This script displays Smith, John.)

For more information, visit this page:

http://developer.netscape.com/docs/manuals/js/client/jsref/regexp.htm

Properties: $1, . . . , $9, $_, $*, $&, $+, $`, $', constructor, global, ignoreCase, input, lastIndex, lastMatch, lastParen, leftContext, multiline, prototype, rightContext, source

Methods: compile(), exec(), test(), toSource(), toString(), valueOf()

Event handlers: None

Reset

Description: A Reset button on an HTML form. This button resets all elements in a form to their defaults.

What creates it: `<FORM NAME="`*formName*`">` . . . `<INPUT TYPE="reset"` `NAME="`*resetName*`"` . . . `></FORM>`

How to access it: `document.`*formName*`.`*resetName* or *formName*`.` `elements[i]`

Properties: `form`, `name`, `type`, `value`

Methods: `blur()`, `click()`, `focus()`, `handleEvent()`

Event handlers: `onBlur`, `onClick`, `onFocus`

screen

Description: Contains properties describing the display screen (monitor) and colors.

What creates it: Automatically created by browser.

How to access it: `screen`

Properties: `availHeight`, `availLeft`, `availTop`, `availWidth`, `colorDepth`, `height`, `pixelDepth`, `width`

Methods: None

Event handlers: None

Select

Description: A selection list included in an HTML form. The user can choose one or more items from a selection list, depending on how the list was created.

What creates it: `<FORM NAME="`*formName*`"><SELECT NAME="`*selectName*`">` `</SELECT></FORM>`

How to access it: `document.`*formName*`.`*selectName* or *formName*`.` `elements[i]`

Properties: form, length, name, options, selectedIndex, type

Methods: blur(), focus(), handleEvent()

Event handlers: onBlur, onChange, onFocus

String

Description: An object representing a series of quote-delimited characters.

What creates it: *aString* = new String("*value*") or *aString* = "*value*"

How to access it: *aString*

Properties: constructor, length, prototype

Methods: anchor(), big(), blink(), bold(), charAt(), charCodeAt(), concat(), fixed(), fontcolor(), fontsize(), fromCharCode(), indexOf(), italics(), lastIndexOf(), link(), match(), replace(), search(), slice(), small(), split(), strike(), sub(), substr(), substring(), sup(), toLowerCase(), toSource(), toString(), toUpperCase(), valueOf()

Event handlers: None

Style

Description: An object that specifies the style of HTML elements.

What creates it: document.classes.*className*.*tagName*

document.contextual(. . .)

document.ids.*elementName*

document.tags.*tagName*

How to access it: See the following Web page:

```
http://developer.netscape.com/docs/manuals/communicator/dynht
          ml/index.htm
```

Properties (Netscape Navigator only): backgroundColor, background Image, borderBottomWidth, borderColor, borderLeftWidth, border RightWidth, borderStyle, borderTopWidth, clear, color, display, font Family, fontSize, fontStyle, fontWeight, lineHeight, listStyleType, marginBottom, marginLeft, marginRight, marginTop, paddingBottom, paddingLeft, paddingRight, paddingTop, textAlign, textDecoration, textIndent, textTransform, whiteSpace

Properties (Internet Explorer only): background, background-Attachment, backgroundColor, backgroundImage, backgroundPosition, background PositionX, backgroundPositionY, backgroundRepeat, border, border Bottom, borderBottomColor, borderBottomStyle, borderBottomWidth, borderColor, borderLeft, borderLeftColor, borderLeftStyle, border LeftWidth, borderRight, borderRightColor, borderRightStyle, border RightWidth, borderStyle, borderTop, borderTopColor, borderTopStyle, borderTopWidth, borderWidth, clear, clip, color, cssText, cursor, display, filter, font, fontFamily, fontSize, fontStyle, fontVariant, fontWeight, height, left, letterSpacing, lineHeight, listStyle, list StyleImage, listStylePosition, listStyleType, margin, marginBottom, marginLeft, marginRight, marginTop, overflow, paddingBottom, paddingLeft, paddingRight, paddingTop, pageBreakAfter, pageBreak Before, pixelHeight, pixelLeft, pixelTop, pixelWidth, posHeight, position, posLeft, posTop, posWidth, styleFloat, textAlign, text Decoration, textIndent, textTransform, top, verticalAlign, visibility, width, zIndex

Methods: borderWidths(), margins(), paddings()

Event handlers: None

Submit

Description: A Submit button included in an HTML form. This button sends the form information to be processed.

What creates it: <FORM NAME="*formName*"> . . . <INPUT TYPE="submit" NAME="*submitName*" . . . ></FORM>

How to access it: document.*formName*.*submitName* or *formName*. elements[i]

Properties: form, name, type, value

Methods: blur(), click(), focus(), handleEvent()

Event handlers: onBlur, onClick, onFocus

sun

Description: A top-level object used to access any Java class in the package sun.*.

What creates it: Automatically created by Java-supporting browsers.

How to access it: `Packages.sun`

(See Packages.)

Text

Description: A text field included in an HTML form.

What creates it: `<FORM NAME="`*formName*`">` . . . `<INPUT TYPE="text"` `NAME="`*textName*`" . . . ></FORM>`

How to access it: `document.`*formName*`.`*textName* or *formName*`.elements[i]`

Properties: `defaultValue, form, name, type, value`

Methods: `blur(), focus(), handleEvent(), select()`

Event handlers: `onBlur, onChange, onFocus, onSelect`

Textarea

Description: A text area element (a multiline text input field) included in an HTML form.

What creates it: `<FORM NAME="`*formName*`"><TEXTAREA NAME="`*textarea* *Name*`">` . . . `</TEXTAREA></FORM>`

How to access it: `document.`*formName*`.`*textareaName* or *formName*`.` `elements[i]`

Properties: `defaultValue, form, name, type, value`

Methods: `blur(), focus(), handleEvent(), select()`

Event handlers: `onBlur, onChange, onFocus, onSelect`

window

Description: A browser window or frame.

What creates it:

`<BODY>`

`<FRAMESET>`

`<FRAME NAME="`*frameName*`">`

` window.open("`*windowName*`")`

How to access it:

`self`

`window`

`window.frames[i]`

`window.`*frameName*

Properties: `closed, defaultStatus, document, frames[], history, length, location, Math, name, navigator, offscreenBuffering, opener, parent, screen, self, status, top, window`

Netscape Navigator only: `crypto, innerHeight, innerWidth, jav, location bar, menubar, netscape, outerHeight, outerWidth, Packages, page XOffset, pageYOffset, personalbar, screenX, screenY, scrollbars, statusbar, sun, toolbar`

Internet Explorer only: `clientInformation, event`

Methods: `alert(), blur(), clearInterval(), clearTimeout(), close(), confirm(), focus(), moveBy(), moveTo(), oen(), prompt(), resizeBy(), resizeTo(), scroll(), scrollBy(), scrollTo(), setInterval(), setTimeout()`

Netscape Navigator only: `atob(), back(), btoa(), captureEvents(), disableExternalCapture(), enableExternalCapture(), find(), forward(), handleEvent(), home(), print(), releaseEvents(), routeEvent(), setHotkeys(), setResizable(), setZOptions(), stop()`

Internet Explorer only: `navigate()`

Event handlers: `onBlur, onDragDrop, onError, onFocus, onLoad, onMove, onResize, onUnload`

Global Properties

Infinity

NaN (not a number)

Undefined

Built-In JavaScript Functions

escape ( )

Description: Returns the hexadecimal encoding of an argument in the ISO-Latin-1 character set. The escape() function and it's reverse function, unescape(), are typically used to send special characters safely from a JavaScript script to another program, such as a Java applet. For example, you can encode a special character by using the escape() function and send the resulting value to another program that can then decode that character by using the equivalent of the unescape() function — and vice versa. (Sending special characters without using this encoding process can result in errors. You can think of the ISO-Latin-1 character set as a lowest-common-denominator language that many programmer languages understand.)

Syntax: escape("valueToBeEncoded")

Example:

```
escape("&") // returns the hexadecimal equivalent of & which is "%26"
```

eval ( )

Description: Evaluates a string of JavaScript code without reference to a particular object.

Syntax: eval("value") where value is a string representing a JavaScript expression, statement, or sequence of statements. The expression can include variables and properties of existing objects.

Example:

```
eval(new String("2+2")) // returns a String object containing "2+2"
```

isFinite ( )

Description: Evaluates an argument to determine whether it is a finite number. If the argument is NaN, positive infinity or negative infinity, this method returns false; otherwise, it returns true.

Syntax: isFinite(*value*)

Example:

```
isFinite(123) // returns true
```

isNaN ( )

Description: Evaluates an argument to determine whether it is not a number. Returns true if passed NaN and false otherwise.

Syntax: isNaN(*value*)

Example:

```
isNaN(123) // returns false
```

Number ( )

Description: Converts the specified object to a number.

Syntax: Number(*anObject*)

Example:

```
alert (Number(d)) // Displays a dialog box containing "819199440000."
```

parseFloat ( )

Description: Parses a string argument and returns a floating point number.

Syntax: parseFloat("*value*")

Example:

```
var x = "3.14" // returns 3.14
```

parseInt ( )

Description: Parses a string argument and returns an integer of the specified radix or base. (Base 10 is assumed if no radix is supplied.)

Syntax: parseInt(*string*[, *radix*])

Example:

```
parseInt("1111", 2) // returns 15
```

```
parseInt("15", 10) // returns 15
```

String ( )

Description: Converts the specified object to a string.

Syntax: string(*anObject*)

Example:

```
aDate = new Date (430054663215)
alert (String(aDate)) // displays "Thu Aug 18 04:37:43 GMT-0700 (Pacific
                Daylight Time) 1983."
```

taint ( )

Description: Adds tainting to a data element or script. (Tainting a JavaScript element prevents that element from being passed to a server without the end-user's permission.)

Syntax: taint([*dataElementName*]) where *dataElementName* is the property, variable, function, or object to taint. If omitted, taint is added to the script itself.

Example:

```
taintedStatus=taint(window.defaultStatus)
```

unescape ( )

Description: Returns the ASCII string for the specified hexadecimal encoding value.

Syntax: unescape("*value*") where *value* is a string containing characters in the form "%xx", xx being a 2-digit hexadecimal number.

Example:

```
unescape("%26") // returns "&"
```

untaint ( )

Description: Removes tainting from a data element or script. (Tainting a JavaScript element prevents that element from being passed to a server without the end-user's permission.)

Syntax: untaint([*dataElementName*]) where *dataElementName* is the property, variable, function, or object from which to remove tainting.

Example:

```
untaintedStatus=untaint(window.defaultStatus)
```

Appendix D

Special Characters

Sometimes you need to represent special characters in JavaScript strings. Common examples of special characters include white space, currency symbols, and non-English characters.

When you represent special characters in JavaScript, you have a choice: You can use escape characters, octal, or hexadecimal representations of the Web-standard character set Latin-1 (ISO 8859-1), or — for versions of Netscape Navigator including 6.0 and later — Unicode.

Together, the ISO 8859 and Unicode standards allow for literally tens of thousands of special characters: enough to represent most of the known human languages! Although I couldn't fit all of them in this appendix, the following tables should cover most of your special character needs. It lists the most commonly used special characters, along with both the hexadecimal and octal representations JavaScript supports.

Character sets are evolving standards. To get the very latest scoop on JavaScript internationalization and supported character sets — as well as to find representations for special characters not listed in this appendix — check out the section of Netscape's JavaScript manual that describes support for special characters at

```
http://devedge.netscape.com/library/manuals/2000/javascript/1.5/guide/
            ident.html#1009568
```

For more information on the Unicode standard, check out the Unicode home page at

```
www.unicode.org
```

The following is example of how you use special characters in JavaScript code:

```
alert("\'JavaScript For Dummies\u00A9\' costs $29.99 in the U.S., 195\xA5 in
            Japan, and \24316 in Britain.")
```

Here are the most commonly used special characters:

Character	JavaScript Escape Characters	Unicode
Apostrophe	\'	\u0027
Backslash	\\	\u005C
Backspace	\b	\u000b
Carriage return	\r	\u000D
Double quote	\"	\u0022
Form feed	\f	\u000C
New line	\n	\u000A
Tab	\t	\u0009

Octal, hexadecimal, and Unicode representations of other common special characters appear in the following lists:

Octal	Hex	Unicode	Description	Character
\240	\xA0	\u00A0	Nonbreaking space	
\241	\xA1	\u00A1	Inverted exclamation mark	¡
\242	\xA2	\u00A2	Cent sign	¢
\243	\xA3	\u00A3	Pound sign	£
\244	\xA4	\u00A4	General currency sign	¤
\245	\xA5	\u00A5	Yen sign	¥
\246	\xA6	\u00A6	Broken vertical line	¦
\247	\xA7	\u00A7	Section sign	§
\250	\xA8	\u00A8	Diaeresis or umlaut	¨
\251	\xA9	\u00A9	Copyright sign	©
\252	\xAA	\u00AA	Feminine ordinal indicator	ª
\253	\xAB	\u00AB	Left-pointing double carets	«
\254	\xAC	\u00AC	Logical not-sign	¬

Octal	Hex	Unicode	Description	Character
\255	\xAD	\u00AD	Soft hyphen	-
\256	\xAE	\u00AE	Registered sign	®
\257	\xAF	\u00AF	Macron	-
\260	\xB0	\u00B0	Degree sign	°
\261	\xB1	\u00B1	Plus-or-minus sign	±
\262	\xB2	\u00B2	Superscript two	-
\263	\xB3	\u00B3	Superscript three	-
\264	\xB4	\u00B4	Acute accent	´
\265	\xB5	\u00B5	Micron sign	>
\266	\xB6	\u00B6	Pilcrow	¶
\267	\xB7	\u00B7	Middle dot	·
\270	\xB8	\u00B8	Cedilla	¸
\271	\xB9	\u00B9	Superscript-one	-
\272	\xBA	\u00BA	Masculine ordinal indicator	º
\273	\xBB	\u00BB	Right-pointing double carets	»
\274	\xBC	\u00BC	Fraction, one-quarter	¼
\275	\xBD	\u00BD	Fraction, one-half	½
\276	\xBE	\u00BE	Fraction, three-quarters	¾
\277	\xBF	\u00BF	Inverted question mark	¿

Uppercase Letters				
\300	\xC0	\u00C0	A-grave	À
\301	\xC1	\u00C1	A-acute	Á
\302	\xC2	\u00C2	A-circumflex	Â
\303	\xC3	\u00C3	A-tilde	Ã
\304	\xC4	\u00C4	A-umlaut	Ä

(continued)

Uppercase Letters (continued)

\305	\xC5	\u00C5	A-ring	Å
\306	\xC6	\u00C6	AE	Æ
\307	\xC7	\u00C7	C-cedilla	Ç
\310	\xC8	\u00C8	E-grave	È
\311	\xC9	\u00C9	E-acute	É
\312	\xCA	\u00CA	E-circumflex	Ê
\313	\xCB	\u00CB	E-umlaut	Ë
\314	\xCC	\u00CC	I-grave	Ì
\315	\xCD	\u00CD	I-acute	Í
\316	\xCE	\u00CE	I-circumflex	Î
\317	\xCF	\u00CF	I-umlaut	Ï
\320	\xD0	\u00D0	D-stroke	–
\321	\xD1	\u00D1	N-tilde	Ñ
\322	\xD2	\u00D2	O-grave	Ò
\323	\xD3	\u00D3	O-acute	Ó
\324	\xD4	\u00D4	O-circumflex	Ô
\325	\xD5	\u00D5	O-tilde	Õ
\326	\xD6	\u00D6	O-umlaut	Ö
\327	\xD7	\u00D7	Multiplication sign	×
\330	\xD8	\u00D8	O-slash	Ø
\331	\xD9	\u00D9	U-grave	Ù
\332	\xDA	\u00DA	U-acute	Ú
\333	\xDB	\u00DB	U-circumflex	Û
\334	\xDC	\u00DC	U-umlaut	Ü
\335	\xDD	\u00DD	Y-acute	–
\336	\xDE	\u00DE	THORN	–
\337	\xDF	\u00DF	Small sharp s	(

Lowercase Letters

\340	\xE0	\u00E0	a-grave	à
\341	\xE1	\u00E1	a-acute	á
\342	\xE2	\u00E2	a-circumflex	â
\343	\xE3	\u00E3	a-tilde	ã
\344	\xE4	\u00E4	a-umlaut	ä
\345	\xE5	\u00E5	a-ring	å
\346	\xE6	\u00E6	ae	æ
\347	\xE7	\u00E7	c-cedilla	ç
\350	\xE8	\u00E8	e-grave	è
\351	\xE9	\u00E9	e-acute	é
\352	\xEA	\u00EA	e-circumflex	ê
\353	\xEB	\u00EB	e-umlaut	ë
\354	\xEC	\u00EC	i-grave	ì
\355	\xED	\u00ED	i-acute	í
\356	\xEE	\u00EE	i-circumflex	î
\357	\xEF	\u00EF	i-umlaut	ï
\360	\xF0	\u00F0	d-stroke	–
\361	\xF1	\u00F1	n-tilde	ñ
\362	\xF2	\u00F2	o-grave	ò
\363	\xF3	\u00F3	o-acute	ó
\364	\xF4	\u00F4	o-circumflex	ô
\365	\xF5	\u00F5	o-tilde	õ
\366	\xF6	\u00F6	o-umlaut	ö
\367	\xF7	\u00F7	Division sign	÷
\370	\xF8	\u00F8	o-slash	ø
\371	\xF9	\u00F9	u-grave	ù
\372	\xFA	\u00FA	u-acute	ú

(continued)

Lowercase Letters (continued)

\373	\xFB	\u00FB	u-circumflex	û
\374	\xFC	\u00FC	u-umlaut	ü
\375	\xFD	\u00FD	y-acute	–
\376	\xFE	\u00FE	thorn	–
\377	\xFF	\u00FF	y-umlaut	ÿ

Appendix E

About the CD

$\bullet \bullet$

This appendix explains what's on the CD-ROM that accompanies this book, as well as how to install the contents and run each of the examples. Here's a sneak-peek at the contents for those of you who just can't wait:

- ✔ Full working copies of each of the HTML/JavaScript listings that appear in the book
- ✔ A wealth of useful JavaScript development tools
- ✔ Sound and image files used in the examples

Getting the Most from This CD

The best way to get familiar with JavaScript is to load scripts and interact with them as you read through each chapter. If it's feasible for you, I suggest installing the contents of the CD before you pick up the book (or at least before you're more than about a quarter of the way through). Then, when you come across a listing in the book, you can double-click on the corresponding HTML file you've already installed and bingo! Interactive learning.

If you really want to make sure that you understand a concept, be sure you take time not just to run each file, but to play around with it, too. Change a line of JavaScript code and see what happens. You can't go wrong because you can just reinstall from the CD.

The examples are also referenced throughout the text. Some were designed to reinforce the concepts you're discovering; others, to be real, live, workable scripts that you can incorporate into your own Web pages. Enjoy!

System Requirements

Make sure that your computer meets the minimum system requirements listed here. If your computer doesn't match up to most of these requirements, you may have problems in using the contents of the CD.

- A Pentium-based PC, or a Mac OS computer with a Power PC-based processor.

- Microsoft Windows 98 or later, Windows NT4 or later, or Mac OS system software 8.5 or later.

- A copy of either Netscape Navigator 7.0 or Microsoft Internet Explorer 6.0. (Chapter 1 tells you how to get a copy and install it, if you haven't already.)

- At least 16MB of total RAM installed on your computer. For best performance, I recommend that Windows-equipped PCs and Mac OS computers with PowerPC processors have at least 32 MB of RAM installed.

- At least 25MB of hard drive space on a Windows PC or at least 10MB of hard drive space available on a Mac OS computer to install all the software from this CD. (You'll need less space if you don't install every program.)

- A CD-ROM drive — double-speed (2x) or faster.

- A sound card for PCs. (Mac OS computers have built-in sound support.)

- A monitor capable of displaying at least 256 colors or grayscale.

- A modem with a speed of at least 14,400 Kbps and an Internet connection (to connect to the World Wide Web).

If you need more information on the basics, check out these books published by Wiley Publishing, Inc.: PCs For Dummies, by Dan Gookin; Macs For Dummies, by David Pogue; iMacs For Dummies by David Pogue; Windows 95 For Dummies, Windows 98 For Dummies, Windows 2000 Professional For Dummies, Microsoft Windows ME Millennium Edition For Dummies, all by Andy Rathbone.

Using the CD

1. Insert the CD into your computer's CD-ROM drive. The license agreement appears.

   - Windows users: The interface won't launch if you have autorun disabled. In that case, click Start ➪ Run. In the dialog box that appears, type **D:\start.exe**. (Replace D with the proper letter if your CD-ROM drive uses a different letter. If you don't know the letter, see how your CD-ROM drive is listed under My Computer.) Click OK.

- Note for Mac Users: The CD icon will appear on your desktop. Double-click the icon to open the CD and double-click the "Start" icon.

2. Read through the license agreement, and then click the Proceed button if you want to use the CD. After you click Proceed, the License Agreement window won't appear again.

The CD interface appears. The interface allows you to install the programs and run the demos with just a click of a button (or two).

JavaScript For Dummies Chapter Files

Each of the chapter listings that appear in the book is contained on the companion CD in the CHAPTERS folder. The naming convention used is list####.htm, where # corresponds to each specific chapter and listing number. For example, you can find Listing 8-1 in the file named list0801.htm.

In addition to the chapter listings, the CD contains multimedia files and additional files for your review. To see a list and description of these items, please see the text file LISTINGS.TXT, located in the CHAPTERS folder.

You may find it more convenient to copy the CHAPTERS folder to your hard drive. To install the files, you can choose the install option from the CD-ROM interface.

What You'll Find

In addition to HTML files containing the JavaScript chapter listings, the following development tools are on the companion CD. Many of the tools are either trial versions or shareware, which means if you like the product and use it regularly, you need to contact the company directly and arrange to purchase a copy of your very own.

Apycom DHTML Menu from Apycom Software, Inc. is a shareware tool you can use to create customized DHTML menus — without coding. DHTML Menu supports Internet Explorer, Navigator, and other browsers running on Windows, Mac, or UNIX. For more details, point your Web browser

```
http://dhtml-menu.com
```

BBEdit (Demo). From Bare Bones Software, BBEdit text editor available for the Macintosh that makes a great HTML editor, too. Get the skinny on BBEDut abd Bare Bones by visiting

```
http://www.barebones.com/products/bbedit/index.shtml
```

Dreamweaver Trial Version. Dreamweaver is an industrial-strength Web development tool that runs on both Windows and Power Mac; it also works hand-in-glove with Macromedia's Web-animation development tool, Flash. To purchase a copy of your very own — or just to get more information on Dreamweaver — visit

```
http://www.macromedia.com/software/dreamweaver/
```

Macromedia HomeSite 30-day evaluation version. HomeSite, from Macromedia, is an HTML editor for Windows with many features that make Web programming a breeze. You can add and check tags, anchors, and formatting quickly. You can find updates at

```
http://www.macromedia.com/software/homesite
```

Paint Shop Pro Evaluation Version. JASC Inc.'s Paint Shop Pro is a shareware graphics viewing and editing tool available for Windows. You can find updates at

```
http://www.jasc.com/products/paintshoppro
```

SmartMenus DHTML Menu. From SmartMenus.org comes this fast, stable DHTML menu creation tool that's free for use in non-commercial Web sites. For conditions of use and sample menus, visit

```
http://www.smartmenus.org/forum/
```

Web Weaver Demo Version. McWeb Software's Web Weaver is a professional HTML editor for Windows platforms. The "gold" version offers spell checking and a few other features not found in the evaluation version. For details, visit

```
http://www.mcwebsoftware.com/webweav.asp.
```

```
http://www.mcwebsoftware.com
```

If You Have Problems (Of the CD Kind)

I tried my best to find shareware programs that work on most computers with the minimum system requirements. Alas, your computer may differ, and some programs may not work properly for some reason.

If you have problems with the shareware on this CD-ROM, the two likeliest problems are that you don't have enough memory (RAM) or that you have other programs running that are affecting installation or running of a program. If you get an error message such as Not enough memory or Setup cannot continue, try one or more of the following suggestions and then try using the software again:

✔ **Turn off any antivirus software running on your computer.** Installation programs sometimes mimic virus activity and may make your computer incorrectly believe that a virus is infecting it.

✔ **Close all running programs.** The more programs that you have running, the less memory is available to other programs. Installation programs typically update files and programs. So if you keep other programs running, installation may not work properly.

✔ **Have your local computer store add more RAM to your computer.** This is, admittedly, a drastic and somewhat expensive step. However, adding more memory can really help the speed of your computer and allow more programs to run at the same time.

If you still have trouble installing the items from the CD, please call the Wiley, Inc. Customer Service phone number at 800-762-2974 (outside the U.S.: 317-572-3994), visit our Web site at http://www.wiley.com/techsupport. Wiley provides technical support only for installation and other general quality-control items; for technical support on the applications themselves, consult the program's vendor or author.

To place additional orders or to request information about other Wiley products, please call 800-225-5945.

Index

Wiley Publishing, Inc.
End-User License Agreement

READ THIS. You should carefully read these terms and conditions before opening the software packet(s) included with this book "Book". This is a license agreement "Agreement" between you and Wiley Publishing, Inc."WPI". By opening the accompanying software packet(s), you acknowledge that you have read and accept the following terms and conditions. If you do not agree and do not want to be bound by such terms and conditions, promptly return the Book and the unopened software packet(s) to the place you obtained them for a full refund.

1. **License Grant.** WPI grants to you (either an individual or entity) a nonexclusive license to use one copy of the enclosed software program(s) (collectively, the "Software") solely for your own personal or business purposes on a single computer (whether a standard computer or a workstation component of a multi-user network). The Software is in use on a computer when it is loaded into temporary memory (RAM) or installed into permanent memory (hard disk, CD-ROM, or other storage device). WPI reserves all rights not expressly granted herein.

2. **Ownership.** WPI is the owner of all right, title, and interest, including copyright, in and to the compilation of the Software recorded on the disk(s) or CD-ROM "Software Media". Copyright to the individual programs recorded on the Software Media is owned by the author or other authorized copyright owner of each program. Ownership of the Software and all proprietary rights relating thereto remain with WPI and its licensers.

3. **Restrictions on Use and Transfer.**

   (a) You may only (i) make one copy of the Software for backup or archival purposes, or (ii) transfer the Software to a single hard disk, provided that you keep the original for backup or archival purposes. You may not (i) rent or lease the Software, (ii) copy or reproduce the Software through a LAN or other network system or through any computer subscriber system or bulletin-board system, or (iii) modify, adapt, or create derivative works based on the Software.

   (b) You may not reverse engineer, decompile, or disassemble the Software. You may transfer the Software and user documentation on a permanent basis, provided that the transferee agrees to accept the terms and conditions of this Agreement and you retain no copies. If the Software is an update or has been updated, any transfer must include the most recent update and all prior versions.

4. **Restrictions on Use of Individual Programs.** You must follow the individual requirements and restrictions detailed for each individual program in the "What's on the CD" appendix of this Book. These limitations are also contained in the individual license agreements recorded on the Software Media. These limitations may include a requirement that after using the program for a specified period of time, the user must pay a registration fee or discontinue use. By opening the Software packet(s), you will be agreeing to abide by the licenses and restrictions for these individual programs that are detailed in the "What's on the CD" appendix and on the Software Media. None of the material on this Software Media or listed in this Book may ever be redistributed, in original or modified form, for commercial purposes.

5. **Limited Warranty.**

   (a) **WPI warrants that the Software and Software Media are free from defects in materials and workmanship under normal use for a period of sixty (60) days from the date of purchase of this Book. If WPI receives notification within the warranty period of defects in materials or workmanship, WPI will replace the defective Software Media.**

   (b) WPI AND THE AUTHOR OF THE BOOK DISCLAIM ALL OTHER WARRANTIES, EXPRESS OR IMPLIED, INCLUDING WITHOUT LIMITATION IMPLIED WARRANTIES OF MERCHANTABIL-ITY AND FITNESS FOR A PARTICULAR PURPOSE, WITH RESPECT TO THE SOFTWARE, THE PROGRAMS, THE SOURCE CODE CONTAINED THEREIN, AND/OR THE TECHNIQUES DESCRIBED IN THIS BOOK. WPI DOES NOT WARRANT THAT THE FUNCTIONS CONTAINED IN THE SOFTWARE WILL MEET YOUR REQUIREMENTS OR THAT THE OPERATION OF THE SOFTWARE WILL BE ERROR FREE.

   (c) This limited warranty gives you specific legal rights, and you may have other rights that vary from jurisdiction to jurisdiction.

6. **Remedies.**

   (a) **WPI's entire liability and your exclusive remedy for defects in materials and workman-ship shall be limited to replacement of the Software Media, which may be returned to WPI with a copy of your receipt at the following address: Software Media Fulfillment Department, Attn.: JavaScript For Dummies, 4th Edition, Wiley Publishing, Inc., 10475 Crosspoint Blvd., Indianapolis, IN 46256, or call 1-800-762-2974. Please allow four to six weeks for delivery. This Limited Warranty is void if failure of the Software Media has resulted from accident, abuse, or misapplication. Any replacement Software Media will be warranted for the remainder of the original warranty period or thirty (30) days, whichever is longer.**

   (b) In no event shall WPI or the author be liable for any damages whatsoever (including without limitation damages for loss of business profits, business interruption, loss of business information, or any other pecuniary loss) arising from the use of or inability to use the Book or the Software, even if WPI has been advised of the possibility of such damages.

   (c) Because some jurisdictions do not allow the exclusion or limitation of liability for conse-quential or incidental damages, the above limitation or exclusion may not apply to you.

7. **U.S. Government Restricted Rights.** Use, duplication, or disclosure of the Software for or on behalf of the United States of America, its agencies and/or instrumentalities "U.S. Government" is subject to restrictions as stated in paragraph (c)(1)(ii) of the Rights in Technical Data and Computer Software clause of DFARS 252.227-7013, or subparagraphs (c) (1) and (2) of the Commercial Computer Software - Restricted Rights clause at FAR 52.227-19, and in similar clauses in the NASA FAR supplement, as applicable.

8. **General.** This Agreement constitutes the entire understanding of the parties and revokes and supersedes all prior agreements, oral or written, between them and may not be modified or amended except in a writing signed by both parties hereto that specifically refers to this Agreement. This Agreement shall take precedence over any other documents that may be in conflict herewith. If any one or more provisions contained in this Agreement are held by any court or tribunal to be invalid, illegal, or otherwise unenforceable, each and every other pro-vision shall remain in full force and effect.

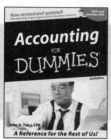

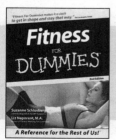

FOR DUMMIES®

A world of resources to help you grow

HOME, GARDEN & HOBBIES

0-7645-5295-3

0-7645-5130-2

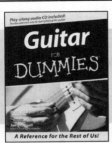
0-7645-5106-X

Also available:

Auto Repair For Dummies
(0-7645-5089-6)

Chess For Dummies
(0-7645-5003-9)

Home Maintenance For
Dummies
(0-7645-5215-5)

Organizing For Dummies
(0-7645-5300-3)

Piano For Dummies
(0-7645-5105-1)

Poker For Dummies
(0-7645-5232-5)

Quilting For Dummies
(0-7645-5118-3)

Rock Guitar For Dummies
(0-7645-5356-9)

Roses For Dummies
(0-7645-5202-3)

Sewing For Dummies
(0-7645-5137-X)

FOOD & WINE

0-7645-5250-3

0-7645-5390-9

0-7645-5114-0

Also available:

Bartending For Dummies
(0-7645-5051-9)

Chinese Cooking For
Dummies
(0-7645-5247-3)

Christmas Cooking For
Dummies
(0-7645-5407-7)

Diabetes Cookbook For
Dummies
(0-7645-5230-9)

Grilling For Dummies
(0-7645-5076-4)

Low-Fat Cooking For
Dummies
(0-7645-5035-7)

Slow Cookers For Dummies
(0-7645-5240-6)

TRAVEL

0-7645-5453-0

0-7645-5438-7

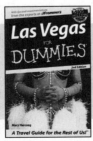
0-7645-5448-4

Also available:

America's National Parks For
Dummies
(0-7645-6204-5)

Caribbean For Dummies
(0-7645-5445-X)

Cruise Vacations For
Dummies 2003
(0-7645-5459-X)

Europe For Dummies
(0-7645-5456-5)

Ireland For Dummies
(0-7645-6199-5)

France For Dummies
(0-7645-6292-4)

London For Dummies
(0-7645-5416-6)

Mexico's Beach Resorts For
Dummies
(0-7645-6262-2)

Paris For Dummies
(0-7645-5494-8)

RV Vacations For Dummies
(0-7645-5443-3)

Walt Disney World & Orlando
For Dummies
(0-7645-5444-1)

Available wherever books are sold. Go to www.dummies.com or call 1-877-762-2974 to order direct.

FOR DUMMIES®

Plain-English solutions for everyday challenges

COMPUTER BASICS

PCs FOR DUMMIES

0-7645-0838-5

The Flat-Screen iMac FOR DUMMIES

0-7645-1663-9

Windows XP ALL-IN-ONE DESK REFERENCE FOR DUMMIES

0-7645-1548-9

Also available:

PCs All-in-One Desk Reference For Dummies (0-7645-0791-5)

Pocket PC For Dummies (0-7645-1640-X)

Treo and Visor For Dummies (0-7645-1673-6)

Troubleshooting Your PC For Dummies (0-7645-1669-8)

Upgrading & Fixing PCs For Dummies (0-7645-1665-5)

Windows XP For Dummies (0-7645-0893-8)

Windows XP For Dummies Quick Reference (0-7645-0897-0)

BUSINESS SOFTWARE

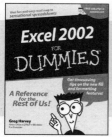

Excel 2002 FOR DUMMIES

0-7645-0822-9

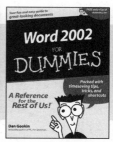

Word 2002 FOR DUMMIES

0-7645-0839-3

Office XP 9 IN 1 DESK REFERENCE FOR DUMMIES

0-7645-0819-9

Also available:

Excel Data Analysis For Dummies (0-7645-1661-2)

Excel 2002 All-in-One Desk Reference For Dummies (0-7645-1794-5)

Excel 2002 For Dummies Quick Reference (0-7645-0829-6)

GoldMine "X" For Dummies (0-7645-0845-8)

Microsoft CRM For Dummies (0-7645-1698-1)

Microsoft Project 2002 For Dummies (0-7645-1628-0)

Office XP For Dummies (0-7645-0830-X)

Outlook 2002 For Dummies (0-7645-0828-8)

Get smart! Visit www.dummies.com

- **Find listings of even more *For Dummies* titles**
- **Browse online articles**
- **Sign up for Dummies eTips™**
- **Check out *For Dummies* fitness videos and other products**
- **Order from our online bookstore**

Available wherever books are sold. Go to www.dummies.com or call 1-877-762-2974 to order direct.

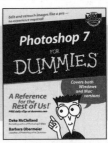

FOR DUMMIES®

We take the mystery out of complicated subjects

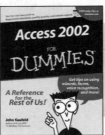